IRELAND'S BANNER COUNTY

Clare from the Fall of Parnell to the Great War
1890 - 1918

Daniel McCarthy

7 V 03

Ireland's Banner County

CLARE FROM THE FALL OF PARNELL TO THE GREAT WAR
1890 - 1918

BY

Daniel McCarthy

Saipan Press

Published by
Saipan Press
Cragbrien, Darragh, Ennis, Co. Clare

Copyright © Daniel McCarthy 2002

ISBN
Hardback   0 9544087 05
Paperback   0 9544087 13

Typesetting and Layout by Hayes Print Ltd., Ennistymon, Co. Clare.

Cover Design by Patricia MacNamara, Oakdale House, Ennis Road, Limerick

Printed in Ireland by Colour Books Ltd., Baldoyle Industrial Estate, Dublin 13.

"It is quite possible to imagine and postulate a unified truth that requires a plurality of consciousness, one that cannot in principle be fitted into the bounds of a single consciousness, one that is, so to speak, by its very nature full of every potential and is born at a point of contact among various consciousness."

Mikhail Bahktin,
Problems of Dostoevsky's Poetics,
Ed. and trans. Cary Emerson.

CONTENTS

List of Illustrations

List of Tables

PREFACE

On 11 July 1917, it was declared that the winner of the East Clare by-election, caused by the death of Major Willie Redmond at Messines on the Western Front, was Eamon de Valera, the senior surviving commandant of the Easter Rising.[1] De Valera was a relative stranger in the County of Clare whom few heard of prior to Easter week 1916.[2] He had defeated Patrick Lynch, K.C., the Irish Parliamentary Party candidate and an Ennis native who was a scion of a well-respected Clare family of 'a long local pedigree and a faultless national tradition', by the vote of 5,010 to 2,035.[3] Prior to the election, de Valera claimed that he 'followed the politics of '98 and the Fenians, that he fought against the same old enemy, that he recognised no other enemy of Ireland and that he would not go over to negotiate with that enemy in his own house beyond'.[4] So coming into this election, de Valera was against Irish participation in the war that was then raging in Europe; he embraced the principle of abstentionism from the British parliament at Westminster and claimed the inheritance of the Republican tradition, which values he openly espoused. In effect, he represented revolution. The democratic majority of East Clare made him their representative.

The most vexing question with regard to this by-election was whether Clare would condemn the Easter Rising as an immoral, illegitimate act and thus vote de Valera down or reject John Redmond's Ireland which pledged allegiance to the imperial crown in return for a limited and suspended Dublin parliament and which supported the allied armies in the World War. This momentous debate raised the odds, especially given that the Parliamentary Party had committed itself towards winning this election and that the eyes and ears of the British Establishment were very much focused on the pending outcome in Clare. The analysis of the practically antithetical stances, of how such stances came to be made in this election, encapsulates much of the study in this book. Although the vast majority of both contemporary and modern commentators on this watershed period, opine that the emphatic nature of the result greatly stultified the mechanisms of the Parliamentary Party not alone in Clare but around the nation,[5] the fact that over one-third of the electorate supported the Redmondite Party's continued commitment to the British cause in the war (even though they claimed that 'nothing but the strenuous opposition of the Irish Party has stopped conscription in Ireland') and that later, in the 1920 municipal elections, there was a strong anti-Sinn Féin polling, would seem to suggest there was a clash of ideologies, and not just perceived party loyalties at work.

The cataclysmic ramifications of July 1917 were to have eventual demoralising repercussions for the old Party and were to contribute in placing the Irish soldiers in the British armies in an actual no-man's land. This book seeks to examine the socio-economic and politico-military factors in Clare along with the political culture of the county in the lead up to the climatic election result and to explore the rise of republicanism in the county up to the War of Independence. It is attempted to give also an accurate depiction of the environment in which Claremen joined the allied armies in their thousands. It is written in the knowledge that history tends to proceed in eras which are contrasted to one another.

ACKNOWLEDGEMENTS

I have many people to thank for helping me through this work and among those I express my sincere appreciation to are; An tOllamh Gearóid Ó Tuathaigh, Roinn na Staire, Ollscoil na Gaillimhe; Dominic Egan, Curator, Cavan Co. Museum and one of Clare's finest; Peadar McNamara, teacher, artist, sean nós singer and a knowledgeable historian who was always generous with his time and advice and his wife Mary, who encouraged me to examine this period of Clare history whilst setting a few bones back in place in the process! Ned Kelly, Keeper of Irish Antiquities, National Museum of Ireland for his encouragement; the staff and design team of the Clare Museum; and Sister Anna Ryan, Presentation Convent, Limerick.

George Harrett, Kilrush and Seán Spellissy for sharing their considerable knowledge of Clare history and sources; the various members of the historical, archaeological and heritage societies in and around Clare who have contributed a rich body of research and scholarship, promoting our local heritage as well as the vibrant Clare associations throughout the world which have continued to foster our identity; Risteárd Ua Croinín of Dysart O'Dea and now County Conservation Officer and my other colleagues who promote our county's culture such as Patrick Maher, Manager of the Burren Centre in Kilfenora, John Keane, chairman, Comhar Conradh na Bóirne, Mary Kerins of Dúchas, Antoinette O'Brien and her former colleague, Senan Ensco in the Clare Heritage Centre in Corofin, Ger Madden, John McMahon and Tom MacNamara from the East Clare Heritage Centre in Tuamgraney, the County Heritage Officer, Conjella McGuire, na teachtaí ón *Clár as Gaeilge*, Nora Daly, Irish Officer, Clare Co. Council, Jaqui Hayes, County Archivist and Cllr. Michael Hillery, chairman of the S.P.C. for cultural development in Clare; Tim Kelly, Denis Canty, Michael Corley, and Seamus Hanrahan, St. Flannan's College, Ennis; John Joe and Michael McCarthy, Plainedge and Rockaway, NY; Francis Meaney, Cathal Talty, the Feeney family of Elmhurst, NY, Veronica Reynolds, Christy O'Connor, Joe Ó Muirceartaigh, Eibhear Mulqueen, Padraig Ó Ruairc, Gerry and Bernie McCarthy, Fergal Ruane, Sinéad McMahon, John Connole,

Taidhg Maloney, Messrs. Troy and Considine, as well as Anne Griffin and Mairín Hill who along with Maura Leyland, Anne Moriarty, Jack Talty and Marie McAllister, all facilitated the researching and production of this history; Kirsten Hayes, Colm Hayes and Anne Kelly of Hayes Print Ltd. for their expertise; Patricia McNamara, graphic designer; Maureen Comber, Peter O'Beirne and Frances O'Gorman of the Local Studies Centre, Ennis - they were Clare's answer to the Oracle at Delphi - one always left the wiser after their professional and courteous advice and assistance; the various staff members of the many museums, libraries, archives and universities consulted with by the author during the course of this research both at home and abroad as listed in the bibliography, with a special mention for the late Commandant Peter Young and Commandant Victor Lang of the Cathal Brugha Barracks, Military Archives Section and Maura Cronin, Lecturer, Mary Immaculate College for her courtesy in providing access to theses pertaining to the 1890-1918 period as well as Marion O'Leary, Audio-Visual Library, Mary Immaculate College, Limerick and Kieran Hoare, Head of NUI Galway, Special Collections Room; various historians and antiquarians, either of the soil of Clare or who have helped to define its people, from the Mac Brodys who were *ollaimh* to the ruling O'Briens, to O'Curry, O'Looney and Westropp right down to Canny, Staunton, Rynne, Harbison, Ní Dhea, Ó Murchadha, O'Connell, Ryan, McMahon, Ó Dálaigh and Sheedy to mention but a selection and one of the great modern Irish historians, Dr David Fitzpatrick, Trinity College Dublin to whom the researcher of this period is indebted. There are many other individuals who I have not referred to here and have aided me along the way and I again extend my gratitude to them.

On a personal note, I would like to salute those who shared and frequented the splendour of our Cherry Park residence in Galway and those who I hung-out and kicked football with, around the 'Valley' in Lissycasey, Mikey, Terence, Tommy Jr., Brian et al. Thanks also to Gearóid O'Sullivan and Liam Ashe of Lissycasey National School and St. Flannan's College respectively who, like Ó Tuathaigh, had the gift of bringing history alive within the classroom; the Clan McCarthy of Clohauninchy, Clohanes, Rockaway and Long Island; my kinsfolk from Cranny and Lissycasey and the Griffins of Cragbrien.

I thank my parents Josephine and Danny for everything down through the years and David, Sarah and Damien also.

Is do mo bhean chéile Siobhán agus ár bpáisti, Seán, Laura agus Dónal Óg a thiomnaím an leabhar seo.

PATRONS

County Clare Patriotic Benevolent and Social Association of New York Inc.

District Council of New York City, United Brotherhood of Carpenters and Joiners

The Local 608, New York, NY

ASC Contracting Corporation, Long Island City, NY

Bayside Fencing Inc., Jamaica, NY

Roche Ireland Limited, Clarecastle, Co. Clare

Corbett Construction, Lisheen, Co. Clare

West End Interiors, Bell Belvd., New York

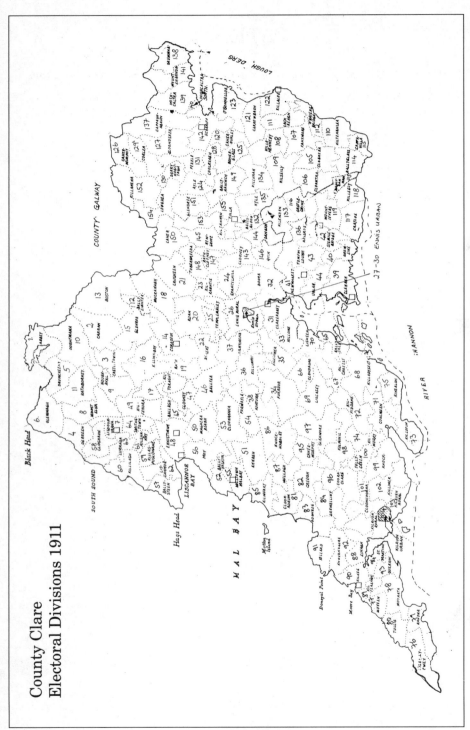

County Clare
Electoral Divisions 1911

SECTION I

County Clare on the Eve of War

CHAPTER ONE

INTRODUCTION

One often hears and reads about the fears of history being hijacked by those who would dictate the social memory and thus the identity of society.[1] While it is not the intention to "aestheticise" this study, it must be emphasised that history loses its raison d'etre when it can no longer be applied in relation to the problems of society. 'Who has fully realised that history is not contained in thick books but lives in our very blood?', Carl Jung queried. Yet very many people only become conscious of their blood when they begin to bleed.

The effect of a much highlighted revisionist schism in Irish historiography had militated somewhat against the effective research of Ireland's role in World War One, for it has created a wedge which too easily categorises historical work into political straitjackets. It is because of our politicised memory of the 1914-18[2] period that it is necessary to apply scholarship to this field. Major William Redmond, the East Clare political representative, was all too aware that the Irish cause for which he was going to die in the Great War was politically bankrupt in the wake of the Easter Rising, when he informed a close colleague: 'Don't imagine that what you and I have done is going to make us popular with our people. On the contrary, we shall both be sent to the right about at the first general election.'[3]

This book focuses on the catalysing impact of WWI on one Irish county in an attempt to convey the greater national complexion during the 1890 - 1918 watershed period in modern Irish history. Professor Finberg claimed that a community is an 'articulation of the larger nation to which it belongs' and Co. Clare was an "insular" community, more so than in any other county in Ireland.[4] Through the medium of local history, the objectives will be to explore and examine the various political and socio-cultural shades in the county. While there will be detailed reference to Clare, inevitably it will be done against the backdrop of changes and shifts experienced nationally during this period of turbulence. Microscopic analysis should lead to a greater telescopic grasp of the scenario unfolding with great haste in Ireland.

It may be questioned whether the neo-colonial complexity of Ireland's recent history has militated against fruitful study of its role in WWI; that the fledgling state needed to have a concise view of itself to project onto the outside world. Commentators like Brendan Clifford have tried to rationalise this tendency; he observed that 'the Independent Irish State originated in the Great War on the anti-British side. But Nationalist Ireland never produced directly out of its own culture a single history of that war.'[5] Yet this is a simplistic observation and one notes that Clifford, armed with the power of hindsight, does not account for the vacuum of the twenty one vital months between the outbreak of the war and the subsequent shelving of the Home Rule Bill up to the Easter Rising out of which was to originate the 'Nationalist' Ireland that he refers to. A cursory glance may corroborate Clifford's view regarding the post-Rising contribution of Ireland to the war (even though on deeper inspection one finds a slight rise in recruitment in 1918)[6] but it is vital to track the evolutionary-cum-revolutionary nature of Irish public opinion from 1914 to 1916 to attain greater comprehension of post-Rising attitudes.[7] This will be examined in the case of Co. Clare through analysis of contemporary sources such as the bulk of local government resolutions,[8] the two main county newspapers, *The Clare Champion* and *The Ennis Saturday Record* (which also appeared twice weekly, Monday and Thursday, in two parts, under the title of *The Clare Journal* and *Ennis Advertiser* until it was discontinued in May 1917), periodicals, national newspapers, the three Irish American newspapers, *The Irish Advocate*, *The Irish World* and *The Gaelic American* (the latter two were particularly inclined to state opinions that would not have been so welcomed by the political orthodoxy pre-1916), diary entries, the Colonel Moore, the John Redmond and the Edward MacLysaght manuscripts, along with the statements and memoirs provided by Clare Republican leaders, detailing the genesis of the revolution.[9]

Where necessary, the above sources will be substantiated by the Monthly Police Reports, Crime Special Branch papers, RIC (which were particularly useful for the study of political activities). Press Censorship Files, Intercepted Letters, Cabinet Reports from the Prime Minister to the Crown, Registered Papers (which included many political and military summaries but were organised randomly) and the Crown and Peace Records, Co. Clare. All of the aforementioned sources will be employed in making contributions to the various chapters.[10]   The Census of Ireland, 1901 and 1911, the Congested District Board Reports and the Agricultural Credit Committee Reports, supplemented by contemporaneous accounts and articles, will provide the backbone of the sociological analysis aided by modern ethnographical commentaries.

There has of late been a growing trend of literature addressing the previously neglected subject of Ireland and WWI, such as the augmenting body of specialist works and monographs in Ireland. Thomas P. Dooley's 1995 *Irishmen Or English Soldiers* gives an excellent account on the socio-economic and political spheres in which Irish Great War recruits operated. Another, Keith Jeffery has asserted that Ireland was entangled within the complex web of being both 'coloniser and colonised', that she has both nurtured and subverted the British Empire simultaneously. He wrestles with the paradoxical theme of Ireland as an imperial and colonial nation through his assessment of the conjoined socio-economic and cultural ties between Ireland and Britain.[11]   However, having pointed to Ireland's role as empire carvers through a study of military statistics,[12] he concludes that during WWI Ireland differed from the rest of the "White Empire" with regard to the whole response (or lack of response), from cultural apathy (from which emerges a theme of distant disengagement, perhaps best captured by the most famous Irish WWI poem, Yeats' "An Irish Airman Foresees His Death")[13] to recruiting statistics that will be later assessed. This disinterested cultural legacy will be contrasted in Chapter Four with the gaelicised tradition, which for a time bound the disparate sections of the country in a cultural tie, and was to inform the republican idealism that was to grip the greater section of Clare society.

One of the failings of the earlier general histories of the period was to overlook the fact that post-Rising republicanism was but a segment of the nationalist tradition, a tradition that had always sought to react to the actions of her British neighbours; and it is by giving recognition to the deeper social and psychological aspects before 1916 that a more thorough analysis may be made of Irish nationalism at a conceptual level. Therefore, Ireland's role in the war was ultimately determined by the subsidiary role imposed upon her nationalist majority by the politico-military decisions made during the 1914-18 period, particularly in the fateful early months of the war. Even David Lloyd George admitted that the War Office's "Irish" policy was 'stupidity amounting to malignancy'.[14]

Yet the leader of nationalist constitutionalism, John Redmond, had crossed the Rubicon at Woodenbridge, Co. Wicklow, when, encouraged by the welcoming of his kinsfolk and friends, he declared 'that Irishmen should go where the firing line extends'. On the day he uttered those words, 20 September 1914, the firing line he spoke of extended through the bloody fields of France and Flanders. By this act, he had nailed firmly to the imperial mast the colours of the Home Rule Party, the Irish parliamentary party which had monopolised the votes of the Irish nationalist population prior to the outbreak of WWI. In the next general election held after the war, the party was annihilated. The tragic consequence of this result was that many Irish nationalists, having followed their hitherto leader's call to arms,[15] became illegitimised in the outlook of the new nation. While one would imagine that another consequence of the downfall of "Redmondism" would be the crumbling of the mechanisms of their system of administration, built up over many years at local government level, this did not actually transpire, and this will be examined in Chapters Three and Eight.

Due to the politicisation of the Great War, which is further accentuated by the ongoing sectarian divide in the North, one must become even more focused on concentrating on the complexity of our past, a past which has seen 49,500 Irishmen registered as dead in WWI memorial volumes, for in doing so, the nationalist culture becomes enriched and more educated on the nuances of Irish society, and therefore better able to appreciate what a great swing of the political pendulum took place during this period.

The above consideration should allow that the Home Rule Party won from the British electorate through passive agitation, the moral concession that Ireland was a free country, by having the Home Rule Bill passed through the Westminster Parliament before a single blow was struck by the Republicans. It was the anti-democratic practices of the Conservative and Unionist Party that lifted the lid off the Pandora's box of physical force which gave renewed impetus to the Republican movement. The failure of Redmondism has highlighted the ambivalence, the gagged language and predilection for the mercurial, which indeed were characteristics of Home Rule politicians. They were also necessary characteristics for the environment in which they operated, because the appearance of unity was always an essential to their existence, so much so that they developed an almost vampiric trait in confronting opposing Irish obstacles. Professor David Fitzpatrick has explored this theme.[16] Unfortunately for them, the Irish nation was destined not to be built on these characteristics but on those which I will assess in Chapter Four, and literary Fenianism made way for active Fenianism in the space of a few years.

While one seeks to explore possible socio-cultural roots of difference between the undercurrent of radicalism that ebbed and flowed within the mainstream nationalist politics and constitutionalism, it must be conceded that there is no single standard for measuring the relationship between culture and politics.[17] Dr Terence Brown, in his work on culture and diversity, asked probing questions on the conflict between the Anglo-Irish/Gaelic Irish dichotomy with regard to recruitment rates being determined by the nature and extent of Anglicisation, with its class and regional variancies,[18] while Erhard Rumpf spoke of such a dichotomy in terms of a national "east-west gradient" concept.[19] These two theories shall be examined in Chapters Two, Four and Seven, where socio-cultural and ethnographical similarities and differences will be contextualised in ascertaining the variations in regional recruitment in the county. It is, perhaps, necessary at this juncture to state that in modern Ireland many citizens feel a certain amount of discomfort when confronted with the question of recognising the mark that Britain has left upon Ireland, because many ask to what extent does such recognition become "West British". Yet by reciprocating the question and asking to what extent has Ireland influenced Britain, a more engaging picture may be framed. The Memorial Rolls of the dead merits this exercise.

Possibly John Redmond's greatest faux-pas was dismissing the importance of Irish radical nationalists, all of whom took their Irishness to be diametrically opposed to Englishness; to these, Redmond and the Home Rule Party became a *mutatis mutandis*, an imitation, following upon their support for the British cause in WWI. Home Rulers saw the Party's policy towards Britain 'as the only logical solution of Ireland's proximity towards her powerful neighbour'.[20] The social theorist, Trinh T. Minh ha, spoke of 'hyphenated identities and hybrid realities' and such a description may be applied to Ireland in the context of competing identities.[21] What is required, therefore, is a scrutiny of inclusiveness and exclusiveness so as to create a greater awareness of the representations of the history of Co. Clare. This theme will feature in Chapter Three.

This book seeks to confront the ugly, thorny aspects of this period in Co. Clare and hopefully provide an accurate picture of the changes that ultimately led to revolution. The nationalists who served at the front were stigmatised because they had no state to embrace their values. Shunned by the imperialists and blighted from the Free State's consciousness because it felt itself obliged to snap the strings of the past, they became incidental casualties, as were most of those who floated between the two transcending ideologies of republicanism and imperialism. These tragic complexities have stemmed from Ireland's 'uncertain constitutional position'.[22] Professor Hayes McCoy summed up this crux quite aptly when he asked why 'we should remain unchangingly, even vindictively, selective of our past, choosing the parts that we deem worthy of us and still spurning the rest'.

The book extends to divide the period to be studied into two sections. The opening section, which will be thematical in approach, will attempt to dissect and project the diversified picture of Clare society as the skies darkened over Europe. The second chapter deals with a comparison of rural life in the county (which 90% of Clare people shared) with the main urban strongholds. The definition retained for what was urban is that employed by the census, which defined someone living in an urban area as a person living in a town of 1,500 inhabitants or more. It is hoped that, from the picture which emerges from this chapter, there will be a groundwork laid for comprehending the actions and reactions of the respective sectors to the events of 1914-18.

The third chapter surveys the structure of local administration in the county, its temperament and make-up and how it interacted with both its political patrons and centralised authority. The objective of Chapter Four is to delineate the various strands of 'advanced nationalism'. Their case will be taken up from the time they wore the cloak of parnellism to the founding of the Irish Volunteers. It is intended to indicate the ways in which advanced nationalists interlocked in various organisations. The extent of the influence of the Catholic Church from the time of the rancorous parnellite fallout, will be scrutinised in Chapter Three.

The second section, which will be more chronologically compact than the first, begins by addressing the lot of the Protestant community that had by 1914 developed a heightened sense of its fragility. Yet its majority remained a class apart as both their socio-economic profile and political activities show. It will be investigated whether there was a peculiarity in the Clare sample of the ascendancy class. This is followed by an analysis of the political and military behaviour of the county in the lead up to the Rising and the direct effects of the war economy on Clare. Chapter Seven looks at the contribution made to the allied war effort by Clare people, including exiles and emigrants, and the origins of the "German Plot" in Clare. In Chapter Eight, the advent of republicanism and revolution will be studied, assessing the actual implications it had for Clare.

CHAPTER TWO

A SOCIO-ECONOMIC SURVEY OF COUNTRYSIDE

2.1 AGRARIAN UNREST

The County of Clare...is a part of Ireland where national feeling is more intense and where political passions are stronger and more ready for action... It is more intensely Catholic, 94% of the population... It is the district where English ideas have the least influence. It's tradition brings alive in it a stronger political feeling.[1]

So wrote Mr. Shaw Llefevre at a time of much turbulence in the county when land agitation was at its peak with the Bodyke evictions of the summer of 1887 and the Vandeleur evictions of the succeeding year gaining national prominence. Within the next twenty years following the strife, the Vandeleur estate, like so many other estates, was to be compulsorily taken over by the Land Commission under the Land Purchase Scheme. It was remarked that there was general uneasiness in the county, owing to the very insecure position of the majority of tenants with much inadequate legislation on the subject but no relief of the tension.[2]

Willie Redmond, who was elected as MP for the East Clare constituency in 1892, told the Westminster Parliament in April 1894 that 'there was less crime in Clare than there had been for a long time. How long that would remain the case he did not know if evictions went on'.[3] Redmond had certainly found a volatile constituency in Clare. In a rather harsh observation, the Royal Irish Constabulary claimed it was 'a county where if a man feels aggrieved with his neighbours, he sets out and burns his hay or fires at him from behind a hedge'.[4] The practice of cattle driving, where a farmer's stock was driven out from his land, if the small farmers and labourers deemed that land to be best employed for sub-division between those in the locality or for tillage or for both, was rampant, and Clare was deemed the most disturbed part of Ireland on numerous occasions.[5] Despite this, the East Clare MP told the House of Commons in April 1913:

> From every point of view Clare was more free of crime than any civilized country in the world. There was very little agrarian crime; but until land purchase was completed there would undoubtedly be *excitement and irritability* (my italics) shown. The nationalist party, however, had done everything in their power to condemn and discountenance crime and outrage of every description.[6]

The descriptions "excitement and irritability" were classic Party-speak, generalising chaotic disorder with understated, understanding words that had the effect of rationalising the high tensions in Clare to the English audience. This speech is particularly ironic in view of the fact that in a local newspaper report in September 1908, when Clare was officially the most disturbed county in Ireland, Willie Redmond, the charismatic nationalist, declared to a boisterous crowd in Ballyvaughan that 'he had no word of blame for the cattle drivers', although admitted 'he had done a lot of queer things in his life but he had never yet driven a bullock'.[7]

Clare was a county badly scarred by the famine. Of the population decrease of 63,996 between the years 1841-1851, an estimated 45,520 died from famine and disease. The small farmers and the landless labourers felt the brunt of this visitation. The 1851 census had shown that all larger farms had increased in numbers.[8] There was in place a whole new agrarian structure, with many farms expanding to over thirty acres and becoming what were regarded as economically viable units. In the 1841-1851 period, the value of stock also increased from £787,556 to £984,785, a 25% increase. The much maligned "rancher" system grew out of this misfortune, and the rapid growth of this sector was to create much rancour, with the cleavage between grazier and peasant becoming increasingly apparent in the post-1890 period right up into the early years of the Free State.[9] In post-famine Clare, political unrest became a symptom of agrarian violence.

It took bad harvests such as that of the 1879 - 1882 period to display the polarities of the economic groupings, fuelling the momentum for political agitation for Home Rule, which was generally held to be the best route towards peasant proprietorship. Some scholars have referred to the average farmer in 1914 as being much better-off than his grandparents ever thought possible.[10] As further scrutiny will show, much of this increase in income can be attributed to the practical extinction of the agricultural labourer class,

11

which resulted in land being distributed between fewer people and livestock replacing rents. Other economic historians have cast doubts on the distribution of economic rewards for the whole period from the Famine to the Great War. Michael Turner claimed that it was the landowning classes that chiefly reaped the benefits of income increase rather than the tenants.[11]

The landlord and the bullock had played a decisive role in triggering the agrarian revolution that was to provide the motor for political change in the 1870s, but it was mainly the larger farmers that won out in the battle for rural independence; and this is borne out by the revival of land agitation which led to the formation of the United Ireland League (UIL) by William O'Brien in 1898 under whose guise the Irish Parliamentary Party reunited following the Parnellite split of 1891. The whole scenario of land reform laid down one fundamental principle; this was the need to contest and to confront the rights of property in order to improve the conditions that prevailed. Land reform was to show itself the narrow end of the nationalist wedge. With the intensification of agrarian attacks, the UIL was proclaimed in most districts of the county in April 1902.[12]

Prior to the Great War, it may be concluded that Clare was a county racked by land conflict. By the end of the nineteenth century, Clare was one of the main ranching areas in Ireland. The West Clare Railway, or the "Kate Mac" as it was locally known, helped to foster the growth of cattle trading or "ranching".[13] Clare was classified as a store grazing region (middleman region) where calves and weanlings were procured from small farmers, and their bone and muscle was developed to be sold to the "fattener" grazier. Certain ranchers with infertile rough pasture specialised in the rearing of young calves up to eighteen months old. The so-called "Ranch War" of 1906-1909 resulted from pent-up antagonism between rancher and peasant, especially after the Land Act of 1903 which failed to satisfy all of the embittered peasants.

Fr. Glynn, Chairman of the West Clare UIL Executive, called for necessary measures to be taken to prevent 'bad blood' between the farmers and labourers of West Clare.[14] The Land and Labour Association (LLA), one of the numerous representative institutions that were fostered by the assimilative Parliamentary Party, refused to send a delegation to the West Clare UIL Executive Convention in July 1904. This protest was lodged because they perceived the UIL as being indifferent to the claims of the agricultural labourers lobby.[15] The Land and Labour Association, founded by D.P. Sheehan, MP,

12

was particularly strong in West Clare, indicating that this area was the poorer economic region in Clare. In July 1905, Fr. Glynn resigned the chairmanship of the West Clare UIL Executive.[16] Before he resigned, he alleged that 'land grabbing is the rock on which we split and smashed'. Later that year in September, P.J. Linnane addressed a joint meeting of the UIL and LLA. Linnane, a grassroots Labour man, reminded the farmers that it was the labourers who had helped them gain possession of their land and that what they sought in return from the farmers was the recognition of their just rights.[17] A picture of an "economic Darwinism" emerges, with unrest resulting from perceived injustices. Public demonstrations, cattle running and boycotting were the main weapons of the smaller peasants.

There was much agitation against the grazing system in North Clare in particular. In the months of September and October 1908, cattle driving assumed very serious proportions in the Ballyvaughan district, but mainly in the Ballyreen, Lisdoonvarna, and Carron sub-districts. Most of the grazing farms in the Ballyreen sub-district were cleared of their stock. In the Lisdoonvarna sub-district cattle driving was carried on extensively, while in the Carron sub-district a good deal of spasmodic driving took place.

An official report described the following incidents in relation to these disturbances:

> On the 12th September the stock belonging to Colonel Tottenham and Messrs. T. McCarthy, James Linnane, and Coleman O'Loughlin were driven off grazing lands about Doolin, in the Ballyreen sub-district, held by them on the eleven months system from Mr. H.V. McNamara. The stock was replaced, but again driven off on the morning of 20 September. On the latter occasion the police patrol on duty at the farms, hearing the noise of a large crowd coming from Doolin, cycled at once to the police barrack for assistance. Eight men immediately turned out, and going through the fields met a crowd of over 100 men driving stock off one of the farms. The police ran in on the crowd and tried to seize some of them, but only succeeded in holding a man named Scales. They, however, identified seven others. A shot was fired from the crowd, but the police did not think that it was fired with the object of injuring them. Despite the efforts of the police the farms were cleared.[18]

Later after warrants were issued for the eight accused, they appeared before court on 22 September. The same report then proceeded to outline the worsening situation:

> Immediately after the rising of the Court on 22 September, a large crowd which had assembled in Doolin was addressed by Dermot O'Brien, United

13

Irish League Organiser, who advised the people present, numbering about 300, to then and there drive off the stock again and deliver them to their owners. This the crowd proceeded at once to do in four parties. The police force present was inadequate to cope with the numbers, but two constables followed each crowd, and noted the names of such as were known to them. The party engaged in driving Colonel Tottenham's cattle and sheep, and those of a man named Frank Cahir, brought them to Kilfenora, where they put Colonel Tottenham's stock in a field belonging to his manager, Mr. Davies. The party delivered Cahir's stock to his herd some distance away, and then returned to Kilfenora, being met on the way by torchbearers who escorted them up and down the village, which was illuminated. Brakes and cars arrived from Lisdoonvarna to convey back the cattle drivers. Before returning a meeting was held, at which Dermot O'Brien and others spoke, advocating cattle driving. Dermot O'Brien, in the course of his speech, applauded the action of the Doolin people in clearing the ranches that day, and advised the people of Kilfenora to follow their good example, and, like them, to do it openly, and in the day time. He referred to Mr. Cullinan, Crown Solicitor, by name, and told the people to drive his cattle to him at Lisdoonvarna, where he was living at the time.[19]

The fall-out from the events led to O'Brien, the UIL organiser, being imprisoned for three months and forty-three of the cattle-drivers were jailed for fourteen days each. The police presence in the area was bolstered by the establishment of an RIC post at Doolin House on 1 October which housed a district Inspector, and Head Constable and fifty constables. There was still a residue of bitterness, in the locality and on 18 October six constables were attacked when returning from a cycle to their post, one of them, severely injured.

A number of government reports were conducted at this time. John Sexton of Lissycasey, when asked by a Parliamentary Commission whether he could distinguish between those who had bought out their land and those who had not, replied:

Yes, for those who have purchased are keeping their farms better and they are better satisfied. They feel it is their home and that it will be free someday.

Mr. M. A. MacNamara, B.L., Lissycasey, when queried by the Departmental Committee for Agricultural Credit about whether there was agitation for land purchase in the wake of a recent Land Act, replied that there was a general agitation, and alluded to the frequent outrages in the county.[20] He explained that the agitation was for the purpose of splitting up the demesnes and that 'they are all disputes about land'.[21] MacNamara went on to highlight the flaws in the recent 1909 Liberal Land Act, claiming that it:

14

virtually put a stop to land purchase. The landlords would be willing to sell as those who sold under the Act of 1903 if they got the three years bonus, and I am sure all Ireland would be purchased in a few years if the landlords had the same terms as they had under the Act of 1903.

One of the adverse effects of the stalling of land purchase was that:

> The tenants are jealous of their neighbours who have purchased under Land Acts and who are entirely better off than themselves. There is no doubt that the rents are low, very low and sufficiently low, but those who have not purchased are disposed to find fault because others have lower rent... because only less than half of the land in the county is purchased, the county will never be settled until the other half of the tenants have purchased their holdings.[22]

Table 1:

Changes in Owner Occupied Land in Ireland, 1870 - 1929 (%)

Year	Owners	Tenants
1870	3.0	97.0
1906	29.2	70.8
1916	63.9	36.1

Source: E. R. Hooker, *Re-adjustments of Agricultural Tenure in Ireland*, p. 120

MacNamara, from this account, seems to be speaking for the more settled section of the Clare agrarian system. A November 1914 *Clare Champion* report would seem to concur with MacNamara's views. It had stated that there were more unpurchased tenants in Clare than in all of Connaught.[23]   Fitzpatrick, in his assessment of the Irish Convention Report of Proceedings, demonstrated that the Clare landlords, who had succeeded in keeping their rents comparatively high, had more to lose in selling out than in other counties for 'tenant purchasers in Clare were not prepared to pay higher annuities than elsewhere'.[24]   The statistics showed that Clare landlords who sold directly to their tenants prior to war had been forced to do so by conceding an average 34% on former rent to set up the new annuities, whereas the rent reduction on a national scale was 28%.[25]   In his analysis of the annual reports of the Congested Districts Board (CDB), Estates Commissioners and Land Commissioners for the period, Fitzpatrick found that 46% of land sold under the Land Purchase Acts, 1870-1919, had been bought by its occupiers by 31 March

1915 and 66% by March 1920. This would confirm the authority of MacNamara's statement and give some credence to the *Champion's* Report (the corresponding national figures for land bought by its occupiers was 58% and 70% for 1915 and 1920 respectively) despite slight variations,[26] when compared with the findings of the Land Commission Report of 1951.

The anecdotal evidence and the statistics indicate that many rural aspirations remained unfulfilled as Co. Clare entered the 1914-18 period, and the Ranch War of 1906-10 never actually died out in Clare, as the economic war against the landlord and the bullock was to resurface time and again in the county.[27] The fact that many graziers were also shopkeepers who had a proclivity towards prominence in local nationalist organisations intimates that there was a hesitancy in tackling head-on the land question in a unified manner. Yet by this stage, the need to interfere fundamentally with the rights of property in order to improve conditions had been recognised. Besides small farmers and tenants who had been evicted during previous land wars, the majority of whom had emigrated, precious little had been done for those who remained until the Evicted Tenants Act of 1907.[28] By 1914, the claims of 3,587 applicants had been met and by 1923 only 191 valid cases remained to be dealt with.[29] By threats of coercion over 170 evicted tenants were reinstated before 1913 on holdings seized from their evictors in Clare. The CDB, which was initially responsible for one-sixth of Irish territory in enlarging and consolidating holdings and improving farming methods, afforestation and the development of fisheries, industry and trade, had its powers extended in 1909. One-third of the land of Ireland was under its control, (69% of Clare) and it had acquired compulsory powers over estates in its zone. Their subsequent actions shall be assessed in Chapter Three.[30]

By comparing and contrasting the various responses of the different sections that made up agrarian society in Clare, the society which 90% of its population lived in,[31] to the intense conflict between landlord/grazier and tenants with uneconomic holdings, labourers and small farmers, it is possible to develop insights into their political preconceptions, ideologies and prejudices. These reactions differed in their reception (or anticipation) of politico-cultural changes, economic shifts and social reforms. This leaves scope for analysis of local leadership and organisation of society and the tensions that existed between local and centralised leadership.

2.2 SOCIETAL STRUCTURES

Around 1914, two-thirds of occupied people were engaged in agriculture and over 90% lived in rural areas in the county.[32] Clare has been the subject of some sociological and anthropological study, both in the 1930s and in recent years. W. M. Williams maintained that 'Co. Clare is an area of small farms, most of which are unable to support a "full" family of parents and children, and since the families are conjugal units, they are likely to have been an imperfect means of ensuring a succession'.[33] He claimed that the complexity of the relationship between family and land is oversimplified by the model of continuity which Conrad M. Arensberg uses for rural Clare in 1937.[34] Arensberg opined that continuity in Clare was inseparable from keeping the name on the land. Children were the link in this continuity and were rendered practically a necessity in rural life.

Within this "stem family" inheritance system, Clare's peasant families had two apparently conflicting aims:

> To pass on the family property as a unit of one heir from one generation to another.
> Providing for all other children in the family.[35]

The second aim was met with good intentions but was not always possible, not in Ireland at any rate. Under this system, the members of the family received money from the son's bride's dowry, which in turn paid for another farm, education or emigration.[36] While the bride and her husband actually saw little of the dowry, it helped to ensure the recognition of her rightful position in her acquired family.[37] S. T. Kimball, along with Arensburg, concurred with this, writing:

> When we remember that the farm is identified in popular thinking with the patrilineal and patronymic family line of the landowner and that the girl is an outsider brought into that group, the money appears as a payment for the girl's inclusion.[38]

It can be deduced that landholding was exclusively associated with men; a woman could only (in customary practice), hold the land in trust for a man. Hillary Hammond describes the regulatory "makeshift devices" which ensured the continuity of the name on the land in her sociological review on Clare.[39] Such regulations represented a conscious attempt to perpetuate social structure. Recent research of statistical material provides a demographic basis that validates Arensberg's model of continuity in Clare.[40] It can be positively asserted that it was not customary to "alienate" the land by sale in Clare. It was a community with a high degree of self-awareness, of sociological insight.

There was around 1914, no indication that the clearly distinctive features of the patriarchal system, with its sexual division of labour, close kinship ties, neighbourliness and self-sufficiency, were in decline.[41] The extended operative kin universe of the farm family in Clare, though highly unusual today, was a distinctive feature of the post-famine period right up to independence.[42] The downturn in Clare's population by approximately 50% in the years 1841 to 1911 put in motion a cycle whereby economic necessity forced social change which led to demographic shifts that forced further social and cultural change.[43] Research has shown that emigration was the single greatest factor in altering the holding of land despite the legislative measures that were won from Westminster. This was accentuated by the fact that fewer marriages were made which meant that fewer children were born to offset emigration, which in turn left fewer people for the land to support.[44] Not even the continued high fecundity rates of marriages compensated for these developments.[45]

A higher frequency of celibacy occurred in the same fifty year period in Clare before the Great War.[46] Under the terms of this unwritten "contract", the non-hereditary members of families, who had chosen not to emigrate, took on the celibate role and the security of a home on a small plot. Usually only one of the boys and one of the girls of big families were contracted into marriage. Those who opted to stay at home knew there was small chance of a wife or husband, as the high proportion of spinsters and bachelors indicate. It may be apt to quote a Clare poet of an earlier century at this juncture, as he lamented what he perceived as one of his community's shortcomings:

> That your men and youths remain unmated
> And your maids in spinsterhood refining.[47]

Table 2:

Celibacy in Ireland
Male and Female. 25-34 and 45-54 age group

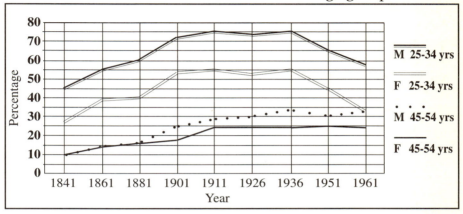

Source: Paul Brennan, *"Ireland, Rural Population"* in **Rural Ireland, Real Ireland?** p. 45

The 1911 census indicates that 53,877 males were living in Clare. Of these, there were 21,693 between the ages of twenty and fifty-four, with 6,451 of this tally either married or widowed. The national average showed that 67% of the male population between twenty and fifty-four were married or widowed. The mere figure of 30% shows that males of the same age category were married or widowed in Clare. It could perhaps be argued that Clare, which was considered by Lord Chief Justice Cherry as the most disturbed county in Ireland in 1913, with a large "undomesticated" population would be more ripe for either recruitment or revolution![48]

One of the most striking characteristics of emigration from Clare for the sixty years leading to 1914 was its rural to urban direction. Most Irish emigrants came from rural areas and located in the industrialised urban areas of the United States and Britain. In 1911, around 14,000 Clare natives had emigrated, with the majority going to America and being particularly concentrated in Boston. Less than 10,000 other Clare natives were living in other Irish counties.[49] Between 1901 and 1911, people were leaving Clare annually at an average rate of 13 per 1,000 whereas the average total for all Ireland during the same period was 8 per 1,000.[50] The irony was that in June 1912, the Clare county surveyor had reported that he had

19

found 'no difficulty in getting workmen. I regret to say the difficulty is in the opposite direction'.[51]

All the demographic sources indicate that emigration was practically a rural phenomenon. A higher number of Irish emigrants were female, with 1,223 females emigrating for every 1,000 males in the 1901 - 1911 period. This can be explained partly by the custom of keeping a son rather than a daughter at home to look after the land and finally to inherit the farm.[52] Emigrants tended to be young and celibate, the vast majority without qualifications and taking on jobs at the lower rungs of the social ladder.[53] They considered the economic and social opportunities of urban areas more important than the relatively better health conditions and familiarity of their rural homes.

Table 3:

Whole of Ireland (32 counties), by Occupational Group in Selected Years from 1875 through 1926 (%)

Occupational Group	Year Ended 30 June					
	1875	1881	1891	1901	1911	1926
Common Labourers	52	67	55	34	26	17
Servants	27	20	31	52	38	30
Skilled Workers	13	7	7	8	19	22
Farmers	5	4	4	1	3	6
Farm Labourers	0	0	0	3	9	13
Entrepreneurs	1	1	1	1	1	2
Professionals	1	0	1	0	2	3
Miscellaneous	1	1	1	1	2	7
Totals	100	100	100	100	100	100
Bases	19446	39232	34621	24192	33575	33170

Source: Robert Kennedy, *The Irish,* p. 76.

The impact of mass rural emigration was firmly impressed on the smallholder/agricultural labourer groups. In 1841, there were 450,000 holdings less than five acres in size. One hundred and twenty years later, there were only 23,000 left. For holdings between five and fifteen acres there were a quarter million in 1841 and only 50,000 in 1960.[54] The vast majority of Irish emigrants came from these holdings, which explains their poverty and lack of qualification. The effect of such emigration was signified by a 20% decline in Clare's population from 1881 to 1891.[55]   They left behind them the most poverty-stricken and isolated areas in the land. The introduction of the agricultural labour-saving practices discussed earlier was resisted by the small farmers and landless labourers who could not afford to adopt the new practices but would be seriously affected by their adoption by the larger farmers. Yet the eventual acceptance of these changes out of economic necessity did come about, albeit to the demise of the agricultural labouring class.[56]   The period of the greatest association between the decline in tillage and decline in rural population was between 1851 and 1881, when this association was directly related to the consolidation of small holdings of less than five acres into larger farms, especially holdings of thirty acres and over.

Table 4:

Percentage Distribution of Holdings Above One Acre, Ireland (32 Counties), 1841-1901.

	Size of Holding in Acres					
Year	*1-5*	*5-15*	*15-30*	*30 and over*	*Total*	*Number of Holdings (thousands)*
1841	45	37	11	7	100	691
1851	15	34	25	26	100	570
1861	15	32	25	28	100	568
1871	14	31	26	29	100	544
1881	13	31	26	30	100	527
1891	12	30	26	32	100	517
1901	12	30	26	32	100	516

Source: Robert Kennedy, op. cit., p. 89.

The social acceptance of leaving agriculture for another occupation (which usually meant emigration) reduced the resistance of the small farmers and labourers to the restructuring of agrarian society. As the previous table shows for Ireland between 1841 to 1901, holdings generally too small even for manual agriculture declined from 45% to 12% of all holdings, while farms generally large enough to support horse-drawn methods (thirty acres and over) increased from 7% to 32% of all holdings. A deciding factor in the high rates of rural emigration was the suddenly widened standards of living between large farmers using new methods and small farmers using traditional methods. The only way most small farmers could increase their standards of living was by vacating their agricultural occupation. Their abandoned land was consolidated into future larger holdings, which were using newer methods. However, another off shoot of this development was that there was a reduction in labour demand for farm labourers and farmers' assisting relatives. Like most of the small farmers, they too chose emigration.

In Clare, most farms were too small and poor to provide work for all the farm family itself, without hiring helpers. In 1911 only 11% of Clare agricultural holdings were valued at more than £30 annually, compared with 16% over the country.[57] Well over half of the manual workers in Clare in 1911 were agricultural labourers according to Fitzpatrick's statistics. The proportion of employees in the agricultural population of Clare in 1911 was 25%, with a proportion of these being farmers' assisting relatives. Fitzpatrick also examined the blurred distinction between smallholder and labourer, stating that: 'Many labourers crept into the legion of smallholders by keeping a cow on their half-acre of government-subsidised garden.'[58]

The Clare rural labourer was hard put to achieve a rise in his real wages, best indicated by his food and clothing.[59] With the coming of the Great War, this situation only improved slightly:

Hunger wasn't inevitable in winter with his plentiful helpings of bread and tea, and also eggs and milk when possible, "yalla male" (Indian meal) as a standby and at times meat in the shape of American salt bacon known as "lad" in some areas. Cheap ready-made clothing enabled him to present a more cheerful appearance, while his children, if still barefoot and liable to be "delicate" (euphemism for consumption, i.e. suffering from pulmonary TB), no longer went practically naked during their childhood. His nominal wages rose to between 20s. and 30s. during the War, when he had the protection of the minimum wage until peace returned. If he still suffered from unregulated hours and spells of unemployment, he was less vulnerable than in earlier years because he had acquired a scarcity value. But for some, seasonal migration was still a necessity, while for others emigration was the preferred and final solution.[60]

The degrading hiring fairs for labourers was by 1914 also a thing of the past. The fact that labourers had acquired a scarcity value seems to be validated by the findings of the Departmental Committee Report on Agricultural Credit in 1914. During the course of an interview with the Departmental Committee, Michael Mescall, J.P., Chairman of the Kilrush Rural District Council replied as follows:

Chairman of Committee: *"Is much land cultivated or much given to grazing there (Cooraclare)?"*

Mescall: *"The majority is under grazing, because labour can't be got there to cultivate it."*

Chairman: *"Labour is hard to get?"*

Mescall: *"Yes, very hard to get."*

Chairman: *"Do the labouring men leave the neighbourhood and go to the towns, or emigrate.....?"*

Mescall: *"No. They retire to the backward parts of the district, and go cutting turf or do some more profitable work - they think it is more profitable than to go and give it to the farmer. There is no use at all for the labouring class in my locality, because nearly all farmers do all the work themselves - the farmers and their families."*

Chairman: *"But their condition is better now than it was?"*

Mescall: *"Far better."*[61]

The findings of the same Committee seemed to indicate that prior to the establishment of Agricultural Credit Societies or Unions, small farmers and labourers were quite often in debt to the shopkeeper. Fr. Anthony Clancy of Ballynacally referred to this credit system in his testimony, and how the shopkeepers provided a very useful service by providing goods on a pay-later basis. Yet he still opined that in spite of labourers working during the winter on the road and being available for the farmers in the harvest, only the formation of a Credit Society could prevent the trend of labourers moving into towns.[62]   The actual statistics bear out the truth of the previous statements. Between 1841 - 1901, there was a 20% decrease in the total male work force engaged in farming; therefore, the fall in absolute numbers of the Irish population was accompanied by a change in occupational distribution. And during these sixty years, there was a notable alteration in the composition of the agricultural work force, for the ratio of farm workers and those assisting was down by 46% and this is a clear indication that small farmers and rural labourers were a class in decline and very much insignificant in terms of their weight in political circles in Clare.[63]

To conclude, as Clare entered the tumultuous period of war, change and revolution, one finds an agrarian community based upon the Irish form of family, family subsistence and familistic custom. Anthropologists and sociologists have outlined the details of a social system they have seen at work in Clare. These have been classified under a master system that articulates five major subsidiary systems comprised of:

1. *The relationships of familistic order.*
2. *The relationships of age grading, or generation.*
3. *The relationships of sex organization.*
4. *The relationships of local division of labour.*
5. *The relationships of economic exchange and distribution in fairs and markets.*[64]

These social patterns as a system determined events in the countryside. The centralised bureaucracies that existed never quite accounted for these local social subsets, and this will be highlighted in the wake of later developments with regard to recruitment.

Even though Clare, as a geographical entity, was almost physically distinctive as an isolated area, from the limestone expanses of the Burren to the north, bordered by the Slieve Aughty Mountains to the north-east, to the Shannon River and its estuary hugging the county lines to the east and south all the way out to the Atlantic which pounded the west coast, the county could not solely function as a self-contained social unit. It had to act and react to forces within and without the county. This can best be observed by examining the geographical-administrative system of the county to gain an understanding of the workings of government at county level against the backdrop of national developments. It is now attempted to demonstrate how the people of Clare were actively engaged through a variety of social, political, cultural and economic strategies in determining their own futures.

CHAPTER THREE

LOCAL GOVERNMENT - "THE SYSTEM"

In this chapter, it will be the intention to present a dissection of the political profile of the county, giving a summary account of its political tradition and of political sentiment within the county (in comparative context) on the eve of the war. Relevant data for this objective will be supplied along with an account of the structure and temper of Clare before 1914. As the urban areas of the county were focussed on by surrounding rural areas for some of their necessities, services and activities, there will be a summary account of the town's role in Clare society. Although governmental and administrative archival data will not fit every projected area of this research, an effort will be made to cull information from relevant sources to emphasise the nature, strengths and weaknesses of the institutional political arena.

3.1 THE TOWN

The four main towns in Clare were Ennis, Killaloe, Ennistymon and Kilrush. Ennis was the county town with a population in 1911 of 5,472. Kilrush, the main western town, followed next with a population of 3,666. Killaloe, the "spiritual capital", had 987 inhabitants with Ennistymon, the key town to the north-west, having 1,204. Although little specialised attention has been devoted to the provincial Irish town, Ennis itself has been subject to some historical scrutiny.[1] The contests over the history and image of these urban areas were inextricably linked to the ways people adapted to the perturbations of their immediate environs. The significance of class and class divisions in town life has also been highlighted.[2] Some scholars have opined that Ennis had a rigid class hierarchy, which was well reflected in the operation of exclusive social clubs.

Ennis was the unrivalled county market town, drawing its economic life-blood from its rich rural hinterland of large farms to the south and east and more numerous small farms to the north and west. It was untouched by the factory system. Indeed in the Factory Act Returns of 1870, it is interesting to note that the only signs of industrial activity in Clare were two mills and a printing press.[3] These employed a total of thirty-one individuals. Such was the extent of the proletariat in Clare forty years before the Great War. Industrialisation was still conspicuous by its absence in Clare by 1914. Ennis was the market centre for agricultural produce and in turn provided many goods and services for farmers. Most people worked either for themselves, their families or for other small employers.

In the absence of manufacturing industry, production was firmly in the hands of local craftsmen or artisans working on their own account to supply local needs. Tradesmen who did not work for themselves or for relatives joined the unskilled building labourers as employees in the construction industry. The principal employers in this regard were the local authorities and small private firms. Many labourers found work only on a seasonal basis. Women workers were typically unskilled and about half of those classified as "gainfully employed" worked in personal service as domestics, cleaners and laundry workers for hotels, hospitals and affluent families.

The work a man did and the tradition to which he belonged was intrinsically linked to the social and cultural pattern of his life. The impact of class on social life was most clearly evident in the operation of "members only" social clubs.[4] There were at least seven social clubs in Ennis around 1914. The County Club was the bastion of the landed "aristocracy" of Clare since the 1840s, therefore, a sanctuary for Unionists as later exchanges between the Club and Edward MacLysaght will show. The Odd Fellows Club and the O'Connell Club served the town's middle and lower-middle class groups. The membership of the former consisted of white-collar workers, lesser government officials, assistants from the largest shops and some of the less important merchants. The O'Connell Club drew its membership from the town's clerks, commercial travellers, shop assistants, some small shopkeepers and other small businessmen.[5]

Social clubs limited their memberships to representatives of certain socio-economic groups, excluding all others from nomination. Socio-economic status was the most important consideration in an applicant's election. The working classes, alienated from these main social clubs, formed their own. The Foresters was their major social club. Founded originally as an artisans' club, it included the large crafts sector, composed of over fifty separate trades. Labour Rooms was the unskilled labourers' club. These "rooms" were unlicensed and worth further investigation. Established in 1910, the Ennis

United Labourers Association, based at premises at Market Street known as the Labour Rooms was more than a mere club but was rather something of a labourers' union. They had a fife and drum band which they marched behind when protesting against employers, and assembled for general meetings at the Labour Rooms.

These members were to play a significant part in World War One. The two other social clubs were the British Legion, whose members were mainly ex-British Army personnel, and the Temperance Hall, where members took the temperance pledge. Both of these were primarily working class outlets.[6] These social clubs permitted class division, and were also locations where political and economic business (especially in the middle and upper class social clubs) could be conducted against an informal background. It is also of interest to note the correlation between the British Legion and the working classes. Later evidence will bear out that urban working classes were in a majority in the British Legion as ex-British Army members in Ennis. As Arensberg and Kimball noted in their study:

> The people of Ennis are keenly aware of the differences that economic interest build, - like many others today, they extend occupational names to cover social classes. They count themselves as members of this or that great economic class, and with the name of labourer or farmer, tradesman or merchant, professional man or government official, they think they summarize the whole pattern of their lives.[7]

The analysis of the connections that shopkeeping established between town and country and family and social class make for fruitful study. Gulliver drew attention to the fact that shopkeepers came to rival landowners and clergymen as wielders of local power and patronage.[8] The process of how the town's shopkeepers became 'socially integrated into rural society' was highlighted by the many marriages which linked farmers and shopkeepers and the number of farmers' sons who became shopkeepers. Such connections were intensified as small Irish towns became 'appendages to the farming population'. Before agricultural credit societies became the norm, shopkeeper-farmer relations often became patron-client ties because of the credit allowed to farmers.[9] As a result of this mutual dependency, shopkeepers were obliged to support farmers in activist movements and to provide leadership. Shopkeepers along with publicans certainly became one of the dominant groups in local administration. No systematic data exists to substantiate whether they were the single most dominant group in Clare, but early twentieth century newspaper evidence would reinforce the view that they

28

were.[10]

Shopkeepers who became involved in politics would naturally favour the farmer therefore. Their over-representation on elected bodies indicated they enjoyed considerably more political power than their small numbers entitled them to, more so than the small farmers and agricultural labourers. Hoppen concurred with this view of their political weight, noting they had a 'significant influence within borough constituencies'. Perhaps the term "gombeen grocer" was derived from those who were disdainful of the shopkeeper's influence. Clare was a county where there was still a high proportion of small farmers to larger farmers despite the previously examined post-famine trends of Chapter Two, which showed the consolidation of larger farms. Henry R. Glynn, a prominent Kilrush politician and a member of the family that owned the mills in Kilrush, stated in his evidence to a parliamentary commission that:

> I do not know of any part of Ireland so thickly populated as West Clare. And they are all uneconomic holdings for it is a congested area. [11]

In such counties, scholars have suggested, the urban shopkeeper has a greater rate of participation in public affairs, due to the nature of their relationships with the smaller farmers of the surrounding rural areas. The implication from this theory is that the bigger farmers did not need 'the assistance of the shopkeepers in their political endeavours'.[12]   However, one finds that the patron/client ties which resulted from the extensive credit system of shopkeepers, may have been losing their strength in Clare if the following evidence to the commission on agricultural credit is anything to go by:

Glynn: *"There are a number of holdings purchased in Clare, greatly to the advantage of the county".*

Interviewer: *"And the small farmers are not now as they were before having bought out - in a position of helplessness as against those to whom they owed money?"*

Glynn: *"No. They are getting into a position of independence. There is no doubt about that. Then the prices of farming produce, including cattle and pigs, butter and other things, for the last few years*

have been at a higher level, and for those
who haven't bought out, the rents are lower...
and naturally the country is improving".

Thomas Gill, member of the interviewing Committee to Glynn:
"That is the story we hear everywhere".[13]

In the county town of Ennis, there were more vibrant commercial
and political activities than in the smaller towns, and there was a
significant population of artisans, non-agricultural workers and landless earning cash wages. Being less constrained by the farmer's
presence, it is quite possible that the majority of the politically active shopkeepers were located here, where they could attain a greater
prosperity and a wider prominence.

In terms of administration, the town ruled its hinterland, for law
and government was centred here (as were the majority of the 487
Royal Irish Constabulary serving in Clare in 1913).[14]   The decrees
and laws of Westminster were channelled through the town.   Ob-
servers have noted that in the turbulence of politics, the countryside
quite often imposed its will on townsmen.[15]   The administration of
law and the promulgation of legislation was ultimately the decision
of the electorate, of which the rural community made up the vast
majority. Political decisions, taxes and appeals were made, and officers chosen in the town. Ennis, as the county town, was the only
common ground for all sides and factions.

3.2 ADMINISTRATIVE STRUCTURE IN CLARE

The modern system of local administration in Clare is mainly
based on the Local Government (Ireland) Act, 1898.[16] The structure
of local administration which emerged from the reform of 1898 was
not fundamentally different from that which had existed before.
What had changed was the membership of local government bodies,
particularly at county level. Whereas before 1898 county administration had been conducted by the grand jury and by magistrates
and ratepayers at presentment sessions, with public health matters
being taken care of by poor law guardians, the new system substi-
tuted county councils for grand juries while rural district councils
took over from baronial presentment sessions and assumed much of
the responsibilities of the boards of guardians.[17]

The Act made the parliamentary electorate (plus peers and qualified women) the local government electorate. Householders and persons occupying part of a house then had the vote. Multiple votes proportionate to the amount of rateable property were abolished. Women, incidentally, could become guardians and district councillors but were debarred from county and borough councils until 1911, when they were admitted by the Local Authorities (Ireland) (Qualification of Women) Act of that year. The next stage in enfranchisement was reached in 1918 when married women of thirty years of age and over got the vote. Proportional representation was first introduced in Sligo Borough in 1918 by a Local Act and was applied generally to local elections by the Local Government Ireland Act, 1919.[18]

The position then was that the Board of Guardians who controlled Poor Relief every year made an estimate of what money they required, and demanded it from the County Council. The Rural District Councils dealt with the cost of the roads in their area, and also such parts of the Public Health Act as applied to rural areas, and they also sent a yearly demand to the County Council. The County Council took these demands into account each year, and also their own expenses for roads, courthouses, asylums, county hospitals, etc. and then struck a rate which was still known as the Poor Rate in the county area. The Urban Councils had to pay their share of Poor Relief and Asylum Charges, but were responsible for the repair of their urban roads and for all town and Public Health Expenditure.

An embryonic welfare state began to develop in the early years of this century. The Clare local authorities were involved with the administration of all these new Acts that contributed significantly to a rise in the standard of living. The first Old Age Pensions Act and the first Tuberculosis Prevention Act was passed in 1908 and the National Insurance Act in 1911. Some of the consequences of these last Acts will be examined below. These Acts were followed by the first School Meals Act in 1914, and the Notification of Births (Extension) Act in 1915, under which mother and child welfare schemes were put into operation. Just after the end of the War, the Public Health (Medical Treatment of Children) Act was passed in 1919 under which provision was made for attending to the health of school children. The Royal Commission on the Poor Law (1909) proposed the abolition of the boards of guardians and the transfer of their powers to the county councils. This followed upon the general outcry against the relief systems under the 1834 and 1838 Acts. As

31

Roche noted: 'the trend was away from the idea of a deterrent poor law with its workhouse test'. Yet the war led to the shelving of legislation.[19]

These local government reforms were widely welcomed in Clare. The Irish Financial Reform League, founded in response to the revelation by the Royal Commission on Financial Relations that Ireland had been over-taxed by Britain,[20] had branches established in Clare. It proved to be an umbrella group for all political opinion in the county, with Colonel O'Callaghan-Westropp, a staunch unionist, seconding Bishop McRedmond of Killaloe's motion that the government relieve Ireland of its high rate of taxation. It provided a wide platform, but eventually passed out of existence soon after Westminster introduced local government reforms and promised a full grant equivalent to the over-taxation of Ireland.[21]

The first election for representative local government in Clare took place in March 1899. Reports in the lead up to the election and actual results indicated an overwhelming nationalist dominance in the county. However, the clergy had spoken out loudly against jobbery and corruption before the vote, with one priest yearning for unity:

> the approaching elections would be the first public act of a re-united Ireland; we should rise above personal interests and private feuds and the promptings of cliques and parties, and consider the best interests in making sure to find the best man.[22]

The newly elected members took up their positions in the following restructured boards and councils:

1. Ennis and Kilrush were upgraded to urban district councils (with municipal functions).
2. Kilkee maintained its Town Commissioners.
3. Ballyvaughan, Clare-Limerick (Limerick District No. 2), Corofin, Ennis Rural, Ennistymon, Kilrush Rural, Kildysart, Scariff and Tulla all became the nine rural district councils in Clare.
4. There were seven Boards of Guardians of Poor Law Unions, located in Corofin, Ennis, Ennistymon, Kildysart, Kilrush, Scariff and Clare-Limerick.
5. The County Council was composed of twenty districts with one member to be elected from each district.

Before the Great War broke, West Clare and East Clare were each represented by one MP in Westminster. Colonel Arthur Lynch represented West Clare since 1909 following a by-election in the wake of James Halpin's death. He was to be their MP for the next nine years, until the end of the war. He was never far from controversy and was to be much maligned in the years ahead. He was, however, a colourful character and possessed impressive credentials. He was an absentee member from Clare. He was an Australian native, his father John being an emigrant from Tiermaclane, Co. Clare, who also took part in the defence of the Eureka Stockade, where four Clare men died in a battle against the Australian authorities who were levying unfair taxes against them. Lynch had been promoted to captain by the end of the engagement.[23] Arthur Lynch was a well-travelled academic, who was on speaking terms with the Kaiser. When the Boer War broke out, he travelled to the Transvaal as a war correspondent but volunteered himself to General Kruger. He was appointed as Colonel of the 2nd Irish Brigade. His service there was to be subjected to much debate and scrutiny; much propaganda came from his political enemies as to his character and courage. This will be examined below, as will his later battles with the clergy and The *Clare Champion* newspaper.[24]

The other Clare representative, for the eastern constituency, was William Redmond, a charismatic figure and one who was very popular with his constituents. From his election in 1892, he served East Clare up to his soldier's death in Europe in 1917, by which time he had been made a major. He had been returned uncontested since 1900. He was a Wexford native and a brother and most trusted confidante of John Redmond, the Irish Parliamentary Party (IPP) leader. He too was an absentee member for Clare and both MPs were also former Parnellites.[25] Fitzpatrick remarked on their responsibilities in Clare as being:

> ...without local affiliations. Their visits were infrequent, ceremonial happenings, in which speeches were delivered, deputations received and complaints against British misgovernment collected for question time in the Commons.[26]

There was frequent correspondence between the MPs and the local papers, but it was those at grass roots level who supported Home Rule and the IPP in the local administrative bodies, who represented the true political power in Clare.

3.3 POLITICS, CHURCH AND REPRESENTATION

We thank John Redmond and his gallant band of followers for having sucessfully steered the Home Rule Bill to victory and that our special thanks are due to our representatives, Mr. William Redmond and Colonel Arthur Lynch for their brilliant services all through the passage of the Home Rule Bill.[27]

Resolution unanimously adopted by Clare Co. Council on 13 February 1913.

Many proposals unanimously resolved by local government bodies in Clare were encomiums to the monolithic IPP. It would have been deemed a form of political hara-kiri for anybody to forswear allegiance to the principles of Home Rule. This constitutional movement had for forty years been the single most dominant representation of Irish nationalism. Its dominance in Irish politics was almost complete save in the northeast corner of Ireland. It seemed almost indestructible. This single political party represented a nation with all of its competing interests and divisions, having uniform local support from all sectors of society. The need to present a united front was the commonly heard mantra in pre-war Ireland. The IPP for all those years in Clare was an umbrella party for various groups in the county. This has been highlighted but one must assess the political climate in which these groups had operated.

For this purpose, the fall-out from the 'Parnell split' of 1891 shall be used as the starting point of this examination. This is because few people could remain apart from the raging debates of that time and these arguments forced people to adjudicate upon issues that had major moral and political implications for the Irish society they lived in. All speeches made by the political figures received full coverage in the Clare press and were scrutinised by the very politically aware constituents. Politics was a serious activity in Clare, and this is borne out by the intense and unique electoral responses of the Clare constituencies, both east and west, at the time.

Their political representatives at local government level had also shown themselves capable of radical, independent action. The takeover of the Boards of Guardians by the electorate from ex-officios by 1890 had been due to political agitation and economic distress, and was seen as part of the local movement for self-government.[28] Many of these new guardians were determined to assert their political views, so clashes with the centralised Local Government Board (LGB) were inevitable. Forster, the chief secretary, and the president of the LGB, gave instructions to the guardians that placed them in direct opposition to the interests of the Irish tenantry. The Kildysart and Tulla Boards of Guardians were two of the four bodies threatened with dissolution in Ireland.[29] They were accused of giving special treatment to evicted tenantry in contravention of regulations.[30] The Tulla Board was amongst the most radical in Ireland and refused on several occasions to recognise the LGB, behaviour which foreshadowed the years of the first Dáil. As far as many nationalists were concerned there were enough boards to make Ireland's coffin.[31] It was also observed that the capture of the Boards of Guardians by tenant representation coincided with a high increase of expenditure. It appeared that peripheralised government bodies were of far more relevance to the people than the centralised authority of Britain. It was altercations such as this that drew pro-Unionists like Robert Buckley, the special correspondent of the *Birmingham Daily Gazette*, to the conclusion that 'rent was at the root of nationalism'.[32]

In December 1889, Charles Stewart Parnell, leader of the IPP and de facto leader of the nation, was cited as co-respondent by Captain William O'Shea, MP, in his divorce case against his wife Catherine O'Shea. It was reported locally in 1890 that the divorce case had caused more surprise in rural areas than in towns, where rumours had been rife of impending litigation for some time. As the infamous case dragged on for eleven months, and revelation after revelation came out into the public domain, Parnell became depicted as a figure of ridicule. Parnell chose not to defend himself and O'Shea had a field day. The tabloids all reported the sordid details. It was recalled that when the Clare representatives of the IPP rejected O'Shea as their MP, Parnell had him foisted upon the Galway electorate.

However, the IPP leader had initial support both in Clare and nationally. The Labour Federation League of Kildysart, Ballynacally and Lissycasey, meeting in October 1890, gave an expression of confidence in the leadership of Parnell and 'his noble band of followers and we promise to resist each and every attack made upon their character whether by professed friends or open foes'.[33] At an East Clare Tenants' Association meeting a week later, Fr. Matt Kenny proposed a resolution 'that we renew our pledge of conformity in the IPP under the guidance of the leader Charles Stewart Parnell'.[34] Parnell was re-elected as chairman of the IPP but there were rumblings in the Liberal party, especially amongst the non-conformists, and Gladstone was worried.

On 17 November 1890, a decree nisi was given to O'Shea and this was uncontested by Parnell (who was privately hoping for a divorce). Yet, one week later, in spite of Parnell's apparent insouciance at the verdict and his subsequent inaction, the Ennis Branch of the IPP passed a resolution promising unfaltering allegiance to Parnell. It was from this juncture on, however, that events began to take what was ultimately a tragic turn. On 24 November, Gladstone delivered an ultimatum to the IPP, which was a clear warning to eject Parnell or jeopardise their alliance with the Liberals. Anti-Parnellites would argue that Parnell should now have done the politically correct thing and fallen on his sword so as to save the Liberal alliance. Defiantly, Parnell lashed out at Gladstone and claimed he was compromising Irish independence.[35] During the fateful IPP meeting in the House of Commons on 1 December 1890, Jeremiah Jordan, the Protestant MP for West Clare, was the first member to tell Parnell that his continuing leadership would damage the party.[36] The acrimonious meeting ended six days later, when Justin McCarthy called on all members who were opposed to Parnell's rule to leave the committee room with him. The two Clare representatives, Jordan and J.R. Cox, the MP for East Clare, were among the forty-three members to leave, with twenty-seven members remaining loyal to Parnell. Parnell declared that the independence of the IPP had been obliterated and he promised to fight to the end.[37]

All the while, the Catholic Church had kept its counsel, but in the wake of the split, a meeting of the Standing Committee of the Bishops and Archbishops of Ireland issued the statement that 'Parnell is decidedly not to be the future leader of the Irish people.' In late nineteenth century Ireland this was a practical decree. The Church in Clare threw all of its weight behind the move to depose Parnell. It can be argued that such a move was not necessarily sectarian inspired, if one alludes to the fact that the Church had not spoken on the affair until it became obvious that, although he was now political "dead wood", Parnell was going to hold his ground. Yet the nature of their avid rejection of Parnell did carry some non-ecumenical undertones as expressed by certain priests. It can be asserted that the actions of the Church were to play a major role in the political polarisation of Clare.

The following examples give a flavour of the strong language used during this period. The first deals with Fr. Murphy, PP, Tuamgraney addressing his congregation at Bodyke Church:

Parnell is a debased wretch and a low scoundrel and Ireland would be very badly off if they could not find a better leader... he is not one of our breed; he is a Cromwellian and not one in sympathy with us in religion; he is the greatest coward that ever lived. When he was put into gaol he was begging and craving 'til he got out; he never did anything for the country... He has been living in sin with Kitty O'Shea since 1880.[38]

The same priest went on to warn his people not to read the *Freeman's Journal* newspaper, which was 'bought over by Dublin Castle and was now corrupting the minds of the people.' He also warned the young men of the parish against involving themselves with 'Parnell's agents' who were 'doing their best to entrap them, as young men would be required to intimidate and frighten the voters when the General Election comes on'. John Kelly, noting that Fr. Murphy also referred to Secret Service money being distributed in the parish, wrote that: 'the priest would have been quite disgruntled to realise that such government money was in fact "buying" one of his congregation that day, passing on the nature of his priest's speech to Dublin Castle.'[39]

Fr. Murphy's diatribe was representative of the stance taken by all sectors of the Church in Clare. Fr. Patrick White, PP, Miltown Malbay, himself a historian, spoke from the altar about 'people going about desecrating the Sabbath and glorifying a man steeped to the ears in sin'; a few days before a meeting which Parnell was to address in Ennis on 1 February 1891, Fr. Molony, CC, Ennis, called on a group of men who were setting up a platform in O'Connell Square to stop, and he described Parnell as an "anti-Christ".[40]

After the April 1891 meeting of the Killaloe Deanery of Catholic Priests in Broadford, a statement was issued repudiating:

the pretensions of Mr. Parnell to the Irish leadership after the divorce revelations, and his subsequent political actions as fatal to the Irish cause; and that we reprobate the methods adopted by his supporters in the press and on the platform as the most pernicious to religion and country. We strongly recommend our people to take the earliest opportunity of forming branches of the Irish National Federation to which we pledge ourselves to give our best support by subscriptions and organisations.[41]

One of the twenty-five priests to sign this statement was Fr. Matt Kenny, PP, Scariff, who had obviously retreated from his October stance held the previous year, which advocated Parnell's leadership.

The newly formed National Federation, also referred to as the "McCarthy Party" had candidates returned in three divisions of the Kilrush Poor Law Elections, as a result of what the *Clare Journal* called 'clerical dictation'. Lady Gregory, while staying at a hostelry in Feakle, related:

> There were portraits of John Dillon and Michael Davitt hanging in the parlour and the landlady told me Parnell's likeness had been with them, until the priest had told her he didn't think well of her hanging it there.[42]

The Church had laid down the gauntlet to its flock in Clare. Arthur Lynch, in his controversial 1915 book, *Ireland-Vital Hour*, painted a tyrannical picture of the Church in Clare and of how they 'enforced their advice on secular matters with spiritual pains and penalties'. However it must be noted that the Church was the sole institution which most of the Irish people owed allegiance to, that had not been conquered. It provided a nationalist identity among the majority of those actively engaged in politics.[43]

C. T. Ó Ceirin from Lisdoonvarna, who was a translator of Irish language literary works, observed the role of the priest in society at the turn of the last century in his introduction to Canon Peter O'Leary's *My Story*, a 1915 autobiography of a priest in the south of Ireland.[44] He concluded that priests like the nationalist Canon Peter O'Leary represented the deeper instincts of the people. Most priests had the desire to protect the 'simple and natural' peasant society from the temptations and vices of modernism.[45]

They abhorred the secularised world they associated with the modern era and Protestant Britain. Such sentiment strongly influenced Bishop Fogarty's outlook during the Great War years. They rejected what they considered to be the Anglo-American popular culture of Irish towns and cities.[46] Many Irish contemporary social commentators concurred with their views. Daniel Corkery, the Cork Gaelic Leaguer and separatist, remarked on the very distinct cultural differences between city and country, which he considered much more striking than the natural differences between rural and civic, differences that were ethnic as well as political; he considered towns as English, and Dublin the centre of English colonial power, whereas he saw the countryside as Irish, Catholic, resistant to city rule and even Gaelic.[47]

The Catholic Church in Ireland had an idealised vision of a self-enclosed peasant community whose whole outlook and culture was solely reliant on local context.[48] Within rural communities the priest played the role of the "intellectual" as a result of his cultural and political influence. He was aware of the broader currents of worldly ideals, and was attached to a church whose centre was outside the country. He was subject to a unique loyalty, distinct from that of political or cultural activists.[49] His church had different terms of reference to such activists and had its own canon law, which may not necessarily have always been in accordance with national aspirations. In the case of Clare, the priest was to become further isolated from the majority of the county's electorate because of the stance the clergy took over the Parnell affair. Yet they were still attached by intimate links to the mass of the people.[50]

The people were sometimes reminded of this attachment by the clergy. Bishop Fogarty was to tell his congregation that 'down through the years your kith and kin have stood side by side with your bishops in the struggle for faith and fatherland', prior to an important General Election in which he was an "interested party".[51] W. P. Ryan, in his account of the Church in Ireland in 1912, claimed that 'the most brilliant thing ever done by the Irish priests was the invention of the legend that they had always been on the side of the people'.[52] The legitimacy of Ryan's statement must be seriously questioned but there is no doubt that the Parnell split in Clare was to take some of the gloss off the 'patriots glory' that the clergy had hitherto basked in.

The 1892 national election resulted in a landslide seventy-one Federation seats against nine Parnellite seats. Yet Clare returned two Parnellite candidates, Rochford Maguire, MP for West Clare, with 65% of the vote, and Willie Redmond, MP for East Clare with 53.5% of the vote. These elections were fought under tempestuous circumstances and Redmond, beginning a political association with East Clare that was going to span twenty-five years, claimed in the flush of victory that the Parnellites 'had put their heel upon clerical influence unduly exercised'.[53]

Willie Redmond attributed his victory to his strong polling in the Ennis vote where he received around 1,300 of 1,500 votes. Some commentators have claimed that people in the countryside were more responsive to clerical influence than "townies".[54] Yet, as the *Freeman's Journal* pointed out, at least half of the Ennis vote on demographic grounds alone must have been from Ennis Rural District as opposed to the Ennis Urban District.[55] In West Clare the pattern of sharp local variation repeated itself, with Maguire actually more dominant in the rural areas such as Feighroe and Carrigaholt than in the towns of Kilrush, Kilkee, Ennistymon and Kildysart. Therefore the claim that the rural voters were more prone to dictation rings hollow in the case of Clare. On the contrary, the response of the Clare electorate both east and west displayed an intellectual and political independence that was precious by contemporary Irish standards.

The theory that the cult of the "personality" or "leader" played a role in the outcome deserves some reckoning.[56] From the time of Boru, the county has been synonymous with "the strong man" or strong personalities from Daniel O'Connell to Michael Cusack and Che Guevara to Ger Loughnane (indeed, research carried out by the Family History Library, Salt Lake City, Utah in 1989, showed that even "the Greatest", Muhammed Ali has Clare blood coursing through his veins, with his mother Odessa Grady Clay being the grandchild of Abe O'Grady, a Clareman, who emigrated to the USA shortly after the American Civil War and married a free coloured woman). The continuity of the strong bonds between the ancient Clare families and their lands, and its throwback to the old clan system, further enhances the theory that Claremen were likely to display a tendency to back a "leader". This theory may lend itself someway towards explaining the county's electoral responses, but the next great electoral issue put before Clare, the 1917 by-election, does not accommodate such an abstract theory as comfortably. By that election, much was to change utterly.

One of the implications of the Parnellite split was that Clare politics now entered a rancorous period over the intervening years, although the feuding factions did vote together for Gladstone's second Home Rule Bill, which was defeated by the House of Lords. The communal solidarity and discipline of the monolithic party had been rocked. The gaping wounds of bitterness left behind from the split initiated a culture of dissension, which persisted even after the re-unification of the party. Fr. Michael Hayes, CC, Corofin, recognised the harm that was being done and pleaded with his fellow clergy members that if they 'cannot see their way to re-unite the rival sections of the party, the next best thing they can do is stand aside and let the people unite'.[57] However, given that the Catholic Church had provided a nationalist identity among the majority of those actively engaged in politics, Parnellites included, (Willie Redmond was a devout practising Catholic), the pastors of Catholicism in Clare were always to be reckoned with despite the setbacks of their anti-Parnellite campaign. Arthur Lynch, West Clare MP, 1909-1918, was to discover this during the Great War. However, there now existed a vacuum in both national and local politics, with Home Rule being a dream that was around the corner.

It was the era of constructive unionism with the Tories instigating government, social and economic reform. It was also during this period that many new labour associations and trade councils sprung up, some of them making their mark in Clare, as previously explained. Trade Unionism was most certainly becoming a factor in Irish society, yet it is difficult to ascertain accurately through statistics how effective it was as an economic and political lobby group within Clare, or how strong was its collective sense of identity. As seen in Chapter Two, there is no doubt that there was an element of class tension between labourers and farmers. Increased literacy levels and an influx of affordable newspapers helped the worker to achieve greater understanding of his world, and facilitated the mobilisation of "Labour" for nationalist advancement.[58] Yet David Fitzpatrick described the pre-war provincial labourer as 'disfranchised, with few public spokesmen, and dependent on goodwill, pleading for a fair deal and grateful when it was offered'.[59]

Such a depiction of the stoical, passive Clare worker contrasts with the idealistic picture James Connolly held of the same class of Clareman and the Ralahine Agricultural and Manufacturing Association, which was an Irish Owenite Commune that thrived during the earlier part of the nineteenth century:

> Had all the land and building belonged to the people, had all the other states been conducted on the same principles and the industries of the country also organised, had each of them appointed delegates to confer on the business of the country at some common centre as Dublin, the framework and basis of a free Ireland would have been realised. And when Ireland does emerge into complete control of her own destinies, she must seek the happiness of her people in the extension of social arrangements of Ralahine or else be but another social purgatory - a purgatory where the pangs of the sufferers will be heightened by remembering the delusive promises of political reformers.[60]

Indeed, as the establishment of the Broadford Soviet highlighted, the Clare labouring class were quite capable of 'organising'.

Within mainstream politics, the Federation Party was faring poorly in Clare with William O'Brien singling out Clare amongst three Munster counties that 'had not sufficient branches to be able to have a voice in the counsels of the Federation'.[61] Another schism occurred within nationalist ranks as T. M. Healy, expelled from the Federation Party, set up the Peoples Rights Organisation in 1897. There were signs, however, of a gradual rapprochement that same year within the county, as all factions responded to Major Jameson's

41

(the West Clare MP) call for action on the over-taxation of Clare, with the MP claiming that 'the financial relations imposed by the Union had been replaced by a system of gigantic fraud'.[62]

The report of the Special Commission on Financial Relations appeared to corroborate the nationalists claims of over-taxation.[63] The Report confirmed that Ireland contributed £2,000,000 more in revenue than it received from government expenditure.[64] The Clare meeting unified the feuding camps, and some branches of the Irish Financial Reform League were established.[65] Ironically, by the time of the next Parliamentary Report on Irish Finance (Primrose Report, 1912), Ireland was to be receiving £1,000,000 more in benefits, mainly for old age pensions and land purchases, than it paid in taxes, as Irish revenue had increased by only 28% between 1896-1911, while government expenditure had soared by 91% for the same period.[66]

Further conciliatory moves were made in 1898, when the Clare '98 Celebration Committee was formed along with a branch of the '98 Club, a non-political organisation set up to celebrate the centenary of United Irishmen's Rebellion.[67] The elections that followed the passing of the Local Government Bill in 1899 threw up new County Councillors, ranging from commercial/pro-grazier representatives to some IRB veterans.[68] The nationalist parties eventually reunited under the banner of the UIL in 1900. The Parnellites were successful in having John Redmond nominated as chairman. The UIL was founded in 1898 by William O'Brien to agitate for the redistribution of the western grass ranches to small farmers. The land crisis was still a burning issue, and as already documented, Clare was rife with agitation.[69]

During the height of land agitation and throughout the Boer War, Irish parliamentarians displayed a proclivity towards using extreme language. Willie Redmond (one Clare IRB veteran actually alleged that Willie Redmond had taken the Fenian oath) was particularly inclined to speak this "literary Fenianism".[70] It was considered honourable and indeed necessary to invoke the venerated names of past patriots, and to claim that the Party now represented the political manifestation of their legacy. Willie Redmond claimed during an election campaign that:

> I would not go to the House of Commons for five minutes to agitate for Home Rule if I thought that the people by putting up a struggle in Ireland, could win for themselves the same national rights and recognition which the Boers had won by fighting.[71]

Speaking in Clare in September 1901, after meeting with Paul

42

Kruger, the Boer President in Holland, Redmond ruled out armed insurrection in Clare; 'we are unprepared for that... but the people could organise and strike for liberty; they could put down the enemy of the people by organising in the UIL'.[72] During his early Parnellite campaigns in Clare, he told a Miltown Malbay audience that he had met twenty men from the area he had met years earlier in Monaghan jail.[73] He told the House of Commons that:

> it has been unfortunately proved now, as always, that when the Irish people are peaceful they get nothing but taunts, and that if they want to get any substantial benefit they have to resort to disturbance.[74]

The above statement is ironic when viewed in the wake of the Party's eclipse by those who would 'resort to disturbance'. Willie Redmond sincerely believed that a Home Rule Ireland could exist comfortably within the British Empire. He claimed in the House of Commons that 'the possession of independent legislative powers had made the British Empire a success in every portion of the globe'.[75] He asked the War Office during the Boer War, to let Ireland raise its own battalions, as he felt it would 'focus rather than diffuse' national sentiment.[76] Redmond felt that the Empire was as Irish as it was British.

Redmond was in a particularly strong political position in Clare in the wake of the first Local Government elections, as his Clare allies dominated the new local councils set up in the county. Probably his closest ally and confidante was Patrick Linnane, an Ennis hotelier who was chairman of Ennis Urban District Council. Both he and Linnane were imprisoned for making seditious speeches, under the Coercion Act in 1902, but were released after a few months. From November 1900 until his death in 1917, Redmond never faced a contested election. He had the backing of the Church now also, particularly since the appointment of Bishop Michael Fogarty of Killaloe, with whom he enjoyed an amicable relationship.

Probably the most difficult situation he faced locally before the war was the criticism he received over his support for the Sale of Intoxicating Liquor Bill in May 1906, which restricted outlets for alcohol sale and granted local government bodies control of the licensing of public houses. The mass Temperance movement, inspired by the Catholic religious revival of the late nineteenth century, which saw the growth of pious devotions, foundation of confraternities and the publication of Catholic newspapers and magazines, had an influence on the introduction of the Bill.[77] The issue nearly led to a vote of no-confidence in Redmond, but eventually the resolution of protest was dropped, but it did highlight the type of pressure the publicans' lobby or "pubocracy" could exert. Perhaps Redmond should have been wary of the fate of Major Jameson, who was accused at a West Clare UIL convention of being 'a Tory in disguise and a trader whose main aim in Parliament was to sell his whiskey' and was promptly ostracised and soon rejected by the UIL Directory and its West Clare branch when he committed the political faux-pas of attending the coronation of King Edward VII.

Some arguments were made at the time of the passing of the Local Government Act, that local politicians would become more susceptible to corruption. D. P. Moran's newspaper, *The Leader*, documented the attempts of local politicians trying to 'get their man' at a Scariff Union meeting in July 1914, and using the cloak of nationalism to do so; a letter was read from the Hibernian Fire and General Insurance Company applying for a transfer of the Board's fire insurances and offering to accept these at the same premium as they previously paid:

Mr. Culloo:	*"I would propose that this insurance be handed over to the Hibernian Society".*
Mr. W. Burke:	(Seconded)
Mr. Holland:	*"This insurance company has nothing to do with the Hibernian Society. It is a mistake to think they are the same".*
Mr. D. Healy:	*"I would give this to an Irish insurance agent".*
Mr. Holland:	*"I think you are making a mistake. A resolution was passed giving this to an Irish company. The Clerk said that on a previous occasion they had decided to insure through the Manager of the National Bank if it was an Irish firm".*
Mr. Healy:	*"What fault have you with Slattery, who is an able man and a good nationalist?"*

44

Mr. Cooney:	*"It is the man Mr. Healy wants, not the company".*
Mr. Holland:	*"The Hibernian Society is not the company at all - it is only a name".*
Chairman:	*"Hibernian is the ancient name of Ireland".*[78]

It was eventually decided to continue the premium with the Patriotic Company, ironically a company that sold itself to an English firm, until the next meeting. One notes the mention of the Bank Manager as agent. D. P. Moran remarked that 'perhaps some of the Scariff Board of Guardians were not anxious to fall foul of a gentleman of such importance in the Scariff economy'.[79] One can also get a sense of jostling nationalist credentials from this exchange and this was typical of many meetings of this kind where the nationalists jockeyed for positions.

The Ancient Order of Hibernians (AOH), mentioned in the above debate, had between 1905, when Joe Devlin took over as President, and the outbreak of the Great War, become a dominant influence on the Clare political landscape as well as on the national scene.[80] It was a versatile patronage, brokerage and recreational association. It served three functions: it fostered the Irish-American link, providing access to money; it provided a new zeal to stoke up Nationalist ambitions as the land crisis began to retract; and it encouraged lay leadership of nationalist Catholicism. It was this last aspect of the AOH that alarmed Catholic Church leaders. Bishop Fogarty of Killaloe was informed by Bishop O'Dwyer of Limerick that he (O'Dwyer) distrusted Joe Devlin who was, in his opinion, 'bidding to become a dictator', and was spreading the AOH throughout Clare, Tipperary and Limerick 'under the guise of a religious association, without making any reference to either priest or prelate'.[81]

In a direct reply to a letter from John Redmond canvassing his support, O'Dwyer sought clarification from Redmond regarding the spread of the AOH. He felt that since they were spreading 'within the regular political organisation of the United Irish League', and, therefore, with the tacit permission of the Party, the politicians were in some way accountable for it. He was convinced that it could very easily become a hotbed for anti-clerical, and even anti-Catholic opinion.[82] O'Dwyer had already told Fogarty that it would only take 'a

45

very slight change in its methods' for the AOH to turn into a secret society, and 'secret societies always attracted their own brand of followers'. The AOH was also seen as 'a cause of prejudice... against Home Rule' amongst the Protestant population.[83]

Such fears of the AOH attracting their own brand of followers were well grounded, if the memoirs of Micheál Ó Muirthuile, a republican activist, are held as standard reflections. He claimed that the AOH was the nearest thing to a paramilitary force until the Volunteer movement developed in 1913 and that the Volunteers had found the AOH as a useful recruiting ground. In Clare, in the early years of World War One, the young men were often AOH and pro-war in politics, but after the Rising, they went anti-war and joined Sinn Féin.[84]

From the time he was elected as West Clare MP, Colonel Arthur Lynch always attracted controversy. He had appealed to the electorate on the back of his record in the Boer War, where General Kruger was persuaded to appoint him as Colonel of the 2nd Irish Brigade.[85] However he was considered 'godless' by the priests, and Lynch had to declare that he stood as a Catholic.[86] In 1910 he had to stand over his comments that claimed the clergy selected 'weak, pliable men' as candidates.[87] In early 1914, Lynch's loose remarks embroiled him in controversy again. The *Sinn Féin* newspaper under the ironic headline of 'Clareshire' published a stinging attack on Lynch. It claimed that 'years ago, Mr. Lynch proffered to the Speaker of the House of Commons an apology for his supposed actions during his flying visit to the Transvaal', and that this was kept from the West Clare electorate.[88] The article then stated that 'their versatile representative informed the English Whigs and Tories that he and the voters of West Clare were willing and ready to fight for England against Germany'. It asked if West Clare had become so ardently attached to English government that it was willing to fight in its defence, yet the article also noted that several Claremen wrote letters to the Dublin newspapers repudiating Lynch's statement, but that these letters were never published. The article ended with the accusation that Lynch was a 'slanderer' and was an 'Irishman never again to be trusted in Irish politics'.[89]

Nearer to home, the *Clare Champion* soon after published more vituperative attacks on Lynch. In his open letter, Mr. Thomas Hayes accused Lynch of fleeing his 2nd Irish Brigade in the face of British fire during the Boer War.[90] John Devoy's *Gaelic American* newspaper also berated Lynch in the same manner. Ironically, Lynch had been commended by President Kruger for his role in the Boer War. The *Clare Champion* also attacked his statement on joining forces with the English against Germany. A supporter of Lynch responded in the *Clare Journal* newspaper:

> Mr. Lynch said nothing which for one moment could be calculated to involve his constituents in a definitive undertaking to take up arms for England, but made a statement which in the opinion of those who are in a position to estimate the true trend of current politics, will go a long way to dissipate the calumnies which have been levelled by the Ulster Orangemen and their friends against every member of the Irish Party. [91]

Lynch denied the charges laid against him, claiming that 'no man in the party is less of an imperialist than I am'. He accused John Devoy, the Fenian veteran, of 'trying to smash the Irish Party and trying to engineer the downfall of Home Rule'.[92] These charges and counter-charges can be seen as the playing out of debates soon to become all the more pronounced within a few months. This coming period may be seen as the militarisation of politics, a process that was influenced by determining forces both without and within.

CHAPTER FOUR

THE FENIANS AND BANBA -
REPUBLICANISM AND A CULTURAL OVERVIEW

4.1 AMONG THE FAITHFUL - FENIANS TO VOLUNTEERS

> We lived in dreams always; we never enjoyed them. I dreamed of an Ireland
> that never existed and never could exist. I dreamt of the people of Ireland as
> a heroic people, a Gaelic people; I dreamt of Ireland as different from what
> I see now - not that I think I was wrong in this.

> **Denis McCullough, IRB leader,**
> **in Garvin, *Nationalist Revolutionaries in Ireland 1858-1928*.**

It is necessary now to delineate the structure of "advanced" nationalism in the county before the Great War and the founding of
the Irish Volunteers. The second part of this chapter will examine
in more detail the ways in which such nationalists interlocked in
various organisations. The range of motives and fierce divisions
beneath the nationalist umbrella of the Party has already been noted.
With the leadership pressing for the passage of the third Home Rule
Bill, however, it was essential for them to project an image of unity
of purpose, the solidity of the nationalist front to the Westminster
sceptics. They appreciated the concept of image over reality. To
obtain their objectives they had to walk a tightrope between the
doubting Fenian hillside men at one end and the British Empire at
the other.

Most Home Rulers accepted the patriotic virtues that inspired
Fenianism, if sometimes only out of a sense of political pragmatism.
Some politicians praised them for devotion, provided that such
Fenians were out of the contemporary picture. William O'Brien MP,
addressing a meeting in Bodyke, claimed:

> I have never said a word against men, against extreme men who don't be-
> lieve in constitutional action, and who are ready to fall back on arms to
> recover freedom... On the contrary (sic) I think Ireland owes a great deal, if
> not most of what she has won to extreme men. But I draw a very broad
> distinction between extreme men and extreme humbugs.[1]

James Halpin, the West Clare MP from 1906 to 1909, joined the Fenians as a young man, and later became chairman of the Ennis Board of Guardians. He was also a member of the County Council, president of the East Clare UIL Executive and involved himself in Newmarket-on-Fergus GAA and athletic clubs. He was amongst the generation who had participated in Land War resistance and the numerous cattle-drives. The British authorities saw a threat posed by the fusion of the INL, IRB and GAA in Clare, which they believed had led to the dominance of the young GAA men within the combined movements, and was to the annoyance of the Fenian veterans.[2]

As already alluded to in Chapter Two, many graziers and shopkeepers in rural society doubled up as being prominent members of local Party organisations, which in turn helped to take the sting out of the Ranch War, because the Party's machine was now, due to vested interests, no longer singularly devoted to the small farmer's cause. There was a groundswell of bitterness left as a legacy of this.

Yet, prior to Thomas Clarke's return from the USA in 1907, the Irish Republican Brotherhood was to a great extent, in Clare, unable to harness the individualistic nature of the hostility against the Party into a concerted drive. However it had been the policy of the IRB to steer away from politics where possible, and instead, build up its conspiratorial network on the ground, asking its members not to be discouraged by defeat or condemnation, 'but rather bear witness to the heroic tradition of revolutionary separatism'[3] and to pass on the separatist ideal to the next generation. They were what James Stephens called 'a few faithful men with a deathless dream'. Few people, regardless of their political ideology, believed that a violent insurrection against the might of the British Empire would have the slightest chance of success. Therefore revolutionary ideology was largely theoretical. It can be argued that the Fenian oath was not anything other than an acknowledgement of the legitimacy of the right to bear arms in the name of the Irish Republic.

The various histories available of pre-Volunteer IRB circles in Clare offer the opportunity to assess the modus operandi of republicans and indicate to what degree they were the moribund organisation of popular belief. Joe Barrett, former O/C of the Mid-Clare IRA brigade and a member of a well-known Clare political family, detailed IRB activities at grass roots level.[4] A native of Ballyea, he had been sworn into the Fenian Brotherhood, which it was known as at that time, in August 1908. He stated that it was the practice in

Clare to invite the oldest son of each old Fenian to become a member of the Brotherhood. He was sworn in by a fellow parishioner at an unoccupied house in Drumquin. There were fifteen men sworn in on the same night, most of them being the oldest sons of Fenians. The fifteen formed the nucleus of a Circle, which represented three or four parishes. This new Circle held meetings every two months, where the ways and means of procuring arms and ammunition were foremost on the agenda.[5]

Andy O'Donoghue of Kilfenora in North Clare, who was to serve in the Mid-Clare brigade, retraced his earliest experiences with the IRB:

> Evidence of the connection of some of my forbears with the Fenian Brotherhood was discovered by me one day when, while searching in a loft for some article, I found a cap and a pistol. I was in my teens at the time and knew enough to realise that what I had found were Fenian relics. I decided to take them to an old man, who, I was aware, had been a member of the Fenians. This turned out to be the case as I had suspected, but he repaired the pistol and gave me a .32 revolver and some ammunition. He did not disclose to me how he had acquired these articles, nor did I ask him. In later years, I brought this gift with me into the Irish Volunteer Movement.[6]

> I wasn't more than sixteen years of age when I made my first contact with the Irish Republican Brotherhood. Some members of that organization, whose names I do not now remember, explained its aims and objects to another young fellow, Peadar O'Loughlin, Tullaha, and myself, and asked us if we were willing to join. We both agreed, and we were told to call a few nights later to Markham's of Clogher, Kilfenora. The IRB centre of the North Clare Circle was Tomás Ó Lochlainn, a native of the Carron district, who was then staying in Ennistymon. We met him at Markham's and we were sworn in by him that night. We were briefed on the following points:

> 1. **Never to discuss the IRB with anyone other than a member.**
> 2. **Never to be seen in public places with other members who were known to be suspected by the RIC as being in the organisation.**
> 3. **Never to speak above a whisper where there was a possibility of being overheard.**
> 4. **Never to sign a statement for the RIC about anything.**[7]

Lieutenant General Michael Brennan, a Meelick native from the East Clare IRA Brigade and one of the most influential revolutionaries of the War of Independence, relaying his first encounter with underground republicanism in 1911, commented on how an IRB member had "worked" on him as a prospective member of the Brotherhood after he joined the Wolfe Tone Club.[8] The interviewer, Patrick Sweeney, at first made references to the old Fenian movement and then progressed to hints that some people thought there was such an organisation still alive in the country. When Sweeney eventually asked Brennan if he would take the oath, Brennan informed him that he was already sworn in by his brother Patrick on account of the approval from Seán McDermott who was on the Supreme Council of the IRB. Michael Brennan was fifteen years of age.[9]

Seán O'Keeffe, a Crusheen native and a former Brigade Quartermaster with the Mid-Clare brigade, related the following, in his account of joining the IRB:

> The IRB circle in Crusheen was in existence prior to 1909, the year in which I became a member. It was started by a Carrigaholt man, Seamus Mór Ó Gríofa, who was then working in Crusheen as a post office linesman. It is my firm opinion that this circle was the first to be formed in Clare after the reorganisation of the IRB, and though I have often heard of people claiming to be members of the IRB circles in other parts of the county prior to 1905, I think they really belonged to what could be described as "unofficial circles" that were kept alive by the remnants of the older IRB organisation in many places in Clare since the Fenians. Unfortunately these "unofficial circles" had, through time, degenerated into groups solely interested in agrarian trouble.[10]

The Crime Special Branch reports before the re-organisation of the IRB in 1907/08 would seem to corroborate O'Keeffe's claims, as it was noted that there was a general tendency for local IRB circles to degenerate into 'mafias' without central authority. The old Fenian movement had taken off in Clare when Edmond O'Donovan, son of the Irish scholar and historian John O'Donovan from Broadford, swore in John Clune of Carrahan, Quin as head of the movement in Clare, while he was organising Fenian cells throughout the country. After the Fenian Rising of 1867, Clune, who had succeeded in helping to make Clare one of the staunchest Fenian counties, was sentenced to be hanged but this was commuted to transportation to Bermuda. He escaped to the USA, where he became a founder member of the Claremen's Association in New York in 1887 and was elected its first chairman.[11] It was Brian Clune, his brother, who claimed he had administered the Fenian oath to Willie Redmond, and who took over the Clare leadership until his enforced exile to New York in 1891.[12]

Another Clare exile who had come to prominence in Fenian circles and was to change the course of modern warfare was John Philip Holland. The Liscannor inventor was the father-founder of today's submarine. His Holland VI model, which used a gasoline engine on the surface and electric motors under water as propelling machinery, was commissioned into the United States Navy on 12 October 1900. Holland, who was educated at Ennistymon Christian Brothers school, had emigrated to Boston, carrying with him submarine designs which formed the basis of his initial submission in 1875 to the US Naval Department, who rejected it as impractical.[13] He had grown up during a decade of famine in Ireland and there was much revolutionary fervour in the Irish-American circles that Holland moved in. At a New York fund-raising social for the *Catalpa* expedition, Holland's brother, Michael, who was a Fenian activist, introduced him to members of the Clan na Gael leadership, who saw the potential of his designs in a covert naval war against Britain's powerful fleet.[14]

The Irish World newspaper launched an appeal fund. The successful testing of Holland's 33-inch model submarine at Coney Island, New York, convinced the Fenian leadership to sponsor Holland's $4,000 construction of a full-sized 'wrecking boat' from its Skirmishing Fund. The success of this 14-foot model led to the $20,000 funding by the Fenians of a second venture by Holland in 1881.[15] This craft, over twice as large as its predecessor and dubbed the *Fenian Ram* by a *New York Sun* reporter, was also successful. While Holland was engaged on a third prototype project, an internal rift developed amongst the Fenians, some of whom were growing impatient about slow progress on the diving boat.[16] One group decided to take the *Fenian Ram* into their own hands. One source suggested that this was primarily to avoid legal sequestration while their monies were in dispute. Led by John Breslin, and using forged papers, they towed away the *Fenian Ram* and Boat No. 3 up the East River into Long Island Sound. Just off Whitestone Point the prototype was sank, while the *Fenian Ram* was taken to Mill river in New Haven where it remained in a shed until the 1916 Rising, where it was displayed at Madison Square Gardens to raise money for dependents of the Rising in Dublin. The *Fenian Ram* is today on display at Paterson Museum, New Jersey.[17]

Holland was furious, declaring that he would 'let her rot on their hands', and thus ended the great "Salt Water Enterprise". Holland went on to eventually sell his designs to the US and Japanese navies and ironically to the very power he had originally intended to employ the submarine against, the British Navy, although, due to the deception of erstwhile litigious colleagues, Holland never bore the financial fruits of his labour. He was, however, honoured with the Fourth Class Order of Merit Rising Sun Ribbon by the Japanese

Ambassador to the U.S. for his distinguished service to the Japanese nation.[18]   In 1904 Holland had told Thomas A. Edison that submarines would serve to end naval warfare, because they were so lethal.[19] When he died aged 73 on 12 August 1914, a World War had just begun, and during it, the submarine was to prove how lethal a weapon it was in modern warfare. In a quirk of history the submarine was to impact directly upon the inventor's very birthplace, as will be looked at in Chapter Six.

The Fenian brotherhood in Clare, even prior to their reorganisation, had regularly been denounced by the Bishop of Killaloe and the clergy. At the close of a mission service in Miltown Malbay, Co. Clare on 12 November 1895, the priest preached on the subject of 'secret societies and moonlighting', in which he warned them against its evils and called upon them to hold up their hands in token that they would not take any part in them in the future.[20]   Later in 1912, Bishop Fogarty of Killaloe issued a condemnation of all secret societies.[21]   This is ironic, given the nature of his May 1916 "condemnation" of the Easter rebels.

British Intelligence was monitoring Clare IRB activities, prior to Clarke's return from the USA, on a regular basis. The spy, *Peter* detailed to the Co. Inspector how IRB meetings were regularly held in Clare and Limerick in late 1905 at which subscriptions were taken up which remained in the hands of the centres. *Peter*, also stated that the IRB had no definite policy at the time but was carrying on an anti-recruiting crusade.[22]   In November 1905, Ennis was among eleven principal towns to stage demonstrations commemorating the execution of the Manchester Martyrs. Anti-recruiting literature was also distributed amongst the crowds.[23]   Examples of open 'disloyalty' that the unionists encountered in Clare will be provided in the next chapter. In fact, some Claremen took up arms against the British military, as opposed to merely dissuading their fellow county men against taking the 'Saxon shilling' during the early 1900's. Pat Fahey, a Clareman and a commando in Colonel Blake's Irish Transvaal Brigade in the Boer War made a lone stand against the advancing British army, shouting and swearing at them until his position was overrun at the Battle of Vaalkrantz 1900. The Boers did fight back and win the battle, and found Fahey's body riddled with bullets and bayonet wounds.[24]

Even by a perusal of the Crime Special Branch reports of this period, one becomes aware of the changing republican scene in Clare. The Fenian suspect, P. F. O'Loughlin, was reported as visiting Ennis in July 1906 as part of a tour organising the IRB in the county. According to *Peter*, O'Loughlin was also arranging for an important meeting of the Munster Council of the IRB to be held in Cork later on that summer, at which some changes in the personnel of the Council would be under consideration.[25] The said meeting was held to consider the IRB leader P. N. Fitzgerald's position on the Supreme Council. He was considered by John Daly (father-in-law to Thomas Clarke) and others as too well known to the police and too apathetic in his work. Yet Fitzgerald held on to his position. However the meeting learned that a delegation from Clan na nGael was about to visit the country, possibly preparing the ground for the return of Clarke, John Devoy's right hand man.[26] In late August 1906, William Fagan from Dublin visited Ennis with a letter of introduction from P.F. O'Loughlin. This visit was probably in connection with O'Loughlin's previous organisation work in Clare.[27]

The recently formed Sinn Féin party was also linked with the IRB in Clare. A branch of the National Council of Sinn Féin met at Carron in September 1907.[28] This was probably at the behest of Carron native Tomás Ó Lochlainn, founder of the Carron Sinn Féin Society and an early member of Sinn Féin National Council, and who was also the IRB centre of the North Clare circle. Diarmuid Lynch claimed later that this North Clare circle was unofficial and there was only one official circle based in Clare and a few minor groups.[29]

Sinn Féin itself had been founded by Arthur Griffith and Bulmer Hobson in 1905 as a radical nationalist party in the wake of the enthusiasm generated for alternative organisations by the Boer War. It was actually Máire Ní Buitléar from Clare who first suggested the name Sinn Féin to Arthur Griffith. Ironically, she was a cousin to Edward Carson, the Unionist leader. The British authorities felt that the IRB in some areas could only be revived under the Sinn Féin movement.[30]

In Clare, however, the IRB was still in operation in the county, and was re-organising itself to a degree after 1907 without strong Sinn Féin grass roots. Fitzpatrick identified the Carron Sinn Féin Society as the one Sinn Féin branch in the county before the Rising.[31] However, two IRA veterans of the period claimed that there was a Sinn Féin club started in each of their respective localities (both outside of Carron) before the Great War. O'Keeffe described the genesis of the formation of the 'official' circle in Crusheen, Co. Clare, in the following account:

In my early youth I came into daily contact with men who had been either members of the Fenian Brotherhood in the sixties or members of the IRB in the intervening years of "Moonlighters" during the Land League days. Though I'm not in a position to vouch for it as a positive fact, a branch of the Invincibles was said to exist in the Crusheen district. It is true, however, that ten or twelve men from the locality were arrested as suspects under the Coercion Acts, introduced after the killing of Burke and Cavendish in the Phoenix Park, Dublin. Another national organisation which functioned in the parish of Crusheen in my young days was the '98 Centenary Committee. Under its auspices parades, concerts and lectures were held, at some of which I can remember being present.[32]

O'Keeffe continued:

The opening decade of the present century saw my native parish with a branch of the Gaelic League, formed before 1900, a senior hurling team, a branch of Sinn Féin, started in 1907 or 1908, which, I believe, remained in existence until the resurgent movement swept the country after the 1916 Rising, and an IRB circle. I was a member of all these organisations. With regard to the Sinn Féin Club, I cannot recall now business was transacted when meetings were held. It was through some of the officials of the club that the official organ of the movement - "Sinn Féin" - was distributed, particularly by members of the McNamara family, by whom I was employed at the time.[33]

Commandant Liam Haugh, of Donaghboy, Kilkee, in his history of the West Clare IRA Brigade, stated that the Sinn Féin movement was first launched in West Clare in the summer of 1909, on which occasion the Dublin HQ of Sinn Féin was represented by Seán McDermott.[34] Nevertheless, however strong Sinn Féin pre-war was in the county, one can discern the interaction of republicanism within various fronts from O'Keeffe's account, and the other contemporary sources. The IRB, both official and unofficial, were also involved in land agitation. Andy O'Donoghue and Joe Barrett outlined such agitation in accounts of their respective IRB activities. O'Donoghue claimed that the IRB took part in the land agitation in Clare and Galway but were prevented from doing so in other areas, and he referred to Clare's population as the 'county of moonlighters'.[35] Perhaps there was a link between Clare and Galway having the highest frequency of 'land outrages' in Ireland and IRB activity.[36] John Moroney, a Feakle native, whose house was used as the HQ for the East Clare IRA Brigade during the War of Independence, was also associated with both the Fenian and land movements as were many of his IRB contacts in East Clare.

O'Donoghue's outline of one of the common cattle drives in North Clare has already been described in Chapter Two. Barrett has also asserted that his IRB circle took an active part in the local agitation for the acquisition of ranches by the Land Commission, and, in the division of such lands, they tried to ensure that their members would get first preference.[37] Barrett identified the owners of the ranching estates as the 'enemies of the Irish national movement' and the reason for the depopulation of the countryside.[38] R.C. Geary, in his study on Labour and the working of the land, did state that from 1881 to 1911 cattle numbers increased by 21%, and the rural population declined by 25%. Yet he also noted that the decline in rural population was also roughly the same in areas where ranching did not occur. Barrett believed that it was through UIL agitation that the Wyndham Land Act was passed but despite seeing the UIL as the successor to the Land League, he viewed the fact that it relied more on constitutional agitation as a flaw.

Obtaining recruits and ammunition constantly focussed IRB attention within the county. Barrett stated that at the IRB meetings he initially attended, ways and means of procuring arms and ammunition were discussed, but that there was difficulty in acquiring these arms.[39] He continued:

> Between 1909 and 1913, the IRB extended its membership throughout County Clare, especially within a radius often of fifteen miles of the town of Ennis, which came to be a meeting place for our circle, as Clarke set about re-organising the whole brotherhood. The question of security occupied a good deal of time at these meetings as did the idea of raiding the ascendancy class, who were of planter stock, for arms and ammunition.[40]

Ironically, some of these members did manage to purchase four or five Winchester rifles from gamekeepers in the employment of landlords.

Andy O'Donoghue, recounting his earliest experiences of IRB meetings, recalled how some outside help was at hand:

> Between 1912 and 1915, meetings of our IRB circle were held from time to time, mostly in Markham's place in Kilfenora. Tomás Ó Lochlainn was usually present and he spoke on a couple of occasions about meetings of the Supreme Council which he attended, and appeared to be on terms of close friendship with Tom Clarke, later executed after the 1916 Rising. At one meeting, he gave us to understand that arms from America might be landed at Liscannor or Doolin in North Clare.[41]

O'Donoghue also related how the North Clare IRB circle had at least obtained four Winchester (.3850) rifles which were procured by Ó Lochlainn through a merchant in Gort, Co. Galway. He also believed Ó Lochlainn paid for all the guns out of his own pocket, as few members subscribed between themselves to pay for one.[42]

An opportunity arrived in late 1913 for the IRB to assert themselves, with the foundation of the Irish National Volunteers on 25 November 1913 at the Rotunda in Dublin. Its setting up was seen as a direct response to Eoin MacNeill's famous 'The North Began' article in *Claidheamh Solais*, where he called upon nationalists to arm themselves in defence of Home Rule, which had been introduced in 1912, but with its enactment delayed for two years by the House of Lords. The Ulster Volunteer Force had already taken up arms in January 1913 to co-ordinate the paramilitary activities of Ulster unionists against Home Rule. Ironically, it was these Ulstermen who provided the IRB with the stimulus of example, and also helped cultivate propitious circumstances for them. John Redmond, who initially conceived of the Irish Volunteers as a militarised body that was not to be trusted, stood aloof of the early growth of the Volunteers, despite the Provisional Committee statement in December 1913 that it was:

> ...representative of every section of national opinion in Ireland, and it stands completely apart from all differences that divide nationalist Irishmen, but it stands without reservation for the Irish Nationalist claim in its broadest sense, and its aim is to secure the rights and liberties common to the people of Ireland.[43]

In Clare, the IRB were hearing the knocking of opportunity and moved towards taking the initiative in moulding the nature of the Volunteers from the outset. Michael Brennan stated that both he and his young associates, who had 'mustered and paraded' in the Fianna (Republican Youth Organisation), and discussed ways and means of infiltrating local organisations and public bodies, found 'progress very slow' until the Irish National Volunteers were formed.[44] He expounded on what was a classical IRB manoeuvre in their infiltration of the Volunteers:

> At our meetings all our members were directed to press their friends and associates everywhere towards having a committee formed to organise a meeting which would launch a branch of the newly-formed Irish Volunteers in Limerick. As there was hostility to us amongst the Redmondites, we were not ourselves to take a public lead, but rather to induce supporters of Mr. Redmond to appear as the moving force. This was managed and a Provisional Committee was formed representative of all Nationalist bodies in

Limerick. We were allotted representation for the Wolfe Tone Club and the Fianna, but in addition, many of our members got themselves selected to represent trade unions and such bodies. As a result, I think we were in a majority on this Committee from the beginning. Actually, several of us attended the meetings not representing anything. As we did most of the work, our right to be there was never questioned and we were accepted as regular members.[45]

Andy O'Donoghue claimed that the hitherto omnipresent Tomás Ó Lochlainn did not openly play a prominent part in the Irish Volunteer movement after its inception, but he still remained as the IRB Centre for North Clare.[46] Seán O'Keeffe stated that it was the IRB element in the Crusheen district which was responsible for the formation of a unit of the Irish National Volunteers in late 1913, and that the first company captain, Con Fogarty was an IRB man, with about sixty men joining at the outset. O'Donoghue also referred to the IRB men becoming officers in the build up of the Volunteers in North Clare.[47]

A company of Volunteers was organised in Killone, in mid-Clare, a week after the Rotunda meeting. Although Barrett's company was relatively small, the majority of men enrolled belonged to the IRB. Barrett claimed that:

The members of the IRB started the Volunteers on their own, without assistance from any outside body or person, that is to say, they had no instructions from the Supreme Council of the IRB on the one hand, or the newly formed Volunteer Executive on the other. Between the end of 1913 and the summer of 1914, volunteer companies were started in most parishes in Clare.[48]

Brennan was based in Dublin for much of 1914, studying wireless telegraphy, but Seán McDermott of the Supreme Council of the IRB asked him to return home, as World War loomed, and work at organising and training volunteers in Clare, as much of their contact with Clare was of an individual nature. Brennan, O'Donoghue and O'Keeffe all referred to their drill instructors as being ex-British soldiers. O'Donoghue traced the development of his Volunteer Company up to John Redmond's intervention in June 1914:

At the big review of Irish Volunteers held in the Phoenix Park on Easter Sunday 1914, a contingent from Kilfenora attended, headed by their brass and reed band. This band included members of the IRB, who during their stay in Dublin met other members of the Brotherhood from different parts of the country, and from them learned of the efforts, which the Irish Parliamentary Party were making behind the scenes to secure control of the Volunteer movement. My recollection of subsequent happenings is that the

Kilfenora unit disintegrated, as such, soon after the Dublin review, and that, on the formation of a company of Irish Volunteers at Cloona following the Redmondite split in the autumn of 1914, a number of Kilfenora men, including myself, joined the Cloona company.[49]

Disintegration of Volunteer companies such as O'Donoghue's in the aftermath of Redmond's nominees being co-opted onto the Volunteers Provisional Executive turned out to be the exception rather than the norm, as will be highlighted in Chapter Five. Now it is necessary to examine the nature of the culture that informed the mentality, and the future political thought of most of Clare's post-Parnell generation.

4.2 A GAELIC REVIVAL

No nation we suppose has been persecuted so severely and so long for the last 700 years. Our history has been a dark record of oppression and misery. It would seem to have been the object of England from the start to crush us as a nation, to eradicate our national characteristics and to totally exterminate us. Yet we have survived all this and, notwithstanding the cruel unmitigated efforts to subdue our spirit of patriotism, our identity has outlived all persecution.[50]

Michael Cusack, *Celtic Times*, 1887

The object of the following is to assess the contribution of culture to the development of nationalist thought in Clare up to the Great War. It must be pointed out that there is no single standard of measurement to assess cultural impact upon a society,[51] but an examination of the correlation between certain aspects of culture and politics may create a greater awareness of the subtext of Irish nationalism. The verse of Patrick Pearse comes to mind in this instance:

O wise men, riddle me this: what if the dream come true?
What if the dream come true? And if millions unborn shall dwell
In the house that I shaped in my heart, the noble house of my thought?

Michael Cusack, of Carron, County Clare, the founding father of the Gaelic Athletic Association and its first secretary, claimed in the above that Irish national characteristics had survived persecution. To 'survive persecution' was one thing; for a culture to flourish and imbue a sense of Irish identity was another. For most nationalists the vision of the future depended on the vision of the past, although some commentators on this period argue that for the politically conscious, the achievement of political independence was the precondition

59

for any more comprehensive 'national independence'.[52]   Yet for the politically informed Fenian, John O'Leary, both culture and nationality were interrelated. He told W.B. Yeats that 'there is no great literature without nationality, no great nationality without literature.'

It is now the intention to assess the contributions various Clare people made to the cultural revival and to indicate the ways in which advanced nationalists interlocked in the cultural organisations throughout the county. As Garvin commented: 'Republican separatism had to trick itself out in the garments of linguistic revivalism to appeal to the clergy, and in the clothes of nationalist athleticism to appeal to the young men.'[53]   A popular case made for why cultural rejuvenation occurred was that the post-Parnell generation became disenchanted with politics. Yet both priests and republicans formed a tacit alliance for the defence of the emotional, spiritual and intellectual properties of Irish-Ireland against the modernising trends of Anglicisation. With land reform being realised, republicans had to force issues like cultural "defence" to keep their own fires burning. As Ernest Blythe claimed:

> If the republican forces had been stronger than they were, they might have been content to allow the Gaelic League to stand neutral; but their numerical weakness made it natural for them to entrench themselves wherever they could do so.[54]

The two cultural organisations that became a part of the social fabric of Clare were the Gaelic League and the Gaelic Athletic Association. Michael Cusack noted that 'the Irish peasant too often wasted his idle hours in smoking and card-playing'[55]   before the GAA was founded. Late nineteenth century Europe was experiencing the blooming of the "culture club". A belief in the characteristics of peoples was manifested in imperialistic mindsets such as in Britain. They projected a "punch-like" stereotyped image onto the Irish nationalist. This contrasted with the "pure Celtic" virtuosity which was being promoted in Ireland, as the impact of Victorian English culture was making itself felt.

One of the earliest historical references to Gaelic games in Clare is in a poem by Lochlann Ó Dálaigh, the O'Brien poet in 1565, which paid tribute to the three hurley-playing sons of Thomond.[56]   Ollie Byrnes, in his history of Clare hurling, made reference to an organised intercounty game between Clare and Galway taking place at Turloughmore in 1759.[57] Cusack, a former cricket and rugby player himself, had become disillusioned with the social exclusiveness of existing sporting bodies and the growing domination of "garrison" games, which he saw as despoiling Ireland of the bricks of nationality. First a codified structure, which could organise and revive native pastimes, had to be established. Such a body was set up when the Gaelic Athletic Association was formed in November 1884.[58]

The GAA had Fenian connotations from its inception. In fact, there are inconclusive claims that Michael Cusack was at the fore of an IRB initiative. One source stated:

> [Cusack] soon found another interest, however, and became a valued member of the Irish Republican Brotherhood and placed before its Council his plan for raising the morale of the Irish people. It was to found a sporting organisation which would bind together all Irishmen, give them pride in themselves and their national games, and serve, incidentally, as a recruiting ground for the IRB and cover for its activities.[59]

What can be asserted is that as the GAA, in the words of Cusack, 'swept the country like a prairie fire', it attracted substantial Fenian support. Cusack himself admitted that 'every social movement in Ireland is to a certain extent necessarily political.'

The RIC authorities in Clare became disturbed by the rapid growth of the GAA in the county. The County Inspector noted: 'a good opportunity of a general communication of all the leading conspirators in the county' was provided by the GAA to 'enable leading members of the IRB to consult together and recruit young men who marched to and from their games in military order and were defiant to the police'.[60] The GAA soon became well enough organised in Clare to be able to take over as a leading nationalist organisation.[61] P. J. McInerney, of the IRB and with suspected connections with the Invincibles, was said to be running the Clare GAA from Ennis as 'a cloak under which meetings of the dangerous characters can take place'. Edward Bennett, a Clare Fenian, was elected GAA President by dubious means at an early infamous convention but was soon ejected.[62]

There was a continuity of interplay in Clare in varying degrees between republicanism and the GAA up to the founding of the Volunteers. Joe Barrett claimed that 'the Fenians had the GAA going well in the county'.[63] The proceeds of a GAA tournament in Ennis in January 1906 were forwarded to the Treasurer of the Allen Fund, (the said Allen was the father of one of the Manchester Martyrs).[64] Seán O'Keeffe said he was sworn into the IRB by a West Clare

Railway official in Ennis, who was on his way to referee a Gaelic football match.[65] The GAA pitch in Kilfenora was also given over for IRB target practice.[66] The ban was in place against RIC and British Army participation in GAA. However, there were instances of this rule being relaxed, such as at a sports meeting held under GAA rules at Doonbeg, where P. J. Hayes, who acted as "handicapper", allowed three members of the RIC to compete.[67] A Mr. Nash, incensed by this, sought to have Hayes censured but his motion was ruled out of order by the Chairman of the GAA Central Council. Yet it was noted in an intelligence report that Nash and many others were opposed to men such as Hayes occupying official positions in the GAA.[68]

The other main auxiliary of cultural revivalism was the Gaelic League, whose aims were to preserve and restore Irish as the national language, encourage Gaelic literature and promote the de-Anglicisation of Ireland. By the mid-nineteenth century, Irish was a dying language. The first real attempt to stop its decline came with the foundation of the Society for the Preservation of the Irish Language in 1877 by Fr. Eoin Ó Nualláin and Dáithí Coimín, a twenty-two year old Kilrush National Bank Clerk working in Dublin. The society had the dreaded "screen" abolished and produced a number of textbooks, such as the *First Irish Book*, which sold 20,000 copies in its first year.[69] The society's monthly journal, *Irisleabhar na Gaeilge*, attracted many significant contributors. In July 1893, at Middleton Hall, of which Martán Ó Ceallaigh, Dysart, Co. Clare was proprietor, the Gaelic League was founded. Ó Ceallaigh was amongst the ten organisers of the League. Dr Douglas Hyde *(an Craoibhín Aoibhinn)* and Eoin MacNeill were its two leading figures.

Intended as an apolitical movement it received ecumenical support. An Irish magazine called The *Gaelic Churchman* was produced by the Irish Guild of the Church of Ireland, on which the founder of the Carrigaholt Irish College represented the Gaelic League.[70] Yet the Gaelic League, which was to become a vital vehicle in the mobilisation of "Irish-Ireland", helped to lay the cultural foundation for outright independence. In Clare, being a Gaelic Leaguer was akin to wearing a badge of identity. As stated in one republican account:

> The Gaelic League became influential in the western part of Clare around 1910-11, and as far as the Clare IRB was concerned, it was the body which catered for people in Clare who had the interests of Irish nationality at heart until the start of the Volunteers in 1913.[71]

This statement is reinforced by Patrick Pearse's claim that 'we never meant to be Gaelic Leaguers and nothing more than Gaelic Leaguers.'[72] Willie Redmond, as he sat in House of Commons lounges, listening to Welsh MPs speaking their native tongue, recognised the sense of identity the Irish language could both provide and stimulate.[73]

The actions and activities of some of the Gaelic League's members in Clare indicate that the issue of language was becoming a politicised issue. In March 1906, Michael Tierney, Ennis UDC, proposed a resolution 'condemning the actions of the Dublin Post Office authorities for the vindictive conduct in connection with the Gaelic League in refusing to accept parcels addressed in the National language'. Peadar Ó Hannracháin was put in jail in 1912 for replying in Irish to an RIC constable when asked for his name. Jim Lorigan of Lack West, Kilmihil, who was an IRA member in the War of Independence, taught Irish to adult classes in his area. Peadar Clancy, a renowned Clare republican, featured in plays organised by the Gaelic League. Clare County Council declared in 1913 that they wanted it to be known that:

> the Irish language is not to be ignored after all the magnificent work of the Gaelic League for twenty years. The O'Curry College and the great Feis at Kilrush proves sufficiently that the language is gaining and Claremen will not accommodate seoinín Irishmen by casting aside the language of the country.[74]

Political groups were lobbied by the League in opposing attempts, led by John Mahaffy, Provost of Trinity College, Dublin, to have Irish removed from the intermediate school syllabus in 1899. They were also lobbied in its campaign to have Irish declared a compulsory matriculation subject in the National University of Ireland in 1908-9 and in its attempts to have St. Patrick's Day declared as a National holiday for Ireland. Each time they were successful.[75]

With regard to the clergy's role as to the revival of Gaelicism in the county, O'Farrell claimed that the popular religious revival that gave much momentum to the temperance movement had 'its real temperamental links with the emerging cultural rebels, not with the Home Rule Party'.[76] However, Fitzpatrick systematically researched (by the statistical assessment of the two local papers) the involvement of senior and junior clergy with the Clare UIL branches and the Gaelic League. It was his assertion from the figures deduced that the Clare priests 'were more inclined to support the Home

Rule cause during the 1913-16 period than the revival of the Irish language'.[77]

Indeed the clergy and the Gaelic League quarrelled over the League's policy of getting Irish into the schools and the new National University. The bishops actually withdrew their support for the Gaelic League.[78] It was noted that many priests were dismayed that under the auspices of the League, 'many more people learned to dance reels well than learned to speak Irish well'.[79] Yet the Church did promote the Irish language in Clare. Bishop Dr O'Dea, who was sympathetic to the language movement, based an Irish-speaking priest in Liscannor, which was in the diocese of Kilfenora in 1907. It served to give a renewed dignity to the native tongue at that time, because 'apart from Latin, English was the language of the Church as much as of the State and in West Clare no value was then set on Irish'. Girls educated at the Ennis Sisters of Mercy Convent sang and danced at Feiseanna organised by the Gaelic League, while at St. Flannan's College, Ennis, the pupils held Irish classes to teach hurling terms and this was the language they used on the hurling fields of Ireland.[80]

Clare Irish had been badly neglected, notwithstanding the brilliant academics the county had produced in Eugene O'Curry and Brian O'Looney. Its dialect only had similarities in Waterford,[81] yet by 1911, apart from the Glininagh district, close to Ballyvaughan, there was no Irish speaking area left in the county. The remaining Irish speakers were generally spread out from each other,[82] (however, many Irish words and phrases did remain in general use). Micheál Ó Gríobhtha, who drew up the Gaelic version of Bunreacht na hÉireann, the Irish Constitution in 1937, listened to Irish spoken by his parents and older neighbours in Lissycasey, even though English was by then the language used. He also spent a year teaching Irish in Scattery Island near the Shannon Estuary.

Ironically, probably the largest Clare Irish speaking area was near Buenos Aires in Argentina, where the extended Carmody family and friends and neighbours from Clare settled in the 1850s! They were Irish-speaking emigrants and it remained as their first language into the 1900s, and Clare Irish was known up to the 1930s, by which time Spanish had taken over.[83] The inroads the timirí (travelling Irish teachers) and the Gaelic League made with regard to reviving Irish and their impact on society and recruitment is examined in Chapter 7.1. Perhaps the following extract from Ó Dálaigh's

Stranger's Gaze, which ends this chapter, best sums up the type of spirit the Gaelic League sought to inculcate in the Irish:

> There is a story of a dying woman near Ballyvaughan, who began her confession in Gaelic. The priest, who did not understand the language, told her to speak in English, as she was able to do so. She replied angrily: "Does your Reverence think I will say my last words to Almighty God in the language of the Sassenachs?" The story does not say whether she received absolution or not.[84]

SECTION II

The Storm Breaks

CHAPTER FIVE

CLARE UNIONISTS AND THE FIGHT AGAINST HOME RULE

5.1 THE ESTABLISHMENT

> *I am only a poor West Briton*
> *And not of the Irish best*
> *But I love the land of Erin*
> *As much as all the rest.[1]*

Anon, 1907.

The lamenting tone of the above verse written by an anonymous Clare unionist shortly before the Great War years, projects the brooding mood of the majority of the poet's fellow county unionists in the immediate pre-war period. It is very tempting to view their lot as a fall from grace, living in a county with the highest percentage of Catholics in Ireland (98.14%, whereas the national proportion of Catholics to the overall population was 73.86%) and about to be abandoned by their northern cohorts. Yet they defended their interests with a gritty determination. In 1911, there was a total of 1,913 Protestants in Clare, 1,709 of them belonging to the Church of Ireland.[2] Analysis of its social structure depicts a tight-knit community.[3] Although this was a very minute social group in terms of numbers, it lent itself towards creating a family-like trust, and in the short term this factor proved a source of strength. The Irish unionist political organisation, the Irish Unionist Alliance (IUA), had a relatively strong and active branch in Clare.[4] The Clare Protestants based their organisation upon close social contacts and there was enough affluence in their community to fund whatever campaigns they wished to raise to support their status quo as the landed 'ascendancy' class and the loyal subjects and representatives of the British Empire in Clare, to which the vast majority of Clare Protestants belonged.

Until the break with Ulster unionism, the Clare unionists had every confidence that the third Home Rule crisis was just another cyclical threat, just another storm to be weathered until it had blown itself out. It had always been a necessity of their position to show both adaptability and endurance. While in common with most southern Irish unionists, they had suffered decline due to the rapid erosion of their landed power base under the Disestablishment and Land Acts, their prestige was still unscathed. As a social and economic elite class, the southern Irish unionists were over-represented in both houses of the British Parliament.

The Irish Unionist Alliance, as their political representation, was engaged mostly in lobbying in Britain, as only token gestures were made at home to give evidence of its existence in the south of Ireland.[5] Part of its work was to offer tours of the south for British electors, so as to press their cause for warding off Home Rule. By 1914, one or two deputations of between ten to fifteen electors were arriving weekly to inspect certain areas illustrating alleged nationalist incompetence and terrorism.[6]

The success of this work in Ireland, particularly of the tours, depended upon the enthusiasm and self sacrifice of local unionists in the small towns and villages of Ireland. They had to give a great deal of time and trouble, and also had to interview the visitors and get others to do so. One such unionist was H.V. MacNamara of Ennistymon House, Co. Clare, honorary secretary of the Clare branch of the IUA. Despite 'living in one of the worst districts in Ireland' he showed 'the very greatest pluck', making 'admirable arrangements for the receptions of tours in Ennis and in so doing splendid work for Co. Clare during the last year'.[7] So went Sir Frederick Shaw's affirmation of the vitality of both MacNamara and the Clare IUA.

Yet during and after the Edwardian period, the southern unionists continued to lose the political ground. The House of Lords' power of legislation was reduced to a suspensory veto of two years under the 1911 Parliament Act introduced by the Liberal/Home Rule Government. This encouraged Ulster unionism to forsake their counterparts in the south and prepare to negotiate for a partition settlement which would thus secure their own interests.

The Clare landlords, deprived of their tenanted lands through the 'kindness' policy of Conservative governments and Liberal legislation, began to adopt a defensive mode. The Local Government Ireland Act had already diluted their local power. Yet, as ex-officio members of Clare County Council, some of the Clare Protestants still continued to stand for their beliefs. At the inaugural Clare County Council meeting a resolution was called for the release of political prisoners. The three ex-officio members dissented from this and two other nationalist resolutions, with Major Wilson-Lynch drawing a distinction between criminal and political prisoners.[8] Some unionists also managed to get elected to local government boards such as the Scariff Rural District Council in 1912 but that was the exception rather than the norm. They were in theory still able to administer the law as JPs, but it was now customary for all the more serious cases to be tried by salaried RMs.

The Clare County Club was an institutionalised part of Protestant society in Clare, with its affluent membership that cost six guineas a year. Edward MacLysaght, a Catholic, thought it exceptional to be permitted entry into the club and saw this as part of an effort by southern unionists to enlist Catholics for their anti-Home Rule cause.[9] Radical nationalism was despised by club members and was a taboo subject.[10] The County Club committee was reorganised in response to the Home Rule crisis in June 1910. It was convened by H.V. MacNamara at Ennistymon House. Robert Studdert claimed that they would not submit to Home Rule, but that if it was forced upon them, they would accept it with bad grace.[11] It was noted that Major Wilson-Lynch (who had earlier spoken out at a Clare County Council meeting against nationalist resolutions) broke ranks and declined to become a member.

The committee was formed with Lord Inchiquin as President, Lord Dunboyne as Vice-President, H.V. MacNamara as Secretary/Treasurer and it also included Captain W. B. Molony, Marcus Keane, Beech Park and O'Callaghan-Westropp of Lismehane, near Tulla.[12] It was O'Callaghan and MacNamara who were the main movers in the committee, which was to comprise around 130 attending members. Clare, notably, was also the first southern unionist committee to reorganise.[13] At a consequent meeting at Lord Inchiquin's Dromoland Castle residence, Inchiquin alleged that 'many farmers who have recently bought their land are not in favour of Home Rule, but as they are afraid to admit it openly, it is all the more reason why those who are not afraid, should declare their opposition.' [14]

The increasing intensity of Protestant sectarianism in Ulster was causing disquiet among the majority of Clare unionists. MacNamara's speech at an Ulster unionist rally in August 1911 at Hollywood, Co. Down, in which he claimed that Protestants were being persecuted in Clare, created both fury and bewilderment among Catholics and

Protestants alike in Clare. Willie Redmond called for reasonable Protestants to disclaim the accusations.[15] Six members of the County Club committee publicly distanced themselves from MacNamara's allegations, among these being F.N. Studdert, Secretary, Clare County Council; W. B. Molony, Kiltannon; Eyre Ievers, Mount Ievers; Fitzgerald Blood, Ballykilty and R.J. Stackpoole. All of these wrote letters to the press refuting MacNamara's allegations.[16]

However, further insinuations of sectarianism were made at the following County Club committee meeting in 1912 at Dromoland Castle. W.W. Fitzgerald accused the AOH of being a secret sectarian society and claimed that the county was full of arms and was held to ransom by the "moonlighters".[17] The Protestant landlord class in Clare was vulnerable to such agrarian attacks, where activity of this nature has already been documented. Even as far back as 1763 and the Whiteboy days, Clare was noted for such attacks against Protestant landowners, these being motivated by grievances connected with the tithe.[18] It was also recorded that Protestant worship was neglected back then in Clare with fourteen parishes out of seventy-six possessing a church. Most of the rectors were non-resident and had not provided a curate, and isolated Protestants could receive no ministration except from Catholic priests.[19]

Another notable aspect of the Clare Protestant landowning class was how unusually integrated it was into society. MacLysaght stated that Clare was remarkable for the high percentage of Gaelic-Irish names among the leading Protestant landlords.[20] Conor F. Clune, in his history of the Clune family in Clare, claimed that Clare had differed from the rest of the country with regard to its landholders. It was asserted that a considerable number of them, while they had abandoned the old faith, were of 'Irish stock' and they could not forget 'their own'. Clune also wrote that it was even known for some 'new faith Irish', having become legal owners of land, to hand it back to the rightful owners.[21] John Kelly also referred to this continuity of family names in Clare, assessed previously, in his history of Bodyke. Fitzpatrick outlined how the Arthurs, Creaghs, Crowes, MacNamaras, O'Briens (Inchiquins), O'Callaghans, Molonys and O'Gormans all traced their lineage back to ancient Clare families.[23] Clare was not subjected to the same intensity of demographic displacement that was experienced in many counties, and this would account for the unbroken links with Gaelic settlement. A cursory glance at the Clare Hunt subscribers' list, which follows below, would confirm the prevalence of Clare family names amongst the unionist community.

The nature of the land violence has already been outlined. Andy O'Donoghue, the North Clare Fenian, described how it was the IRB that 'squared up' to the local landlords in his district, Inchiquin and MacNamara. He related how it was the County Inspector of the RIC (who was married to MacNamara's daughter) that ordered a baton charge against unarmed civilians who were protesting a court sentence in Ennistymon and that the British Government, to protect the landlords' interests, established a number of auxiliary RIC stations all over Clare.[24] He referred to the aforementioned landlords as being

> harsh and very much out of sympathy with the people, with each of them owning large tracts of land throughout the district which was strictly preserved for the protection of game. The gamekeepers they employed were alleged to have frequently poisoned the tenants' dogs to further protect game.[25]

Other Protestants in Clare made much contribution to the Gaelic language revival. They boasted of the Clare Protestant poet Micheál Coimín and his contribution to the county's literature.[26] As already observed, the Church of Ireland produced a Gaelic hymnal, or *Duanaire*, and magazine called *The Gaelic Churchman*, which was the organ of the Irish Guild of the Church (Cumann Gaodhalach na h-Eaglaise), which had been founded in 1914 'to provide a bond of union for all members of the Church of Ireland inspired with Irish ideals'. [27] The Gaelic League was represented on the Guild by Nelly O'Brien, grand-daughter of William Smith O'Brien and founder of Craobh na gCúig gCúigí and of the Irish College in Carrigaholt.[28] A Clare woman, she also later endeavoured to organise Protestant support post-1916 for Sinn Féin, but support was slight. *The Gaelic Churchman* did not survive her death in 1929. Along with her sister, Lucy, she had raised funds (especially from her Spring Rice relations) to enhance the Gaelic League.[29] Bishop Berry of the Killaloe Protestant Church was actually the Irish Guild's President until 1918 and later formed a new Irish language society, Comhluadar Gaodhalach na Fiadhnuise.[30]

Many from the Protestant community, away from their political world, retired into their Edwardian leisurely lives, hunting, shooting, fishing, playing games and gardening. In this world, politics did not enter into the equation. Their social life on the whole continued to be centered on social events such as the Lough Derg Regatta, spring rook shoots, tea-parties and above all the Clare Hunt.[31] An outline of the subscribers to the Clare Hunt and the expenses of staging such an event provide a useful social document on contemporary Protestant society in Clare.

Clare Hunt

SUBSCRIPTIONS FOR SEASON 1912-1913

	£	s	d		£	s	d
Ball, W. H.	3	0	0	Brought Forward	147	6	0
Blood, Honble. Mrs.	2	0	0	Maunsell, Herbert	3	0	0
Blood, Fitzgerald	8	0	0	Maunsell, Miss Ivy	2	0	0
Brady-Browne, Captain	5	0	0	Molony, B. (Ennis)	1	1	0
Brady-Browne, Mrs.	3	0	0	O'Brien, The Lady Beatrice	5	0	0
Burton, W. C. V., D.L.	5	0	0	O'Brien, R. Vere, D.L.	2	2	0
Butler, Lieut. Col. W. B.	4	0	0	O'Brien, Captain, (Cratloe Woods)	8	0	0
Carey & Co., Ennis	1	0	0	O'Brien, Mrs. (South Hill)	3	3	0
Creagh, Miss	5	0	0	O'Dea & Co. (Ennis)	1	0	0
Crowe, Mr. R. Hume	3	0	0	O'Callaghan-Westropp, Mrs	4	0	0
Crowe, Captain George	3	0	0	O'Gorman, Thomas A.	5	0	0
Crowe, Thomas, Junior	5	0	0	O'Grady, Captain S. B.	3	0	0
Dunboyne, Lord. D.L.	10	0	0	O'Halloran, P. F.	3	0	0
Ellis, R. G. E.	1	1	0	O'Loghlen, Sir Michael Bart, HML	3	3	0
Fitzgerald, W. W. A., D.L.	5	0	0	Parker, A. J.	5	0	0
Fitzgerald, W. H. W., D.L.	3	0	0	Parker, Major r. G.	5	0	0
Gore, Reginald, R. N.	5	0	0	Paterson, Marcus	2	0	0
Gore, The Lady Viola	5	0	0	Pilkington, Thomas H.	1	1	0
Greene, Arthur, M.D	1	0	0	Regan, John M., D.I.	3	0	0
Henn, Miss M	2	0	0	Roberts, A. A., C.I.	1	1	0
Hickman, Major S. C., D.L	4	0	0	Scott, James W.	3	0	0
Howard, P. J., V.S.	3	0	0	Scott, F. W. A.	1	0	0
Honan, M. S	1	1	0	Stacpoole, Miss	1	0	0
Ievers, James Butler	10	0	0	Studdert, Miss K. A.	3	3	0
Ievers, Major Eyre	3	0	0	Studdert, R. R.	3	0	0
Inchiquin, Lord, D.L.	10	0	0	Studdert, Mrs. T.	3	0	0
Joynt, R. Lane	5	0	0	Studdert, Mrs. Hallam	4	0	0
Kelly-Kenny, General Sir T., D.L.	3	3	0	Studdert, F. N.	4	0	0
Kelly, Mrs. (Ballintlea)	2	0	0	Studdert, F. N.	2	0	0
Kelly, M. F.	3	0	0	Studdert, R. O'B., D.L.	5	0	0
Keane, Charles O	1	0	0	Studdert, Captain G.	3	0	0
Kenny & Co., Ennis	1	1	0	Studdert, Loftus A.	5	0	0
Leconfield, Lord, D.L.	10	0	0	Tottenham, Lieut Col., D.L.	1	0	0
MacNamara, H. V., D.L.	5	0	0	Vandeleur, Captain A. Moore	10	0	0
MacNamara, W. J.	1	0	0	Walton, George H.	5	5	0
McMahon, James	3	0	0	White, Patrick	3	0	0
MacDonnell, C. R. A., D.L.	3	0	0	Willis, G. de L.	1	1	0
	£147	6	0	TOTAL	261	6	0

Source: Wilson-Lynch Papers, Belvoir, Sixmilebridge.
L.S. Breise, Douglas Hyde Files, Nos. 111-113, NUIG Special Collections.

ACCOUNT OF CLARE HUNT BALL – 1908

RECEIPTS

	£	s	d
103 tickets at 10s.	51	10	0
3 " at 10s. 6d.	1	11	6
Contributions to Supper	1	15	0
	54	16	6

EXPENDITURE

	£	s	d	£	s	d
Band:						
Piano & 3 men (Pigott)	6	0	3			
Carmody's Hotel	1	9	8	7	9	11
China:						
Miss Clancy				2	0	4
Cutlery:						
Mrs. Goodwin				2	16	3
Draper:						
Messrs. Kennedy, rosettes	0	2	6			
Do. Glass cloths, hairpins, &c.	0	5	1	0	7	7
Floor:						
Shanks	1	10	6			
Lambert, Brian	0	3	4			
Boric powder	0	0	6			
Porter for polishers	0	1	0	1	15	4
Furniture:						
Messrs. Cannocks & Co.				2	4	3
Lighting and Heating:						
Kenny & Co.	4	0	0			
Ennis Gas Co.	1	2	8			
Kennedy (coal)	0	3	0			
Candles	0	1	0	5	6	8
Printing:						
Messrs. Hely Ltd.	1	0	11			
Nono	0	4	6			
"Clare Journal"	0	10	0	1	15	5
Rail and Cartage:						
S. S. and W. Railway	0	11	1			
Messrs. Howard	1	10	0	2	1	1
Stamps &c.:						
Cheque Book	0	2	1			
Stamps, 1d and ½d.	0	12	8½	0	14	9½
Supper and Refreshments:						
Miss Smith	3	6	0			
Messrs. Knox	0	6	1½			
Messrs. Hassett	0	6	0			
Messrs. McDonagh, ice	0	6	3			
Messrs. Honan	4	11	6	8	15	10½
Waiters, Maids, Court and Door Keepers:						
Thomas O'Leary	1	0	0			
Lynch, 10s., Fletcher, 10s. Greene, 10s., Moroney, 10s.	2	0	0			
O'Neill, 7s. 6d; Moloney, 7s. 6d; and 6 maids, 7s. 6d.	3	0	0			
Egan, 5s; Rice, 5s; Kenny, 5s; and the Cook, 5s.	1	0	0			
Two Women Washing Up	1	5	0	8	5	0
TOTAL EXPENDITURE				43	12	6
Balance in Bank				11	4	0
				54	16	6

Audited and found correct: JAMES W. SCOTT.
10 March 1908.

W. WILSON-LYNCH, Hon. Sec.

Source: Wilson-Lynch Papers, Belvoir, Sixmilebridge.
L.S. Breise, Douglas Hyde Files, Nos. 111-113, NUIG Special Collections.

The Ulster Unionist Council had, by June 1913, decided to raise an Ulster Volunteer Force. This fateful decision, legitimising the use of physical force to attain an objective, was to open up a Pandora's box of conflict. The Protestants of Clare had always provided military officers for the British Army. The lure of adventure had seduced the younger generations of the landed classes, more so than working for Dublin Castle. They had established a tradition of servicing the Empire as soldiers and sailors. In the late nineteenth century the local press noted of the Clare Regiments of Militia who marched through Ennis:

> There is undoubtedly good stuff in the Clare Militia which could be made available for the line regiments and we hope not a few of the muscular young men who marched so proudly through our streets on Saturday may find it advantageous to themselves and their country to join some of those famous regiments whose gallant deeds will excite praise and admiration to the end of time.[32]

The arrival of a British Naval battleship into the Shannon Estuary during the Boer War and its passing by Kilrush, carrying ten large guns created much excitement. The ship's captain gave his permission for public visits to the ship as it lay anchored for ten days.[33] During the Boer War also, the Clare Artillery was the first militia artillery regiment in Ireland to be called by the War Office for garrison service.[34] However, Lieutenant Colonel O'Callaghan-Westropp of the Clare artillery,[35] previously mentioned, took it upon himself to notify General McCalmon from the Cork district, of the disloyalty he perceived in County Clare during that war and the damage it would do to his men if they were not soon deployed:

> Last May, the Clare Artillery volunteered for special service and was accepted and has a special service section including officers and permanent staff about 350 strong. The disloyal UIL will probably tamper with my men to prevent them coming up if the Regiment was mobilised. Police (three weeks prior) had reported to Lord Inchiquin, Lord Lieutenant of Clare, that "a very bad feeling" existed among the peasantry and that the more dangerous among them were ripe for a rising.
> About the same time, a large flag was hoisted near the village of Bodyke, in the centre of a very disturbed district, inscribed "success to Transvaal Republic" and it was saluted with volleys of rifle shots and I also heard that some of Dr. Leyd's money was finding its way into the country. A few days later, I was informed that two Transvaal agents were known to have been in Ennis. I don't think I have got hold of the "mare's nest". I have too many ways of gauging the local feeling and, therefore, I felt it my duty to acquaint you, as it seems to me that, if my regiment is wanted, the sooner it is called

up the better. So far, I believe no harm has been done, the temper of my men has been excellent, and I have had frequent inquiries from them as to their prospects of employment but I cannot answer for the consequences if they are left scattered amongst a thoroughly disloyal population.[36]

Yet when General McCalmon approached the Clare County Inspector, RIC, about the content of O'Callaghan's letter, the Inspector totally repudiated the allegations:

On the whole the UIL has been very inactive in the county since the war broke out. There is no doubt many of its members sympathise with the Boers, but it is absurd to say that they would tamper with the Clare Militia in the event of their being mobilised... There is not the most remote probability... under any circumstance, of any of the peasantry rising. They are quite unprepared for anything of the kind; and notwithstanding the apparent pro-Boer sympathy, the great bulk of the people have no desire for the Boers to succeed. I know for a fact that some who are believed to be "Boerites" are most anxious for the success of the British, from selfish motives (if from no higher), as they hold a large number of shares in South African mines. I conclude that the information was supplied by some person who was anxious to ingratiate himself with some ulterior object.[37]

However, Inchiquin, who was the Lord Lieutenant of Clare and O'Callaghan's ally, felt that the 'embodying of the Clare Artillery and its removal to England from their present disloyal surroundings' was desirable and that O'Callaghan's proposal should be laid before the military authorities for their consideration. It was eventually 'embodied and removed'.[38]

Ambiguity is an apt word to describe the War Office's dealings with Irish affairs prior to the War. All through, it persistently held doubts about the susceptibility of the home-based Irish regiments to the potential disaffection of the general populace in the event of war. Lord Roberts had a definite belief that it was necessary to keep an army corps in Ireland in case any disaffection arose, with the militia units raised in Ireland being transferred to Great Britain. When the militia was superseded by the Irish Special Reserve Battalions in 1915 the stationing of these units in Ireland was again been debated. The London War Office refused to entrust even the unionist classes with the responsibility of enrolling a National Reserve in Ireland for the purpose of defending the coasts from possible invasion. Sir Neville Lyttleton, who actually was in favour of a National Reserve, assessing the political situation in Ireland in 1912, wrote that 'it would be most undesirable to completely denude many parts of the country of all troops even for a few days, for were a raiding party successful in landing at that critical period, the temper of the civil population in any part of Ireland might be such that an extremely dangerous situation might arise.' [39]

So wrote Lyttleton in 1912 of the temper of the people, at a time when the Home Rule Bill was embarking upon its arduous passage through the Westminster Parliament, a Home Rule Bill that was intended to satisfy nationalist aspirations. The factors that contributed to the insecurity of the British military regime with regard to the possibility of civilian disaffection in the event of war, have already been examined. Ironically, Ireland never seemed so close to developing a working relationship with Westminster. Even Padraig Pearse had envisioned an oppositional role for the radical nationalists in a Dublin parliament and he actually spoke on a Home Rule platform with John Redmond in 1912.[40] Yet skies would darken before any form of Home Rule was realised.

5.1 WAR CLOUDS

Let Irishmen come together in the trenches and spill their blood together and I say there is no power on earth can induce them to turn as enemies upon the other.[41]

John Redmond, 1914

We must accustom ourselves to the thought of arms, to the sight of arms, to the use of arms... bloodshed is a cleansing and a sanctifying thing, and the nation which regards it as the final horror has lost its manhood. There are many things more horrible than bloodshed and slavery is one of them.[42]

Patrick Pearse, 1914

John Redmond had underestimated the seriousness of the Ulster Volunteer Force's intent. He believed in the supremacy of Westminster parliamentary procedure. However, the Curragh Army mutiny of March 1914 and the spectacular April 1914 gun-runnings staged by the UVF at Larne and Donaghadee, along with the rapid growth of the Irish National Volunteer Force, (INVF) forced Redmond's hand, as he was alarmed at the increasing militarisation of Irish society. He therefore delivered an ultimatum to the INVF, and was allowed impose his own nominees on the organising provisional committee in June 1914. The Volunteers did not initially resist Redmond as the Home Rule Bill had just completed its passage through the House of Commons and their stated function was to defend Home Rule, even though there was unease amongst the IRB element that had infiltrated the INVF at this turn of events.

The unionist community in Clare, before they had become fully aware of the designs of the Ulster Orangemen, declared their 'heartfelt gratitude to the brave men and women of Ulster for the stirring and gallant fight they are waging in defence of the Union and to their loyal and intrepid leaders'.[43] Now in April, anticipating the threat of partition, the Clare County Club passed a motion from H. V. MacNamara calling for the establishment of military garrisons for the protection of unionists from attack upon the passing of the Home Rule Bill.[44]

The Irish Home Rule Bill which the Clare unionists feared, was in itself a humble enough proposal. The Irish parliament was to have no influence on foreign affairs, no part in the fixation or collection of customs and excise, very little control over finance and no control over the police for six years. She was to have no army or navy of her own. In all of these matters, the dominions had by this time achieved practical autonomy with the exception of foreign affairs. Compared with the bills of 1886 and 1893, the Home Rule Bill of 1912, that was intended to satisfy Ireland's aspirations and to indirectly lead her representatives to bring her into the Great War to defend it, gave Ireland less immediate financial autonomy but control of her police at an earlier date. As regards representation at Westminster (she had 103 representatives under the Union), she was to have only forty-two members under the 1912 Bill, rather more than half of what would have been appropriate on a reckoning according to population. Of course, there was also the Oath of Allegiance.[45] These proposals seem quite tame in comparison with the Irish Volunteers demands in October 1914. F. S. L. Lyons commented that it was 'little more than glorified local government'.[46]

Clare republican accounts refer scathingly to Redmond's 'take over' of the Volunteers. Barrett claimed that the 'Redmondite Party' usurped the Volunteer Executive Council in June 1914.[47] As already mentioned, the Volunteers in Kilfenora actually disintegrated after Redmond's takeover.[48] The republicans claimed that Volunteer companies had been formed in most parts of the county prior to the co-opting of Redmond's nominees in June. The Clare County Inspector's report for April 1914 stated that seven branches of the INV were formed and several others were in contemplation.[49] On 26 April, 580 Limerick Volunteers with contingents from Sallymount, Castleconnell, Ennis, Sixmilebridge, Killaloe and Newport, numbering 1,285 in all, marched from Killaloe to Kincora, Co. Clare and held a meeting there.[50]

In June 1914, the Volunteer movement was 'proceeding actively' with membership over 3,000, according to the County Inspector's report for that month.[51] He also noted that 'the want of influential leaders is marked and will probably lead to dissension later on'.[52] In Kilkee, during the same month, a meeting attracted 220 Volunteers. However, Liam Haugh, in his account on the West Clare IRA, stated that 'ninety per cent of the able bodied population joined the Volunteers after Redmond's takeover and leadership of the various units was accepted by professional and influential classes'.[53]

By the time the Great War broke out, Colonel Maurice Moore of the Irish National Volunteer Force, who documented the strengths of the various Volunteer companies, stated that there were over sixty companies in Clare with over 2,500 members.[54] In June 1914, there was a Volunteer review held in Ennis at which Willie Redmond informed the Volunteers that their function was to defend Home Rule.[55] Barrett stated that Volunteers from all over the county were present for this review.[56]

The clergy availed of a Volunteer parade in Kilrush to renew old acquaintances with Colonel Arthur Lynch, MP, who had recently criticised their role in Irish society in a US newspaper. In dismissing 120 Kilrush Volunteers, Fr. O'Brien directed the instructor to tell them they were not to parade for inspection by Lynch. After dismissal most of the Volunteers went to a nearby hotel where they were addressed by Lynch, who in the course of his speech said that before long every Volunteer would be provided with a rifle.[57] Both Willie Redmond and Arthur Lynch had become aware of the vibrant possibilities of the Volunteer movement and sought to control the reins at local level. In a militant tone, Redmond told a Volunteer meeting that if the occasion warranted it, he would come back and take his place 'shoulder to shoulder with the young men of Ennis'.

At a meeting in Miltown Malbay, a few days after the Ennis review, Colonel Lynch told the Volunteers assembled there that they (the Volunteers) were necessary for securing the country. He claimed that 'a free man is a man who has a vote and a rifle. We have the votes. It is now our task to get the rifles'. He also rejected partition, which was mooted now in Tory circles as the alternative to Home Rule, and which he felt Asquith was now leaning towards, asserting that 'no final peace is thinkable which does not give us a United Ireland'.[58] A few weeks later at a meeting of the Clare companies of the Irish National Volunteers at which fourteen areas were represented, there seemed to be general agreement when John Kerin,

Ennis, insisted that the Volunteers should not be used for 'imperial purposes', as Britain was edging closer towards war in Europe.

References have already been made to the lack of guns and ammunition among Clare Volunteers. P.J. McNamara, on behalf of the Clare Volunteers, wrote the following letter of protest to chief secretary, Augustine Birrell, on 27 July 1914, regarding the Arms Proclamation the British Government had put in place:

> I am directed by the INV, Clare County Board and by Ennis Brian Boru Volunteer Corps to forward you the accompanying resolution in the hope that you may use your influence in having the objectionable act herein mentioned repealed and help to place the southern portion of Ireland in a position to possess the right to carry arms as the people in the Northern Province are. By doing so you will be acting up to the wishes of the County and all nationalist Ireland.

> That we the members of the Clare Co. Board and the Ennis Brian Boru National Volunteers call on the Government to repeal the Arms Proclamation Act as we think it an insult to Nationalist Ireland, considering that the Volunteers of the North are allowed to carry arms without being in the least way challenged or interrupted. We are strongly of opinion that the Proclamation should be immediately withdrawn, in as much as the nationalists of Ireland are acting constitutionally and within the meaning of the law and order and are a body formed for the protection of life and property. On this account, we think it is only reasonable that this objectionable Proclamation should be rescinded.[59]

Gun-running was reported at Kilkee at the end of July 1914.[60] The 'successful coup' was said to have imported 1,200 rifles and the town was 'seething with excitement' as rumours spread of ships carrying contraband of war. At the same time as this gun-running, the *Sinn Féin* newspaper advertised a 'Volunteer Holiday Camp' that was, coincidentally, running in Kilkee at the same time as the reported gun-running. Camp routine included squad, company and skirmishing instruction, swimming lessons, rifle practice and physical drill.[61] The newspaper added that 'we wish the camp well and hope that the drawbacks will be few'.[62] A week later 150 guns for the Irish National Volunteers were claimed to have been landed on several places on the Shannon from a yacht seen on the river for some days.[63] The Volunteers of the district were appraised beforehand of the landing and 'made arrangements to have the landing effected without intervention by the authorities'. The rifles and bayonets landed were said to be 'the gifts' of Limerick and Claremen domiciled in New York.[64]

Despite the reports, most Clare units drilled mainly with wooden dummy rifles.[65] To all intents and purposes, John Redmond was at the head of an unarmed political army, when World War broke out. When Britain declared war on Germany, John Redmond committed this same "army" towards supporting the British war effort. This act was to set in motion a chain of events that was to annihilate the party. Yet it can be argued that there was no other way for Redmond to steer the Home Rule ship, for he had already embraced the concept of imperialism so as to secure the passage of Home Rule.[66] It could be argued that by committing Ireland to the course he eventually took, Redmond was taking the last throw of the dice to preserve the unity of the island. He felt that the War offered the opportunity of cementing, through the bloodshed of Irish Catholics and Irish Protestants for a common cause, a lasting union between the two traditions in Ireland.[67]

Redmond initially committed the Volunteers to defending the coasts of Ireland - alongside the British. In a communication from Willie Redmond to Michael McNamara, an Ennis urban district labour councillor and the commander of the Ennis Brian Boru Volunteer Corps, the MP wrote:

> Please tell Ennis and Clare Volunteers from me that they may be called upon to protect their country and their homes. I trust that Claremen will be ready, Protestant and Catholic, to stand shoulder to shoulder, for the benefit and protection of all the people irrespective of class, creed or party.[68]

Redmond's offer to the British had impressed some Clare unionists; Colonel O'Callaghan-Westropp, one of the most notable of them, wrote a letter to the press praising the 'creditable' offer. He thought it God's blessing that 'during this emergency and for all time our local differences should be forgotten for men who have served together find it hard to think unkindly of old comrades'. He called upon the retired Clare military officers to fall into line and to help train the southern volunteers and also added that their co-operation would encourage the Government to provide arms, equipment and training facilities.[69] O'Callaghan-Westropp's view that the Volunteers in Clare were ill-equipped for modern warfare and best suited to coastal defence or "home guard" purposes was shared by those who had considered the situation of utilising the Volunteers' resources. Yet as events worked out, the Irish Volunteers were not even granted home guard duty. J.J. Lee has argued that Redmond's pledge was merely theatrical, for the Volunteers as they stood were simply raw and under-equipped and distrusted in high places in the

War Office.[70] Such distrust has already been highlighted with regard to the Clare Militia in Chapter Five.

The *Clare Journal* editorial took a jingoistic tone in its assessment of the declaration of war by Asquith:

> The Mother Country has, in fact, never embarked upon a more righteous cause.. Let us then have confidence in our defenders and in our allies - free men all, who are fighting for that very freedom of right and conscience which we have enjoyed longer than they, but of which they are proving themselves no less tenacious than we. Let everyone help. We cannot all go to war: we can all assist in the less exciting duties which compel us to remain at home - to give aid and assistance, personal or pecuniary, to those who are damaged by the inevitable working of the war-machine, to give courage to the despondent, and to help, so far as in us lies, to consolidate the brotherhood of nations to whom the written promise, the given word, are sacred to death.[71]

The Clare county inspector noted that 'great interest is being taken in the War, with public opinion on the side of England and a bitter hatred and fear of Germany exists', but he also recorded that the INV movement, gaining ground with membership at 5,200, 'do not all drill and not many of them would join the army'.[72]

Edward MacLysaght referred to the 'clever propaganda of German atrocities' that the Clare people heard from the spin-doctors of the British authorities and asserted that there was initially a rush to the colours.[73] Amidst this early rush of moral indignation, *The Leader*, D.P. Moran's extremist newspaper, cried out for calm and recollection:

> In a manner of speaking nothing has happened at all. Outwardly a change appears to have swept over the country; a new state of affairs seems to have arisen. Superficially, this is so; but to those who keep their heads and use their judgement, things remain as they were. Ireland is Ireland still. [74]

The *Clare Champion* also sounded a cautious note about the war, stating that 'the wisdom or unwisdom of her (Britain) final action can only be tested by time and results'.[75] Following upon mobilisation orders, a large number of reservists left Ennis to join their regiments at Athlone and Fermoy and various other stations. The portion of the regular army stationed in England was part of the first wave of the British Expeditionary Force to arrive in France, and Ireland itself was to be defended by battalions of the Territorial Army sent over from Britain.[76] The Munster Championship hurling semi-final between Clare and Limerick in 1914 was originally fixed for the Markets Field, Limerick, but was transferred to Mallow as the

Limerick pitch was occupied by British troops mobilising for the War (this Clare team went on to beat Limerick, Cork and Laois to claim the Munster and All-Ireland Championships).[77]

Clare INV Board chairman, J.J. O'Shea, presiding over a smaller than usual attendance of a specifically convened meeting of the Volunteers, announced that:

> there were circumstances which had changed since the last meeting. It was often said England's difficulty was Ireland's opportunity but a great change has occurred since that was said...We need no reminder of the cruelty of the Hessians in 1798, and of Claremen who died later at Fontenoy. We extend a welcome to Protestants and Unionists to join the Volunteers.[78]

O'Shea's comments indicated the relaxed attitude many Home Rulers had towards past grievances against Britain. The meeting was also informed that as a result of the departure of the army reserve men who were drill instructors for the Volunteers, consideration would be given to the use of police sergeants to fill the vacancies.[79] The secretary, Michael McNamara, stressed that the role of the Volunteers should be limited to the defence of the Irish coasts and that they should not be used for any imperial designs outside Ireland: 'we have not yet got Home Rule and we should see that Home Rule is passed before a single Volunteer is stirred for any reason whatsoever. It must be peace with honour.' McNamara also argued that a successful Britain would be in a stronger position to suppress Ireland, and a message was sent to John Redmond insisting that the Home Rule Bill should be placed on the Statute Book.[80]

In a published letter to the Miltown Malbay Volunteers, Arthur Lynch claimed that Germany was the obvious aggressor and he would like to get to the Front to help France if he could get the troops to come with him.[81] He toured his constituency at the beginning of September and expressed his intellectual and idealistic motives and fears vis-à-vis the war and warned how German victory would be detrimental to the hopes of Irish independence. He spoke further of his desire to lead a troop of Volunteers, to fight side by side with the French, arguing that the Volunteers would become a well-trained efficient force and that war was the best school of actual training.[82] However his call to arms in west Clare was met with indifference, as the majority of the Volunteers preferred to sit tight and pressurise the British into the deliverance of Home Rule.

Most of the local government bodies expressed confidence in John Redmond. The Kilrush Urban District Council endorsed Redmond's offer to the British Government, whilst also passing a resolution that the authorities should equip Volunteers not already armed.[83] A further resolution of the Kilrush UDC was that the 'responsible members of government should be implored to at once adopt stringent measures to put an end to the tactics of dishonest traders who are endeavouring to inflate the prices of the necessaries of life which will ultimately result in the dire distress of the working classes'. Indeed there were some troubled incidents in Kilrush regarding the objections of the workers of the Railway Company and Steamship to the forwarding of consignments of eggs and butter destined for the British market.[84] Kilrush UDC also sanctioned the tillage of the cricket field.[85] The Ennistymon Board of Guardians adopted the Limerick County Borough Council's resolution for the conservation of food supplies for Ireland.[86] Kilrush Rural District Council also adopted this resolution.[87]

As assessed previously, the procuring of arms was an important goal for the Clare Volunteers. P.J. McNamara informed Willie Redmond in September 1914 that the Volunteer treasurer 'is sending on nine rifles for the £20 sent to him from some time back, and there is hope for more rifles from the "American Grant".'[88] Robert Barton of the Provisional Executive was informed in a communication from the Clare INV Board of the main question posed at their most recent meeting in September; the majority of the Volunteers wanted to know what steps were going to be taken to arm them, what portion of the American aid were they to receive and when. There was also the matter of provisions being made to defray the expenses of the Board. The Board claimed that they could not lay down any levy on any corps as they were not in a position to do so.

Seemingly there was a lack of clarity on the jurisdiction and responsibilities of the various bodies within the Volunteers. Another indication of this was the confusion over the appointment of Captain James Corless as inspector officer for Clare. The Clare INV Board wanted to know if he was appointed officially by the Executive, and if so, why they were not informed of such an action, while on the other hand if he was not officially appointed they desired to be informed of who leaked the information to the Dublin press. The acting secretary of the Executive, Miss Mary Spring Rice, replied that a misprint between "Clare" and "Carlow" in a recent press release was the cause of the confusion.[89]

The Provisional Executive also informed the Clare INV County Board that it was through the chairman of the Party (i.e. Redmond) that rifles were to be obtained. P.J. McNamara hoped that brotherly understanding would clear up the problem in Clare, because, he asked Willie Redmond that if he could 'do anything in this line for us, we would be obliged, for without the rifles, the people are getting sick of the whole idea'.[90] MacNamara also required ample notice from Willie Redmond of any proposed inspection by Colonel Moore, the inspector-general of the INVF, as the county was 'very disorganised'.

The continuing delay of an inspection of Volunteers in Clare by the INV Provisional Executive irked McNamara. He wrote to Redmond:

> You yourself can inform him that visiting on a weekday would be altogether out of place, as we in Clare cannot leave our work for a review. It is puzzling that Moore has visited north, south, east and west on a Sunday but not Clare. I wonder are they afraid of being shot. If so you can vouch for their safety and urge them (officers of the INVF) on in this matter and oblige your Clare constituents.[91]

McNamara also informed Colonel Fitzroy Hemphill, the assistant inspector of the INVF that an urgent inspection was required because the Clare Volunteers needed prompt attention as to Battalion formation. He expounded upon the difficulties of weekday inspections as being 'out of the question as the majority of Volunteers were labourers and workers'.[92] By the time the review did take place, events had taken a different course.

John Redmond's supreme hour of triumph came on midday, 18 September 1914 when the Home Rule Bill was placed on the Statute Book. Its implementation was suspended, however, until the War was over and a clause was also included which would give special consideration to the north of Ireland. Despite these inserted stipulations, the county rejoiced for what was ostensibly a great victory and bonfires blazed in most areas. Redmond and his party received many resolutions of gratitude. The Kilrush RDC congratulated them on their 'great victory in getting the Home Rule Bill placed on the Statute Book... the fight for liberty has been a long and strenuous one and to the credit of the great democratic parties, has been honourably won'.[93] Kilrush UDC congratulated the IPP and our 'English allies on the consummation of Ireland's hopes'.[94]

Mr. Dan O'Brien, chairman of Ennis RDC, in a meeting at the Trade and Lecture Rooms, Clarecastle on 24 September 1914, addressed the Volunteers of the Clarecastle corps:

I consider it our duty to pass a resolution of congratulation and confidence to our able leader of the Irish Party, Mr. John E. Redmond, on the historical occasion of the Home Rule Bill receiving the Royal Assent. The 18th September will be singled out as one of the memorable days in the history of our country. On that day the terrible strife and turmoil between Great Britain and Ireland for the past hundred years, a quarrel that seriously affected this country and which kept Ireland so dissatisfied is happily ended by the placing of the Home Rule Bill upon the Statute Book. The true remedy to make Ireland a contented and loyal country was to govern Ireland by Irish ideas.[95]

The parliamentary leader upon his return to Ireland was buoyed by the many encomiums both he and his party had received. While touring Wicklow with his entourage, they made an unscheduled stop to watch the East Wicklow Volunteers drill in Woodenbridge. After an inspection, Redmond addressed them and said:

I am glad to see such magnificent material for soldiers around me, and I say to you: go-a-drilling and make yourselves efficient for the work, and then account yourselves as men not only in Ireland itself, but wherever the firing line extends in the defence of right, of freedom and religion in this war.[96]

Redmond had gone from advocating a home guard policy to a recruitment policy. The advanced element within the Provisional Executive immediately denounced Redmond. The split in the Volunteer movement technically began with the removal of Redmond's twenty-five men from the Executive following upon the action of the IPP chairman who, according to the remaining members of the Executive, had tried to use his position to direct the Volunteers into a channel that was not in accordance with the constitution of that body. Before the IPP proceeded to start a new body that became known as the National Volunteers, the most that a Volunteer who supported John Redmond could do was to resign as a protest against the exclusion of certain members of the Executive.[97]

The National Volunteers retained the support of around 155,000 people while the Irish Volunteers or "MacNeillites" had a small but hard core following of around 5,000 people. This figure was to increase to around 15,000 before the 1916 Rising. It was also noticeable that many Volunteer officers remained with MacNeill. At local level, confusion reigned with many units being neither pro nor anti-Redmond.[98] Others, like in Kilfenora, simply dropped out. For John Redmond and his party a vacuum was left that was open to exploitation, as will now be examined.

CHAPTER SIX

FROM VOLUNTEER SPLIT TO PROCLAMATION OF INDEPENDENCE

6.1 THE HOME FRONT

The twenty months between the outbreak of World War I and the Irish Proclamation of Independence is a pivotal period in Irish history. An analysis of the main players and events in Clare against the backdrop of national and international crisis projects the deeper social and psychological aspects of the county before the outbreak of sympathy for the 1916 rebels.

The reality was that there existed a hardcore element who envisioned Ireland's future as totally separate from that of Britain and who regarded any calls of allegiance to Britain and its army as anathema. The development of events over the course of the First World War was to both corroborate and enhance their position. This was vital, as the republican movement moved from token voluntarism to determinism during this period while the fabric of the body politic of the Parliamentary Party was gradually eroded. As the urgency of wartime recruitment into the British army became more pronounced, nationalists reassessed and questioned their relationship with Britain. The facade of IPP unity was not to hold in the wake of Redmond's Woodenbridge call to arms.

Some of the volunteers who did not take sides in the split soon laid down their interpretation of what their role would be in the war, such as the Bunratty unit:

> Having fully deliberated upon the condition and prospects of a united Ireland in the present painful crises, we, the representatives of upper Bunratty Corps of the Irish National Volunteers unanimously resolve that whereas Nationalist Ireland has already contributed to European strife, much more than her share and vastly more than gratitude demands of Irish blood and treasure, we recognise ourselves bound by no other military obligation than the defence of our own shores; and that in furtherance of this national object, we call upon those who have not already joined the volunteers to do so immediately.[1]

The Redmondite followers soon became known as the National Volunteers after the split. Its secretary's report for 1915 stated that 'in a short time, the work of organising on an efficient military basis, the companies and battalions made decisive progress and a Co. Board was properly established'.[2] The Clare county representative on the National Committee was Edward MacLysaght, Raheen. Their motto was 'defence not defiance'. The formation of the County Board consisted of three representatives from three battalions attached to the County Board, with the National Committee having the power to nominate two to the County Board. Each company of a battalion was represented on the battalion committee by the company captain and one elected delegate, Willie Redmond, was also on the National Committee.[3]

P.J. McNamara, in a letter to Colonel Moore regarding the October 1914 volunteer review, wrote that:

> I must mention that in regard to the volunteer corps mentioned herein, we have not got definite information that all will attend because the County has taken sides more or less in the present dispute, but at all events I think we will have the majority.[4]

A week before the review, MacLysaght wrote to Colonel Hemphill: 'I hope all will go well, but I am afraid of this split, especially in West Clare'. Michael O'Shea, Kilrush, communicated to Hemphill at the National Volunteers Headquarters: 'I regret to say that the volunteer enthusiasm in the west is somewhat dormant, but I am confident that on the days in question there will be a good muster of volunteers'. Bishop Fogarty of Killaloe, wrote to Willie Redmond: 'As far as I can gather the Clare Volunteers stand thus; Ennistymon, Carron have unanimously refused to come to the review; in the other battalions, there is a division more or less. The greater number have a majority for the Party and while the recalcitrants will not come to the review, the others will come... the parade will be an accurate account of this division. McNamara and nearly all Ennis are now right and will be there.'[5]

Patrick Linnane claimed that the Volunteers in Clare were practically all supporters of the Irish Party, including the majority of the Ennis Brian Boru Volunteers, who owing to the action of their leader Michael McNamara, had decided not to take sides at the time. He then added:

> for various reasons they object to volunteer for active service, one reason being I suppose is that they think it is safer in the "firing line" at home.[6]

89

On 25 October 1914, Colonel Moore accompanied by Willie Redmond reviewed a parade of 100 Volunteers in Ennis on a terribly wet day. Moore rejected the idea that the Volunteers would be forced to serve in the British army. Yet he added that any Volunteer who wished to enlist would not be stopped and that large numbers of young Claremen had joined regiments and were receiving training before being shipped to France.[7] Edward MacLysaght agreed with Moore's sentiments about the Volunteers existing for Ireland only; he claimed that the Volunteers could not be forced to serve abroad by any power in the world. Coincidentally, MacLysaght had a brother who was killed at the Front and Moore was a former colonel in the Connaught Rangers. Joe Barrett, the author of the Mid-Clare IRA brigade statement used in Chapter Four, had a brother Jack, who was killed in action at the Front also. That a number of the leading republicans in Clare were veterans of the Great War became a feature of the guerrilla struggle in Ireland from 1918 on.

However, dissenting voices were accumulating among the National Volunteers as the war went on. John de Courcy wrote to Moore complaining of the men getting tired of drill, and that among them were some who were not in sympathy with John Redmond.[8] The Ennis Brian Boru Volunteers, the largest corps in the county, had just over two-thirds of its Volunteers armed as McNamara revealed to the INV Headquarters in February, 1915.

> Our corps at present number 150 members, with 100 sets of equipment, including belt, bandoleer, cap, putters (blue) and haversack, khaki colour. We also have 100 Italian rifles, a few marten rifles and one Lee Enfield, along with one miniature rifle for rifle practice.

Elsewhere, all corps continued to experience a great shortage of guns.[9] On 5 November 1914, a shipment of arms designated for the NVF was detained by the British military authorities. The British replied following representations to the chief secretary and under secretary, that only such consignments as were not required for their own use could be delivered, but they tried to sweeten the dose by stating that efforts would be made to give the NVF, in exchange, rifles not using service ammunition which would 'equally well serve for purposes of training'. They justified their actions by alluding to successful 'Sinn Féin' raids on a number of rifles belonging to the loyal section as they were being conveyed under insufficient protection.[10] The military authorities urged Moore to obtain reports from local Volunteer units of the steps taken by them to store and guard the rifles and to take steps to secure uniformity in the mode of addressing consignments intended for the NVF. Moore agreed with these recommendations and reported that he was carrying them into effect. Only shotguns and genuine miniature rifles and accompanying ammunition, therefore, were permitted to be for NVF use. All else was to be allowed only with the consent of the military authorities.[11] This incident indicated the scepticism held of the NVF by the British military, although they would have had 'no objections so long as the firearms go to the charge of responsible people and are not required by the military authorities for their own purposes'.

Edward MacLysaght gave his house and grounds for the purposes of holding an NVF Training Camp in the winter of 1914-15. Previously the question of effective winter training had been a problem. A force whose members exclusively consisted of men who had to pursue their civil lives could only spare moments for training and the short days of winter inevitably led to difficulty in keeping up training. Yet MacLysaght succeeded in organising a training camp.

An average of twenty five NCOs and men were provided for in camp for two weeks and an average of thirteen officers for the same time. A number of local Volunteers attended the camp regularly but were not accommodated there, except when on guard duty. Bad weather necessitating the use of a very large quantity of fuel, the road transport of all supplies for ten miles (the canal service around Raheen Manor being stopped by floods), the abnormally high price of food and the large quantity of light required in the dead of winter all added to the expense of the camp. With the exception of an NVF camp which failed due to lack of sufficient support in Dublin, Clare was the only such camp run.[12]

The *Clare Journal* reported at the time:

Great interest has been aroused recently in East Clare by the establishment of a training barracks at Raheen Manor for the INV. For this purpose, Mr. Edward Lysaght, County Organiser, has lent his house for a period of between two and three weeks and upwards of 70 volunteers have undergone training there under the command of Captain Lysaght and the work carried out was comprehensive. Four Church parades occurred during the training period and the volunteers heard Mass at Tomgraney, Bodyke and Scariff. Though weather was not good, on the whole, no time was lost; four days were spent in the field manoeuvres, in which both officers and men had an opportunity of using intelligence and originality... As far as we can judge, perhaps the most useful lesson has been the inculcation of a spirit of discipline...It is generally agreed that the volunteers have had at Raheen Manor a better opportunity of learning the life of a soldier than has been offered to them up to this.[13]

A unionist associate of MacLysaght wrote to him upon hearing of MacLysaght's initiative, and in a patronising tone stated:

> You appear to be doing well with the Volunteer Camp, but I think the political articles in the paper are somewhat ungenerous to England to put it mildly... As it is I believe that a really generous response from your side to English efforts to do you what you call justice, a little less of the emphasis on Ireland being the sole object of your admirable efforts with the explicit corollary of "To Hell with England" and the Empire would help to convert a large number of lukewarm unionist opinion to your side and what is more give your friends a rather better opinion of Irish generosity.[14]

ILLUSTRATION

Raheen Manor National Volunteer Training Camp Schedule.

Sir,

I have the honour to report that on January 5th;

At 7.20 a.m.	I relieved the guard.
At 7.45 a.m.	I attended first parade.
At 8.15 a.m.	I inspected the breakfast of the men and found no complaints.
At 9.00 a.m.	I inspected the officers' and men's quarters and found all in order.
At 1.00 p.m.	Dinner; no complaints.
At 2.30 p.m.	I attended shooting practice.
At 7.00 p.m.	I saw guard mounted.
At 9.10p.m.	I inspected the canteen and found it closed and all in order there.
At 10.00 p.m.	Last post, the guard was turned out and inspected.
At 10.15 p.m.	I saw all lights out.
At 12.15a.m.	I inspected the guard and found all in order.
At 1.00 a.m.	The sentry man was taken off.

There is no incident to report. All fieldwork was carried out in a satisfactory manner and discipline maintained.

Yours etc.

Diarmuid Ó Coffaigh,
On duty officer, January 5-6, 1915.

To Capt. E. Lysaght,
C.O. Raheen Manor.

Source: *Mss. Moore, (10544), NLI.*

ILLUSTRATION

Raheen Manor National Volunteer Training Camp A/C.

A/C

RECEIPTS				EXPENDITURE			
Grants from National Committee	65	0	0	Ammunition	2	5	0
Officers' contributions at 17/6 p/w	21	17	6	Groceries	40	7	0
Balance debit	7	11	11	Meat	13	0	3
				Butter and Milk	8	10	0
	£147	6	0	Eggs, Fish & Vegetables	3	3	4
				Fire and Light	12	12	6
				Newspapers		18	0
				Printing of Circulars, etc.	1	7	0
				Cook's wages	4	0	0
				Wages paid for work done in repairing barracks	2	15	6
				Hiring of bedding, hardware, etc.	6	12	6
				Freight	1	1	2
				Transport	3	17	2
				Sergeant's Pay for two weeks	2	0	0
					£103	9	5
				Less provided by private subscription to cover support of Band	9	0	0
	£94	9	5		£94	9	5

*Source: **Mss Moore (10544), NLI.***

In the initial stages of the war effort on the home front, Captain O'Grady and Captain Moloney were commissioned to purchase horses throughout Clare for the army and they were assisted by Dr P.J. Howard, Ennis and Dr Kelly, Kilrush.[15] Large numbers were being purchased and trained every day, so much so that when Ireland became rife with dissent in the latter stages of the war, complaints were raised about the dearth of thoroughbreds throughout the counties at race meetings. However, in the initial stages, Clare horse dealers were jubilant with the prices they had received from the military authorities for over 200 horses by September 1914 (the price of horses rose between £25 and £45 between August 1914 and September 1914). Dr Patrick Howard who became a purchasing agent for the British army supplied horses and transport for the RIC in the barracks next door to his house which became known as "Remount Castle".[16] Potato acreage went up by 6.5% in Clare between 1914 and 1915 compared with a 40% drop between 1881 and 1914 in the same county, as tillage became more utilised.[17]

The Clare unionist community threw itself whole-heartedly in behind the war effort. Protestant women were kept busy organising the seven war charities in Clare[18], as the flower of the manhood of their class, as became their military tradition, joined the British regiments. Lady Aberdeen, the wife of the Lord Lieutenant, made the faux pas of writing a letter to the editor of the nationalist *Freeman's Journal* alleging that there was a bit of a plot amongst the unionists to capture the Red Cross society in Ireland. This letter was later published in another paper. The unionist ladies resented her suggestion that they were 'guilty of the use of a great public calamity for political purposes'.[19] The ladies of the ascendancy in Clare helped the wounded by collecting sphagnum moss, which was renowned for its healing properties and used in hospitals for dressing wounds and they also grew other such herbal remedies.

A number of the Clare country houses closed for the duration of the war. Some commentators have remarked upon the apparent fatalism or death wish shared by the sons of the Clare unionists - 'a fatalism as though they knew that their world in Ireland was dying and saw little point in surviving it.' [20] Some non-serving members showed great generosity, such as Lord Inchiquin who provided two houses for Belgian refugees who had fled the German army's occupation of their native land.

Many of the Clare unionists rowed in behind the Volunteer Force to lend assistance believing that it was for the greater good of the imperial cause. Colonel Butler of Dangan, Quin, offered his assistance to the local Volunteers corps via Colonel Moore. Butler also referred to the gross shortage of equipment, thought it would be impossible for the Volunteers to get on until the problem was remedied, although he acknowledged that they were 'really keen, well disposed and anxious to get on'.[21] Mr. Brown of Clonlay, O'Brien's Bridge, making the observation that the Volunteers, with most of their instructors called up to the army, would have no-one left to guide them, offered his help, claiming 'that it is most necessary that there should be proper control of the Volunteers. The central body must get into touch with all the branches, many of which are quite impossible'. Major Hickman, Fenloe, Newmarket-on-Fergus, claimed that:

> ... the INV scheme is badly done I think, in fact, not done at all. If I could take up the job and organise it a bit here, I am willing to do so...they know me pretty well and I think I could get the best out of them all.[22]

Yet within a month, Hickman wrote to Colonel Moore the following report:

> After seeing the report of a meeting of the Co. Board of the INVF in Ennis and that seemed to wish for an Inspector Officer of their own choosing, I sent in a wire to appoint whoever they wanted in my place - it is better so - though I could work under and with you, I do not think I could stand taking orders from some of the people who appear to be in authority on the Co. Board - I am very sure that you would not care to be under their orders... I confess I am a bit afraid of the whole thing, if it is to be run by some people I hear about here - good fellows in their own way - but it wants a different class of man at the head or it seems to me the movement will lead to great trouble in the future. I was undertaking the job to work under you and be a sort of restraining force as well as working it - but from what I gather that seems impossible. The idea among the country people here is that the National Volunteers are to be trained and armed with American rifles to be ready to fight Ulster any day! ...and the way people later encourage all this is too much I think.[23]

Hickman, whose extended family were to provide seventeen officers to the army during the Great War, continued:

> I feel awfully ashamed of us all in the south, not enlisting in the Irish divisions and this movement has a lot to do with - you should hear what people say in England - relations of mine too! But I would not mind that if I was working with you, but how could a soldier work under the class of the Co. Board - and perhaps have to take orders from 'Col.' Lynch - you know his record no doubt. I did not realise this at first but I may tell you now this is a difficult county for anyone in your or my position. I had planned a tour in the motor to every place in Clare each week to find out everything but things were too strong and I had to chuck it all.[24]

Moore asked that Hickman would not fuss; yet some members of the Clare unionist community evidently saw themselves as a type of *herrenvolk* who had to keep the disorganised and potentially dangerous, uninitiated nationalists in check. Colonel Butler, applying to Colonel Moore with regard to becoming inspector officer for the Clare NVF, wrote:

May I offer a few suggestions which I trust are in accordance with the latest 'declarations': -

1. Let us all join Lord Kitchener's army for the war;
2. As to keeping together, it might be arranged that we form one or more companies of some units.[26]

There was an obvious difference between the respective interpretations of Colonel Butler and the majority of nationalists on the role of the NVF.

During the course of the president's address at the Protestant diocesan synod of Killaloe and Kilfenora in early 1916, the bishop spoke thus:

We meet under the cloud of war still overhanging many nations and mourn the loss of many brave sons of our Empire, who, in obedience to the call of duty, counted not their life dear unto them, in order that they might fulfil the task to which their patriotism and loyalty summoned them. From our own diocese not a few have fallen, and to those mourning for them we offer our heartfelt sympathy. After two years' experience of the awful tragedies of this war we lift our hearts with added earnestness to Him, the Author of Peace and Lover of Concord, to give unto His people again the blessing of peace.

Continuing, the bishop said that it was proposed to unite the parishes of Tuamgraney and Iniscealtra, and also Kildysart and Kilmurry:

Both amalgamations are most desirable. The principle upon which, with our diminishing Church population in this part of the country, we must henceforth work to provide the clergy with a reasonable number of people to look after, with an adequate income for the clergy.[27]

J.M. Wilson made a tour of Irish counties during the war so as to represent his findings to Walter Long, the Unionist leader. He observed how local unionist organisations were flagging in the 1915-17 period, but observed of Clare that the unionists had not 'weakened in their resolve and faith and that the same fighting spirit as ever lasts, they have not thrown up the sponge but are firmer than ever.'[28] During his tour through Clare, Wilson wrote that the basis of southern unionism was a particular interpretation of the Irish and British situations in relation to Anglo-Irish interests. Asquith's government's placing of the Home Rule Bill on the statute book caused these southern unionists to lose confidence in the utility and efficacy of the British connection. There was a sense of betrayal and grievance, seemingly confirmed by the government's refusal to take a firm line with the Irish Volunteers and 'bitter feeling was engendered by the fact that little or no acknowledgement had been given by anyone in the Houses of Parliament, that the bulk of recruiting in the South and West has been from the two classes, the landlord and the lowest'.[29]

The following is a transcript of the interviews on topical subjects Wilson carried out while in Clare:[30]

CO. CLARE   23. 1. '16

PARTIES INTERVIEWED.

Lord A.   **Large Landowner.**
Mr. B.   **A land owner in extreme West.**
Mr. C.   **Local resident gentleman.**

SYMPATHY WITH ENGLAND IN THE WAR

Lord A.   *They did feel that England had committed a terrible error, but now have changed, and see what brutes the Germans are.*

Mr. B.   *Would vote exactly as their Priests and political bosses told them. Follow their leader slavishly.*

Mr. C.   *Absolutely not, there is a general disloyal feeling. General idea, it is England's war, and has nothing to do with Ireland.*

REDMOND IN FLANDERS

Lord A.   *I think it was approved, and they were very glad to read his speech in England about it, but he never came over and spoke here. I think he is more or less honest.*

Mr. B.	I think they were indifferent. The town of Ennistymon took it very philosophically. Didn't care two-pence about it. Exercise no individual opinion.
Mr. C.	Nobody bothered over his visit or showed any interest.

SUPPOSING THE BILL EMPOWERING THE RAISING OF IRISH VOLUNTEERS BECAME LAW, WOULD THEY: (A) TAKE THE OATH OF ALLEGIANCE? (B) GIVE UP ARMS AT CONCLUSION OF WAR?

Lord A.	To defend shores of Ireland would probably take Oath of Allegiance, but not much use unless good officers were appointed, no value. I think they would go to Kinsale. A percentage of arms might be given up. Great danger of an influx to escape service. I hope the Government won't take up the Volunteers. Certain amount of arms, loosened off at night.
Mr. B.	The Redmondite army, although there are splits among them, is the predominant section. If Redmond gave word would take Oath of Allegiance. Ninety percent of them might go, or might not, to Kinsale. If taken on of course they would be given good officers. As to giving up of arms, much would depend on whether they were under a proper discipline if they would give up their arms, and no one could foresee what would happen. A risky procedure. O'Callaghan-Westropp joined at the first in helping and going in with them but had to give it up, and found the idea was the officers should be promoted from their own ranks.
Mr. C.	The National Volunteers would not, I think, take Oath of Allegiance, would not leave. A danger instead of protection, no arms would be given up.

HAS RECRUITING BEEN A SUCCESS?

Lord A.   *The County has done shockingly ba[...]*
who have gone in a small way are Prot[...]
what is greatly required is to have so[...]
seen and a band on occasions, in Ennis,[...]
Clare Castle had men in the old days. [...]
loss of old Militia is a great drawback.

Mr. B.   *Co. Clare has done very badly. Even the tou[...]*
are indifferent, whole system of recruiting[...]
extremely extravagant and wasteful. The da[...]
of Volunteer is over. It is the most Roman
Catholic county in Ireland, and the most
disloyal and disaffected towards English
connection. If a tighter hand from
Government were adopted by getting rid of
four-fifths of JPs, the general tone of society
would improve and respect for the law grow
up. The Co. Court Judge personnel ought to
be changed; fifty percent of his decisions are
reversed.

Mr. C.   *Case of O'Regan, prominent Nationalist, etc.*
was prevailed upon to attend Lord Wimborne,
but would not speak, and said he could not
do so because his business would be damaged,
thus showing his feelings. I said all I could to
my workmen, only two came forward, none of
the other men responded. One yardman, said
to one of our Sergeants who is English,
referring to the King's letter: "I see your King
wants troops." Nobody hardly except corner
boys and married men, went for benefit of
their pockets, not for Patriotism. Everything
that has been done for the Empire has been
by the loyal section, and got small credit for
it.

*the National politicians were arrested in
ase they opposed, the bulk of the population
would not really resist, but they would have
to imprison half-a-dozen leaders under
Defence of Realm Act. Any man a great
firebrand ought to be "Jugged".*

*If Defence of Realm Act were put in force, and
a few leaders arrested it would be easily
carried out. Only possible machinery for
enforcing Act would be the Military
Authorities, and then there would be no
difficulty.*

*Ought to have been done long ago. I can't say
as to resistance, in the village here all are a
quiet people. It depends on the order they get
from Dublin. If shown to be a Military
necessity it would be all right. Never, never,
never could be done through the Irish Office.
Quite impossible. Birrell is hopeless. A strong
man sadly needed.*

UNIONISTS

Lord A.

*No meeting since War, if the problem arose
again the same men would turn up again.
Have not weakened in their faith. Before War,
at every meeting here all enthusiastic about
it, say 120 present.*

Mr. B.

*We are very small, but agree with above. A
bitter feeling engendered owing to little or
no acknowledgement by anyone in the House
that the bulk of recruiting in South and West
has been from the two classes, landlord and
the lowest. The former claims no special
kudos, but surely the fact ought to be
mentioned and rubbed in. I feel too disgusted
for words at times.*

Mr. C.	Very weak in this County. Intimidation is awful, not a decent shopkeeper in Ennis but is a Unionist at heart.

REDMONDITES

Lord A.	Majority are his followers. But the opponents are increasing somewhat.
Mr. B.	Sinn Féiners increasing. I would prefer a Sinn Féiner to a Redmondite, because he is an open enemy.
Mr. C.	All more or less Redmondites.

O'BRIENITES

Lord A.	A negligible quantity.
Mr. B.	O'Brien would not get a hearing. No supporters in Ennis.
Mr. C.	Very little following and could not get on a platform.

SINN FÉINERS

Lord A.	Increasing slowly.
Mr. B.	Do. do. do.
Mr. C.	Round Ennis a good few, but not many at Newmarket.

AGRICULTURE

Lord A.	Only way would be a minimum price, or a bonus, no farmer will do it out of patriotic motives. I grow a good deal of wheat but the sample is not as good as American, too wet.

Mr. B.	*Do. do. do.*
	Oats grow very well, and a big trade.
	Mangels, oats, beans, all do well.
Mr. C.	*Only if you prove to him 'twill be a benefit to his pocket, and only by doing so.*

Wages had not maintained balance with the cost of living and by early 1915 rising prices were beginning to tell on the poor. A meeting of the Clare County Relief committee heard that the hardship and distress felt in Kilkee in 1915 was primarily due to the want of employment on account of the war:

> Consequent on the outbreak of war there is no employment except for a few men who are engaged in stone breaking. The month of August has always been the month when hotel-keepers and lodge-owners made their most plentiful harvest, but on the 6th August when the news had reached Kilkee, that all Banks had closed their doors, there was a great exodus of visitors, and the majority of them didn't return. Then military men and their families left on the declaration of war. The principal hotel in Kilkee shut its doors and the other hotels and lodges did a poor and profitless business and this had fallen on the poor who lived by visitors.[31]

There were some philanthropists amongst the Clare unionists. George McElroy, RM, who could not attend a meeting held to relieve the poor of their distress, wrote to Mrs Hickman (of the officer family), 'the poor are with us always, but our sympathy with them is dormant until war comes, then they need to defend their homes, their trade and their wealth. Why should distress be allowed in Clare at present? They speak of war and hard times but the fact is that there was never more money than now'.[32] At a meeting of the County Relief committee for the distribution of relief in cash and kind, the main sources for funding, employment and relief were specified:[33]

(a)   The Prince of Wales National Relief Fund;

(b)   Grants by the Development Commissioners for schemes of improvements;

(c)   Grants from the Road Board for constructing and improving main roads.

Fr. Glynn, Kilkee, stated that due to inflation as a result of war, what a poor labourer purchased for 9s in 1914 would cost him 12s in 1915. Bishop Fogarty asserted that the ruinous circumstances amongst some of the poor people could be directly traced to the war. Clarecastle was instanced as such a place. The industrious poor were largely dependent on work connected with the shipping which came into their port, and were badly hit as this shipping had practically ceased.

Canon Bourke, P.P., Clarecastle, expounding on this point, stated that the community of Clarecastle was divided into two classes - workers and shopkeepers. Of the workers, there were twenty two men in two quays who earned their livelihood in connection with the discharge and loading of the boats, there were eleven carters dependent on the removal of goods and there were five families employed in connection with the quays, pier and the local coal store, so that they had a total of forty families dependent on this harbour. The discharge of each boat meant an expenditure from £40 to £60, the amount varying ascending to the call vessel. On an average, two vessels arrived in the harbour each month and that meant there was a loss to the village of £350 from 1 November up to late February as no vessel had, during that time, arrived in the harbour.

The poor had subsisted in this period by being practically dependent on the credit they had received from the shopkeepers, and this credit had now reached a breaking point. He felt an immediate money grant was necessary and if the shipping continued to be interfered with, steps should be taken to provide employment by means of relief work. He implored the committee, in spite of critics in Clarecastle, who called these people improvident, to grant relief to them.[34] The claim that Clarecastle had suffered as a result of the loss of shipping trade is substantiated by newspaper claims of the presence of floating mines off the Clare coast with one exploding off Doonbeg, near Johnson's Bay, which of course greatly menaced navigation to and from the Shannon.[35] Mrs. Vere O'Brien referred to those in her neighbourhood of Killaloe who were anxious to get some of the Canadian gift flour that was being distributed.[36]

In one of the ironies of history, it was noted during the war that on parts of the west coast of Clare, some of the population had become used to making a living off the flotsam, jetsam and oil from sunk ships.[37] The submarine ship which sank most of these ships, was, as previously recounted, the invention of west Clareman, John Philip Holland from Liscannor. The flagstone trade from Holland's native village also collapsed during the war years.[38] The civilian casualties arising from U-boat activities off the Irish coast impacted upon the public imagination. Bernard Hynes, who served as a

103

doctor in the Royal Army Medical Corps in the Great War, lost his father and his sister Claire, who both drowned following the sinking of the *SS Leinster* which was on its way to Manchester, where the Hynes family had interests in the drapery business (they also owned a drapery business in Tulla, Co. Clare). Locals remembered Claire saying 'she was packing her bags for the fish' when she learned that she was to accompany her father to Manchester. It was also recalled how the wailing sounded out from the women at the telegraph office as the news of the sinking came through.[39]

There was an influx of Belgian refugees into the county since the German invasion. In November 1914 a concert was held in Ennis to aid them. There were by January 1915 eleven Belgian refugees resident in Clarecastle, the Nissens and their three children and the Van de Veldes, their three children and their grandmother. They were of an artisan class and were natives of Antwerp.[40] They spoke Flemish and broken French. As well as Lord Inchiquin providing two houses for the refugees, another house was provided in Sixmilebridge. By March 1915, the Ordnance House was accommodating refugees. Several of the refugees offered classes in French to make a living and the boys who reached military age returned to their native land to fight.[41] In November 1915 another fund-raising concert was held in Ennis.

Natives of the Central Powers were apprehended for not registering with the relevant authorities and were promptly dispatched to Cork where Germans and Austrians had been detained since the opening of the war.[42] Two such emigrants were arrested at the Golf Links Hotel, Lahinch where they were employed as chefs. In Lisdoonvarna, the chefs employed at the Imperial, Queen's and Atlantic, along with four other German and Austrian residents in Lisdoonvarna, were all brought to Ballyvaughan under police escort where they were formally registered under the New Order. This meant that they could not leave their places of residence, unless on permit and this pass was only valid for twenty-four hours. Similar internments also occured in Ennistymon and other towns in the county. On 23 October 1915, Mr. Joseph Maurer, the principal jeweller in Ennis and Mr. Clement Dilger, a local watchmaker, both of whom were Germans, were removed by the local police for internment in Oldcastle, Co. Meath. Mr. Maurer had been about twenty eight years resident in Ireland but had never taken out naturalisation papers. Mr. Dilger had been living in Ennis for about thirty years. [43]

The British military authorities were wary of the threat of invasion along the west coast and by the Shannon. Notices were given to the people on evacuation procedures, indicating where they were to proceed to.[44] The inhabitants were informed that in the event of a hostile landing being attempted or effected, the farmers would remove their stocks, provisions and all implements that would be of use to the enemy immediately.[45]

On the recruitment issue, Willie Redmond had announced that he was joining the "Irish Brigade". 'I can't stand asking fellows to go and not offer myself, he told his friend J.J. Horgan.[46] Expressing his three principal reasons for enlisting, Redmond firmly believed first of all, that Ireland's best interests were bound up with the allies; secondly, he did not want Ireland's name disgraced and, thirdly, Ireland had to be true to her treaties, which he believed the Home Rule Bill to be.[47] Expanding on this, Redmond referred to the state of peasant proprietorship that now existed in the country. In February 1915 he joined the Royal Irish Regiment and wrote to his ally, P.J. Linnane:

> I am far too old to be a soldier but I will try my best. I believe the men of Clare will approve of my action. If they should not, then I shall part with nothing on my side but the warmest gratitude for the unvarying kindness shown to me by the people I have done my best to serve for twenty-three long years.[48]

Another prominent local politician who enlisted, in March 1915, was Lieutenant Daniel O'Brien, Clarecastle, a National Volunteer officer, a member of Clare Co. Council and chairman of Ennis RDC. A rumour circulated that he was wounded in the buttocks while training.[49] It was notable that the local media was gagged with regard to this embarrassing affair for fear of adverse propaganda. Each of these politicians were not to survive the war.

The *Lusitania* was sunk on 7 May 1915. There is much contemporary debate on this ship today as to whether or not it was carrying military supplies from the USA to the British mainland. In any event, there was gross loss of life. One of those from Clare who drowned was Dr Joseph Garry, brother of Dr M.P. Garry, the well-known Irish international rugby player. He was the tuberculosis sanatorium doctor for Clare. A report said he gave away his lifebelt and attended to the wounded while the ship was sinking.[50] MacNamara has claimed that recruiting for the forces was at a high point in Clare in 1915 and that following the sinking of the *Lusitania*, recruitment rose in

Ennis to forty a day and that Major Wilfred Dulcken had recruited over 2,000 men at the Ennis Depot between 3 February and 14 June 1915. The *Clare Journal* depicted an image of the diabolical "Hun". It printed a letter from an Ennis man in the Army Veterinary Corps at the Front, with scaremongering obviously in mind; an extract read that 'some prisoners were brought in here last week and on being searched by one of our fellows, one was found to have in his haversack, wrapped up in a handkerchief, a lady's hand, with five rings on the fingers.'

The aforementioned Lieutenant Daniel O'Brien, who was now serving with the 8th Royal Munsters, which was the battalion reserved for NVF recruits, made a poignant appeal for recruits. 'Many Claremen,' he said, 'who were in the flesh a few months ago, who are now living under foreign soil, must be honoured.' The enlistment of John Fox, Newmarket-on-Fergus, a member of the 1914 All-Ireland hurling winning team, was a minor propaganda coup as was the enlisting of P.E. Kenneally, the man who had succeeded O'Brien as chairman of Ennis RDC. [51] Ironically Fox was no longer eligible to represent his county due to the ban on the British military playing GAA games. The band of the 8th Battalion of the Royal Munster Fusiliers visited Ennis twice, while the Irish Guards Fife and Drum Band also paraded. The Canadian Prince of Wales, Leinster Regiment, marched through the county and the military authorities made much of the propaganda value of the award of the Victoria Cross medal to Sergeant Michael O'Leary who was fêted on his return to Ireland from the Front.

Patrick Lynch, KC, in seconding a resolution that the Solicitors Apprentices Debating Society was worthy of support by the government due to sacrifices made by its members in the war, said:

> It is difficult to speak of the outrages committed by German Armies but it is not now a question of talking (applause). I am satisfied that wherever there are men who are worthy of the name, they will draw the sword in defence of right and justice and avenge the outrages that have been committed during the last 15 months by the devastating hand of German oppression.[52]

Lynch was to be de Valera's opponent in the 1917 by-election.

The war had also managed to rouse some enthusiasm in old veterans. One such veteran wrote to the Lord Lieutenant on 27 October 1915:

> My Lord Lieutenant, I trust you will excuse me for applying to your Excellency for some possession (sic) in the army under the new conditions. I beg to

state I was discharged by purchase twice from the Army (sic) the second time I had two years, and 168 days I left a non-Commission Officer with an exceptional good discharge. I am in good health thank God. I am an all round handy man would take any job about barracks or stores to relieve younger men - or would do better - carrying, willing to join any core (sic) for term of war. I beg to state I have a son and daughter with Canadian Army, my daughter is a nurse. I also have six nephews serving. I am over 60 years of age.[53]

Some Clare farmers resented the tag of slackers with which the recruiting bodies and military authorities labelled them. At a Clare County Council meeting in mid-April of 1915, voluntary recruiting was on the agenda and a deputation of the County Clare Recruiting committee was received, amongst them Lord Inchiquin, Colonel Sir Charles Barrington, DL and P.J. Linnane, JP. The deputation wanted a resolution passed which would assist them in getting recruits in the county. Opposing this motion, Mr. Crowley, cllr. (and farmer) stated:

I'm sorry to hear that the farmers are put down as slackers. The duty of the farmer is to till the land. Well how is he going to till the land if the Council advised him to join the army? To my mind, the resolution is wanted on paper for the purpose of holding up before the Government and proving there are men available in Clare. There are no available men in the County of Clare. If the number of farmers who had joined was compared with the number of shopkeepers' sons, the farmers would have doubled and trebled them. I ask the Council not to pass the resolution, as if they do, it would be calling for conscription purely and simply. Home Rule has been promised when the war is over but "get a horse and you will get grass". I do not believe any resolution they adopt would be responsible for a single man joining the army. The men are wanted in the country and it would be an everlasting disgrace to the Clare County Council if the resolution is passed.[54]

A resolution was passed by thirteen votes to six by the County Council expressing sympathy with the objects of the deputation and agreeing to form a Central Committee of Voluntary Recruiting for Clare, to consist of the members of the council and members of the existing committee. Crowley, a native of Tullagower, Killimer, in the course of his statement (which was inadvertently contradictory because he first said there were no men available, and then proceeded to attack the shopkeepers' sons for not contributing their fair share) expressed what was the consensus of the majority of the rural population.

A motion of sympathy was passed upon the death of Major Hickman in March 1916 by Ennis RDC and following the death of Captain Gore-Hickman, a similar motion was passed in September

1915 by Kilrush RDC. Further motions of sympathy were also extended towards the family and friends of O'Donovan Rossa by Kilrush RDC and Clare County Council in mid-1915.[55]   In April 1915 the East Clare UIL Executive passed a vote of confidence in the policies of John Redmond and, at a Dublin rally for the NVF, companies from Ennis, Barefield, Miltown Malbay, Lahinch, Ennistymon, Killaloe, Mountshannon and Scariff attended. On 25 May 1915, a wartime coalition was set up in Britain which included Carson and Bonar Law, sworn enemies of Home Rule. John Redmond had previously rebuffed the opportunity of joining. Yet, given Redmond's previous course of actions, to have joined the Coalition would have been a natural progression. The move did not gain him any more admiration in Ireland, whilst it excluded the party from all vital politico-military decisions that were being made. Colonel Lynch stated that 'certainly my task does not appear difficult to point out the danger to the Home Rule cause, considering that a Government is in power that reckons as one of its ornaments, Sir Edward Carson himself'. He maintained that the Liberals had become subdued by the 'vain threats' of the Conservatives.[56]

In October 1915, Colonel Lynch published his book called *Ireland-Vital Hour,* which surveyed in his idiosyncratic manner the cultural history of Ireland. The author himself admitted that his book was to some extent a departure from his usual style in that he claimed he never dwelled too much on history, because, like his many fellow nationalists who now had a tolerant view of perceived grievances, he felt the past was irrecoverable.[57] Having condoned the Fenian movement, Lynch went on to describe Parnell as a 'cold-blooded sensualist and a dictator' despite having once been a Parnellite himself. Yet it was his views on the role of the priests in Irish society and his criticism of the *Ne Temere* decree that was to set in motion the process of Lynch's ostracisation in West Clare. The *Clare Champion* led the chorus of condemnation:

> We regard Mr. Lynch's bitter and insulting attack on the Irish Catholic priests as wholly undeserved and sufficient to oblige any decent nationalist to turn from his false doctrine in disgust.[58]

The paper went on to claim that he was 'totally unworthy to represent a Catholic constituency and that it did not expect such an action from a member of the Irish Party'. Against these weekly bombardments, Lynch pleaded in turn that he was misunderstood by his critics. He felt that Ireland's future was greater 'than that of even the brightest pages of the past... a live Irishman of 1916 was worth more than a dead Cromwell of a century previously'. However, the *Clare Champion* dismissed Lynch's claims as 'not washing' with Claremen. It found in Lynch's historiographical essay 'a slobbering tenderness for Ireland's worst oppressors and a very different spirit when dealing with the most honoured names among Ireland's mightiest dead'.[59]

Fr. Monahan, Crusheen, who was one of Lynch's earliest advocates, denounced Lynch and publicly apologised 'to the honest nationalists of West Clare for foisting him on them'. Lynch paid his first visit after the publication to his constituency in early February 1916. It was remarked that 'never in political history has an Irish MP received such an icy reception by a body of representative constituents'.[60] His coming went unannounced in the local press. Despite sending private wires to some of his supporters, informing them of his pending visit, no attempt was made to welcome him at the railway station in Ennistymon, the frontier town of his constituency. On his house-to-house visits he was totally on his own. The chilling nature of his reception indicated the offence taken by nationalists to his book, which some local satirists lampooned as 'Ireland-Fatal Hour'. His reception at a meeting of the Ennistymon Board of Guardians was 'distinctly frosty and his presence created an awkward and uncomfortable situation'.[61] Lynch was informed by some of the members at that meeting that he had abused their confidence, offended their feelings, and merited their censure. When Lynch claimed that a great deal of Englishmen who figured in Irish history had good intentions towards Ireland, the chairman claimed that 'the good intentions were to wipe it out', and he went on to add that Lynch 'had thrown mud on every good Irishman and has even gone so far as to question morals. Our priests, our heroes did not escape'.[62] Lynch's desire that Ireland should ultimately 'reach a position of entire friendliness with England.. .whilst advancing the flag of Ireland' was to become an unfulfilled hope,[63] and his future actions were to complete his alienation from the people he represented.

6.2 INDIFFERENCE AND RESISTANCE

The Clare County Volunteers Board never officially split. According to Liam Haugh of the West Clare IRA, the professional and intellectual classes who initially accepted leadership, accepted

Redmond's declaration in favour of Britain, but when they 'endeavoured to impose their views' on rank and file, the Volunteers simply deserted en masse, and the Volunteers, as such, disintegrated.[64] Joe Barrett estimated that about one-third of the Volunteers in Clare gave their allegiance to the Irish Executive under Eoin MacNeill. They opposed recruitment by every means possible.[65] However for seven or eight months after the split matters did not go too well for the Irish Volunteers in Clare; but they gathered strength while the Redmondite section of the Volunteers weakened. These Redmondite Volunteers carried on in their own units. Early in 1915 they were said to have deteriorated to such an extent that some of them handed over arms to the Irish Volunteers.

Barrett remarked that not many of these rifles were of much use for action and from the Mid-Clare IRA brigade's experience only twelve to fifteen of the guns from this hand-over were to be of any further use - these mainly being Martin Henri rifles. During 1915 the Irish Volunteers in Clare absorbed many ex-Redmondites. The Volunteers sought to procure guns by removing them from the ownership of soldiers home on leave who were allowed to carry their rifles and equipment into their homes. In this way, they collected another dozen rifles until the authorities banned soldiers from bringing their rifles home while on furlough.[66]

Peadar Clancy was a prominent gaelic leaguer and republican, who was to meet his death at the hands of his captors during the War of Independence. A native of Cranny, he referred to the divide in Irish society over the war issue in a letter to his brother M.J. in Chicago:

> There is a very vast range of subjects on which I should like to write to you about; particularly with regard to the great European war. There has been a very pointed and sharp division of opinion in Ireland with regards to it, created to a very great extent by the attitude that Mr. Redmond has taken up. I understand that diversity of opinion obtains to a very great extent in America too, but our sources of information from America are altogether one sided in this country since the Government has prohibited the circulation of the Irish World and the Gaelic American in Ireland. As I write the one hope is the American note to England and France. It is evident to everyone that it raises very serious complications for the latter countries. Germany is making a very great struggle and with the co-operation of America it is difficult to hazard an opinion as to the ultimate result of the war. I expect America is pretty much agitated by now. Please write soon and let me know your opinion on the whole affair.[67]

After the Redmondite split, the IRB cemented itself as a strong organisation in Clare. Some republicans opined that the Volunteers

110

would have had a hard time overcoming the opposition were it not that the IRB was the backbone of the Volunteer force and that practically all officers belonged to the IRB. The IRB had a ban imposed on it by the Catholic Church and republican veterans opined that this ban would have had a serious effect on both the Volunteers and the IRB if the IRB members had not been advised that 'any action taken by men for the freedom of their country was no sin and that they need not disclose their membership to their confessor'.[68]

Michael Brennan organised a Volunteer company in his home parish of Meelick in 1914. To his surprise he enrolled many recruits. He organised another company in Oatfield, about three miles from Meelick. As there was nobody else with sufficient experience, Brennan had a hard time training three companies (Limerick was the third company). In 1915, he began using existing units as organising agencies. The procedure was to march them on Sundays to suitable points such as centres where sporting events had gathered crowds. None of the men were in uniform but many of them had shotguns. Brennan often borrowed a piper from Limerick for these occasions. Once a tin whistle was even used.[69] Yet all this promoted interest. One Sunday, after "softening up" (marching and drilling in the village occasionally and having talks with prominent locals), they marched about ten miles to principal Mass in Kilkishen. After Mass, they formed up outside church, and following an appeal for recruits, over one hundred names were handed in. He (Brennan) arranged for drills and he cycled there frequently after that to carry out these drills. In a similar manner Irish Volunteer units were organised in Clonlara, Cratloe and Sixmilebridge and then with bicycles they went farther afield and established units in Newmarket-on-Fergus, Tulla, Scariff, Ogonnelloe, Clarecastle, Ennis, Crusheen, O'Callaghan's Mills. In Feakle, Thady Kelly established a Volunteer company and as an act of defiance against police prosecution for drilling, about 150 young men flocked into it.[70]

In June 1915, Ernest Blythe visited Clare. According to British intelligence, Blythe had boasted that he enrolled 5,000 members of the IRB in Ireland. The chief secretary, Augustine Birrell described him as 'one thousand times more dangerous than newspapers and spouters of sedition at the street corners'.[71] He came to Clare as the Irish Volunteer organiser - a job for which Barrett praised him. The RIC followed him everywhere and they advised hotel proprietors not to take Blythe in.[72]

Andy O'Donoghue recalled Blythe issuing each Volunteer with a membership card and establishing new Irish Volunteer companies in Doolin and Liscannor, yet having no joy in establishing a company in the town of Ennistymon, as most of the old company followed Redmond into the National Volunteers.[73] Blythe was eventually deported under DORA because of his activities in Clare. Liam Haugh referred to organisers from Dublin setting west Clare up as a battalion area with Art O'Donnell, Tullycrine, as C/O. Training was most intensive in the Carrigaholt area where the Fenian tradition was strongest. About a dozen rifles were landed here towards the end of 1915, off a cargo boat. They were encased in a coffin and were secreted at night in the local curate's house.[74]

Bishop Fogarty in an Episcopal letter to the clergy and laity of the diocese of Killaloe outlined the Church's stance on the war from the outset of hostilities:

1) On Sunday and on the first Sunday of every month, until further notice, the Litany of the Saints be recited after public Mass for the cessation of the war, the safety of our friends, the welfare of our country and let the congregation join in aloud in these prayers.

2) ...Finally, we beg our people, unlike the thoughtless Press we daily read, to be charitable in their language about the enemy in the war, remembering that in big struggles of this kind, there is always something to be said on both sides and that each nation is fighting for that which, according to their lights they consider essential for their national life.[75]

It was the influence of Dr Fogarty that was to help to accommodate the inter-changing between the political and the Irish-Ireland movements and also to keep the fine line between the two in check, as the Volunteer movement seeped through the various political bodies and strata in the county. Fitzpatrick's research indicated that of the twenty-two known Volunteer priests in Clare, two were associated with the Hibernians and three with the UIL. Of the 311 lay leaders of the Volunteers identified, twenty-five were also prominent in the Hibernians and twenty-one were United Irish leaguers. Among the Volunteer rank and file, the proportion of leaguers and the Hibernians was much higher.[76] But it was the leaders, more than the rank and file, who were the pipers of the three organisations and they all ensured that these would march to the one tune.[77] The Volunteers did not have to become an overtly political organisation.

Bishop O'Dwyer of Limerick was stung by Redmond's refusal to associate himself with Benedict XV's efforts for peace. Furthermore, the omission of any mention of either the Pope or Ireland in

The Carrahan Banner, one of the earliest known GAA artefacts, dating from 1888. In a nod to military tradition, it was played for as a trophy, with the Tulla hurling team winning the first Carrahan tournament as gaelic games became regulated accross the country.

(Courtesy of Micheál King, Tulla, Co. Clare)

Clare World War I veteran, Private Joseph Molloy, with his combat medals which included Boer War medal, Service medal, WWI medal and Victory medal.

(Courtesy of Christina Finn, Ennis, Co. Clare)

Douglas Hyde addressing a rally in Ennis, 1909

(Courtesy of Peadar MacNamara, Inch, Co. Clare)

Subs.—JOHN RODGERS, Tulla;   PATRICK McDERMOTT, Whitegate;   PATRICK MOLONY, Feakle.

THOMAS McGRATH, O'Callaghan's Mills;   JOHN FOX, Newmarket;   ROBERT DOHERTY, Newmarket;   MICHAEL FLANAGAN, Quin;   JAMES CLANCY, Newmarket;   JOE POWER, Quin.

J. GUERIN, Newmarket;   PATK. McINERNEY, O'Callaghan's Mills;   W. CONSIDINE, Ennis;   AMBY POWER (Capt.), Quin;   M. MOLONY, Ennis;   ED. GRACE, O'Callaghan's Mills;   J. SHALLOO, O'Callaghan's Mills.

BRENDAN CONSIDINE, Ennis;   SHAM SPELLISSY, Ennis.

Training Committee—Rev. Father W. O'Kennedy, Rev. Father M'Creedy, C.C., Quin; James O'Regan, J.P., Chairman Clare County Council; Dr. Fitzgerald, Dr. M'Donagh, John Jones,

Clare 1914 All-Ireland Hurling winning team

(Courtesy of John Ryan, Cratloe, Co. Clare)

Royal Munster Fusiliers on a recruiting tour in Ennis, 1915

When the Russo-Japanese war broke out in 1904, the five Japanese submarines seen here, which formed the first Japanese submarine force, were ordered by the imperial government from John Philip Holland. They were built in Massachusetts, dismantled and shipped to Japan where they were reassembled at Wokosuka., near Yokohama.

(Courtesy of the National Maritime Museum, Dun Laoghaire)

Clare volunteers in the Red Cross pictured on St. Patrick's Day
during the Great War.

Willie Redmond's grave at Locre, Belgium

(Courtesy of the Somme Heritage Centre)

Pappy Neville, the last surviving Ennis soldier of WWI, at his home in Beechpark during the 1930s. A pre-war regular soldier with the Royal Irish Regiment, he entered the trenches on Christmas Day 1914. He was not relieved for several days and suffered frostbite, which necessitated the amputation of his feet.

Many veterans developed drinking habits having been plied with rum in the trenches. It was remarked upon that Mrs. Neville would sometimes threaten to take Pappy's leg if he was about to indulge himself! His last years were very comfortable as he was one of the last beneficiaries of British Legion funds.

(Courtesy of Peadar MacNamara, Inch, Co. Clare)

Eamon de Valera during Clare 1917 by-election.
Note the RIC presence in foreground.

(Courtesy of the Keogh Collection, NLI)

Clare hunger strikers pictured with Eamon de Valera.

(Courtesy of Peadar MacNamara, Inch, Co. Clare)

Redmond's reply, regarding this initiative, he found particularly offensive. He wrote to Fogarty to express his displeasure with the Irish leader, who, 'like a true Imperialist, had referred to the Germans in his letter as "our enemy".' The Bishop of Killaloe agreed with his colleague's appraisal of Redmond and stated that 'the Party had bent very low when they were afraid either to mention the name of their own country or of the Pope, lest they should offend "our allies".' However, to some extent, O'Dwyer seems to have sympathised with the dilemma in which Redmond found himself. Writing again to Fogarty he defended Redmond insofar as he had been caught in a 'cleft stick' and could not budge. If he had mentioned the Pope he would have been considered a 'genuine Catholic' by his English allies and, as such, would not have been trusted to implement Home Rule impartially.[78]

Only four priests spoke out openly against recruiting before the Rising. These were Fr. John O'Dea, CC, of Bodyke, Fr. Culligan, CC, Carrigaholt, Fr. Marcus McGrath, CC, Ballyea and Fr. Maher of Killaloe and Garranboy. Fr. John O'Dea on 13 June 1915, from the altar, **advised members of the hurling team to go to the bank in Scariff and buy guns and learn how to shoot straight, and resist conscription by every means in their power instead of being led like sheep to the slaughter.** No action was taken against him for this outburst. Fr. Culligan was known to have identified himself with the Sinn Féin movement in his locality (one bears in mind the coffin of rifles said to have been hidden away at his house by local republicans), while Fr. McGrath, during Mass on 4 October 1914, told the congregation that they should not believe 'all the stories of German atrocities and that the victory of the Allies might not be helpful to Catholicity'. Fr. Maher of Killaloe and Garranboy was also alleged to have given a seditious sermon.[79]

When it seemed that Redmond had been out-manoeuvred after the formation of the wartime coalition, a disgusted Bishop Fogarty wrote the following to the IPP leader, which Redmond in turn showed Asquith how 'intelligent' people were thinking in Ireland:

This coalition with Carson on top is a horrible scandal and an intolerable insult on Irish sentiment, and greets the efforts of coalition to make a place for Campbell; 'such hideous jobbery'! The English having got all they wanted from Ireland, didn't care two pence about her feelings. Such is our reward for her profuse loyalism and recruiting. The people are full of indignation. The Party, to my mind, a great mistake, have taken the whole thing lying down without a bit of fight. Worse still, in their proclamation immediately after it, they declared they would support coalition and Carson and indulged in the usual nonsense about England's struggle for small nations. Little she cared for small nations as far as Ireland is concerned. There is nothing to choose between Carsonism and Kaiserism, of the two the latter is the lesser evil; and it almost makes me cry to think of the Irish Brigade fighting, not for Ireland, but for Carson and what he stands for. Orange ascendancy here.

Home Rule is dead and buried and Ireland is without a national party or national press. The Freeman is but a government organ and the national party but an Imperial instrument. What the future has in store for us, God knows. I suppose conscription with a bloody feud between people and soldiers. I never thought that Asquith would have consented (to this ruin). There is a great revulsion of feeling in Ireland...this you should feel yourself, I am sure, without my sad and angry tale.[80]

Fogarty had become disillusioned with the Party and he despaired of the war:

It was a pity this outbreak of war upset things. ...Perhaps it was all God's will that things should be like this, so that people would again be brought back to the simple life, and that the war and the consequences of it would burn to ashes the luxury, sensuality and extravagance which had begun to over-run the whole of Europe.[81]

When enclosing a subscription to the radical newspaper, *The Leader*, Fogarty also wrote:

Without The Leader, what is left of Irish sentiment in Ireland just now would be badly off for an honest spokesman.[82]

Anti-war sentiment was growing rapidly by late 1915. The undercurrent of discontent that was to manifest itself in the wake of the 1916 executions can be seen in the shape of various incidents taking place in every part of the county. Patrick MacNamara was arrested under DORA on the occasion of the return of the Royal Munster Fusiliers band under Captain Roche from a recruiting tour. As the band proceeded through Ennis, MacNamara, from Ennistymon, shouted - 'Are there any German recruits among you?' and was subsequently taken into custody. Billposters, Thomas Crowe and Patsy Carey, were respectively fined £5 bail and two sureties in £2 10s each in Ennis and Kilrush for covering recruiting posters. Carey argued that 'others did it and got away scot-free'. A big exodus was reported from west Clare in 1915, principally the young men of the farming class, leaving Kilrush terminus en route for America on account of rumours of imminent conscription.[83]

G. R.

A PROCLAMATION!

By GEORGE V., King of England

To Our Faithful Irish Subjects,

We are at present engaged in war With Our first cousin, the Emperor of Germany. We hate the Germans, because Our father, Our grandfather, Our grandmother, and all our ancestors were Germans, and every sensible man now-a-days hates his ancestors!

YOU, ALSO, OUR BRAVE IRISH, HAD ANCESTORS blood-thirsty rebels, who wanted to own Ireland for themselves, and be separated from Our Glorious Empire ; but our predecessors on the Throne of England (who were all Germans by birth o rby descent) got rid of these narrow-minded savage ancestors of yours. They flogged, hanged, and burned them in '98. They starved them in '48, and brought the food across to feed our Free-born Britons (for Ireland was England's larder then as now). They shipped a few millions who survived the Famine out in Coffin-ships across the Atlantic, and most of them were thrown overboard, and their bones lie whitening at the bottom of the ocean. A few weeks ago, in Dublin, We managed, with the aid of Our Own Scottish Borderers, to let all who had any recollection of ancestors left, know that We were prepared to clear them out root and branch, and to spare neither women nor children in the clearance.

NOW, OUR BRAVE IRISH, We know you don't want to be reminded that these men were your ancestors, anymore than Our Royal Self do that We are German by blood.

WE WANT MEN TO FIGHT THESE GERMANS, and We know from history that the Irish are a Fighting Race. A large number of your Countrymen have been sent to the Front to fight the Germans. THE MOST OF THEM HAVE BEEN KILLED, BUT THEY DIED NOBLY FIGHTING FOR US AND OUR EMPIRE. We want more to fill their places, and ONLY IRISHMEN WILL GET THE POST OF HONOR. Come and volunteer for the Army at once and We will arrange that you will be sent to the Front and Killed ; if you are not killed, when you are no longer of any use for fighting, Remember the British Laws—the Poor Laws—have provided for your up-keep in the Workhouses of Ireland.

Remember the Empire comes first and the Poorhouse after, you survive the War. GEORGE R.I.

GOD SAVE THE KING

Anti-Recruitment Poster, 1914.

Source: National Archives, Registered Papers 1914, no. 22394

115

Table 5:

Return of number of young men of military age who are believed to have emigrated to USA owing to rumours of conscription.

	To end Oct 1914	Nov '14	Dec '14	Jan '15	Feb '15	Mar '15	Apr '15	May '15	June 1-15th	Total
Clare	5	3			2	3	4	47	64	128
Munster	108	56	1	17	11	24	84	76	111	498
National Totals	885	156	19	39	44	106	189	367	405	2211

Source: National Archives; Crime Special Branch Reports, 1913-17.

There were some Claremen who defected from the British army before the Rising for various reasons. In June 1915, an Ennis youngster, who had been arrested for desertion, escaped from the Ennis Barracks and was at large. The police paid a surprise visit to his house in the Market, Ennis and caught him there. As they were about to remove him in custody, his father had a sudden seizure and died.[84] A Lissycasey native, was charged with being an absentee under the Military Service Act at the Ennis Petty Sessions. Sergeant Gunning said that in April 1916, the defendant told him he was registered at Stamford St., London, but claimed exemption from the Military Service Act on the grounds that he left London in October 1915 and came home to work on his father's farm. He had worked six years in London as a clerk in a drapery establishment. Eventually when the evidence closed, Mr. McElroy, RM, said he would avoid sending the defendant to Limerick Prison if he agreed to join an Irish regiment. The defendant refused to reply and an order was then made that he be handed over to the military authorities in Limerick.[85] The only Clareman executed during the war was Private Thomas Davis, Ennis, 1st Battalion, Munster Fusiliers. On the dawn of 29 July 1915, Davis was summarily shot for abandoning his post during the Gallipoli campaign, despite having endured three months of heavy fighting. Ennis RDC resolved on 8 December 1915:

That we, the members of the Ennis Rural District Council, while we have no objection to any person or persons who care or wish to join the British army to do so, we are opposed to conscription in any shape or form. That conscription if applied to Ireland would mean a repetition of the Famine and Plagues of 1847.[86]

Fr. Tomás Ó Maolmuidhe presided at a conference of Clare Irish Irelanders in Ennis during the first year of war. The business of the conference was to review the work done for the language revival in Clare and to frame a scheme for cooperating with the Coiste Gnótha in its efforts to avail of the enthusiasm for the movement.[87] The Gaelic League made its own sardonic contribution to the war effort by passing a resolution for the preference for Irish over German.[88] The GAA's continuation of its ban on men who joined the British Army and Navy annoyed Redmondites in the county.[89]

Limerick city was the divisional centre of the IRB in Munster. Joe Barrett, as one of the representatives of the IRB in Clare, attended the biannual meetings. He noted that the main subject matter was the Council's desire to ensure that the IRB was in control of the Volunteer organisation, because through such control, 'it would be in a position to handle any situation that might arise'. Other Clare men to attend these meetings were Pakie Ryan, Art O'Donnell, Seán McNamara, Con Kearney and Ned Fennell. The Brennans would have attended these Limerick meetings also. Between May and September of 1915, Barrett was informed that the situation which 'might arise' was going to happen sooner rather than later.[90] Liam Haugh and the Irish Volunteers were also aware of the coming rebellion and took appropriate measures. Some weeks prior to the Rising a lookout was left on the Shannon coast by them. This was on instructions of GHQ, which was represented in West Clare by Seán Ó Muirthille. The possibility of Roger Casement's arrival or another landing from an outside agency in support of the forthcoming Rising was presumed. However no such landing took place.[91]

Andy O'Donoghue was uninformed about a Rising taking place in Easter 1916.[92] Even Barrett did not expect the Rising to take place until about June or July of 1916.[93] Michael Brennan was given instructions by the IRB Limerick centre to mobilise on Easter Sunday 1916 and to hold the roads leading into Limerick from Clare, which entailed blocking six roads spread across five miles of country. He was also unaware as to what direction he was supposed to face - whether he was to prevent people getting in or getting out.[94] Yet he was too excited at the prospect of action to ponder such a logistic.

Sean O'Keeffe recalled his encounter with Bishop Fogarty on the eve of the planned Rising:

On Holy Saturday, 1916, orders came to the Crusheen Company to mobilise that night with all available arms and that each Volunteer was to be instructed to have with him a couple of days' rations. Seán McNamara, who at that stage held the rank of Battalion Commandant, sent me early on that day with a dispatch he had received from GHQ in Dublin to the Bishop of Killaloe, Most Rev. Dr. Fogarty. I met his Lordship at the Cathedral gate in Ennis and handed him the envelope. When he had read the communication he passed the remark 'Good man', tapped me on the shoulder and walked away. Later on I heard that a similar dispatch was sent to every Catholic bishop in Ireland, and that it asked for the appointment of chaplains to administer to the spiritual needs of the Irish Volunteers as soon as they went into action in armed rebellion against the English government. Though I can't say so with certainty, it was rumoured in Irish Volunteer circles at the time that the Bishop of Killaloe selected Fr. Michael Crowe, then C.C. in Dooragh, as chaplain to the Clare Irish Volunteers.[95]

Clare's part in the Rising was negated by countermanding orders from Limerick HQ and the failure of the gunrunning plan in Kerry. The county inspector noted that it was the intention of the 'Sinn Féiners', as the Volunteers were called, to 'take part if arms had been forthcoming, or if the rebellion had lasted longer, and their numbers would have increased three-fold'.[96] The *Clare Champion*, which was issued on Saturday, 29 April 1916, when the Rising was practically over, referred to the county as bewildered by 'the maze of rumours'.[97] A week later the *Clare Champion* wrote:

The Dublin Revolution has come and gone - gone to join the shades of many another attempt on the part of desperate Irishmen to establish an Irish Republic...It is not for us to sit in judgement, and useless would it be to weigh the evidence which has as yet filtered through. History alone, in the clear cold light of time can do it justice and to it we leave the task.....we would appeal to those who are now in power to be merciful to the misguided masses who were drawn into this conflict. Now that the danger has passed, we must all look to the future and let us not forget that justice finds a truer and grander vindication in mercy than in force. We believe that a wise, prudent and paternal administration just now would effect far more permanent good in the country than an example of strict and stern justice...The majority of the English and Irish people have begun to understand each other.[98]

The *Champion's* pleas for 'wise and paternal' justice fell on deaf ears as widespread arrests and internment followed throughout the county. Peadar Clancy was promoted to lieutenant during the Rising. He was among the volunteers who repelled an infantry attack at Church Street Bridge. Clancy also captured Lord Dunsany and burned out a sniper single-handedly. Spellissy's *The Ennis Compendium* lists eleven Clare internees: Michael Brennan (Meelick), Daniel Canny (Tulla), C. O'Halloran (Tulla), Mick Dinan (O'Callaghan's Mills), Denis Healy (Bodyke), Timothy Kelly (Feakle), J. Malone (Ard, Feakle), Patrick O'Connor (Killaloe), Patrick Brennan (Meelick), Art O'Donnell (Tullycrine) and Tómas Ó Lochlainn (Ennistymon). Other internees were William and Hubert Hunt and Martin Crowe, all from Corofin, as well as Thomas Kierse, Peadar Clancy (Cranny), Martin Lynch (Coolmeen), John Murnane (Liscannor) and Peter Moloney (Meelick). Cornelius Colbert, who had close ties with Clare, was executed for his part in the Dublin Rising.

Martin Lynch, of Coolmeen, Co. Clare, who later became a general and was to be in the forefront in organising the establishment of the civic police force, the Garda Síochána after independence, fought in Dublin during Easter week. The following is his account of his experiences during the uprising:[99]

G.P.O. AREA - EASTER WEEK

1 (1)	Post or Subsidiary Position (2)	Officer in Immediate Command (3)	Duties Performed Incidents of special interest recalled (4)	Hour (approx) (5)
Monday	-	-	Mobilised No. 2 Section DCD Coy, 2nd Battalion to report for Duty at Stephen's Green.	10.30 a.m.
	Holohan House	Capt. P. Daly	Reported for special Duty in mufti and with short arms to Capt. P. Daly.	11 a.m.
	Magazine Fort	Do.	Proceeded with Capt. Daly and party - took Magazine Fort, disarmed Guard and evacuated Fort after laying fuse to Magazine. All members of this Party are well known.	12 Noon
	G.P.O.	Commdt. Sean McDermott	With Sean O'Callaghan reported for Duty to Commdt. Sean McDermott at G.P.O. and was placed on Duty at front window at right of main entrance. Took charge of Party with two cars to commandeer provisions etc., for use of G.P.O. Garrison on direction of Sean McDermott. Party passed Customs House under heavy fire about 3.30 a.m. Sean O'Callaghan assisted me. Bill O'Reilly was one of the Party.	2 p.m. to 5 p.m. (5 p.m. to 4 a.m. Tuesday)
Tuesday	G.P.O.	Do	Proceeded to Kennedy's Bakery, Great Britain Street and secured delivery of 4 or 5 vanloads of bread for Garrison. Paid in cash for order.	6 p.m. to 7.30 p.m.

119

1	Post or Subsidiary Position	Officer in Immediate Command	Duties Performed Incidents of special interest recalled	Hour (approx)
(1)	(2)	(3)	(4)	(5)
Do.	Do.	Commdt. Jas. Connolly	Granted two hours leave to return home for Uniform and Equipment.	8.30 p.m. to 10.30 p.m.
Do.	Do.	Commdt. Sean McDermott	Resumed Duty on defence position at window of G.P.O. Was engaged on this duty and also in arranging supply of provisions for Garrison for remainder of day and night.	11 p.m. to 5.30 a.m. Wednesday
Wednesday	Do.	Do.	Detailed to establish contact with Stephen's Green and Jacobs Posts. Returned to G.P.O. with information sought. Travelled in commandeered car. Driver not a Volunteer but afterwards interned in Stafford. Car was under fire in Stephen's Green and College Green.	6 .m. to 8 a.m. Thursday
	G.P.O.	Commdt. Sean McDermott	Assisted in defence of G.P.O. on ground floor from 12 noon on Wednesday. Two Norwegian Sailors reported to O/C G.P.O. and took up defence Post alongside me at front window. I understood they escaped on evacuation.	8 a.m. to 4 p.m. Thursday
Thursday	Do.	Do.	Detailed for Duty with three others under Lieut. Michael Collins at Hoyts, O'Connell Street. Collected Arms and Uniform left by men posted there and conveyed same to G.P.O.	4 a.m. to 4.30 a.m.
Do.	Hoyts Chemist Shop	Do.	Detailed by Sean McDermott to return with four others to take charge of Post at Hoyts, O'Connell Street and hold same until ordered to leave. Held Post until burned out and ordered to leave. Returned to G.P.O. under machine gun fire without casualties. Commdt. Tom Clarke complimented the party on bravery saying men were getting V.C.'s for less in Flanders. He excused each man from duty for remainder of night. Moran of Kerry, one of London Refugees, and a Boy scout Officer from Drumcondra - I think Moloney was his name - were two of this Party.	6.30 a.m. to 6.30 p.m.
Friday	G.P.O.	Do.	Rearmed Defence of G.P.O. Post on ground floor. Vols. Dennehy, Cooke and myself were amongst the last to be called our prior to roof falling in.	10 a.m. to about 5.30 p.m.
Do.	Moore Lane	Lieut. Plunkett	Sec. Comdr. Sean Russell and myself under Lieut Plunkett covered the retreat of wounded from G.P.O. in Moore Lane to Moore Street.	5.30 p.m. 7 p.m.

Do.	Moore St.	Commdt. Pearse	After evacuation of G.P.O. was completed, I billeted with Frank Henderson, Paddy Dennehy and others in house at corner of Moore St. - Moore Lane.	7 p.m. 8 a.m.
Saturday	Moore Street	Commdt. Pearse	Moved through Houses in Moore Street up to Price's. J. J. Walsh mobilised all men having Rifles and bayonets for a bayonet charge through enemy lines to Williams & Woods. Commdt. Lynch was to take charge of this Party of which I was one. Commdt. Pearse postponed the bayonet charge till 3 p.m. to afford the men time to eat and rest.	8 a.m. 3 p.m.
Do.	Do.	Do.	When Party re-mobilised at 3 p.m. we were informed that Commdt. Pearse had surrendered. I, with this Party under Commdt. Myles O'Reilly surrendered at Parnell Monument at 7 p.m. Remained the night in the Green outside Rotunda and were conveyed to Richmond Barracks on Sunday Morning. We were deported on Sunday Evening arriving in Stafford Gaol on the 1st May, 1916.	

Clare Co. Council, meeting on 29 May 1916, placed on record their 'abhorrence of the drastic punishment meted out to the patriotic but misguided leaders of the late attempt to set up an Irish Republic'.[100] Bishop O'Dwyer of Limerick and Bishop Fogarty both took a compassionate stand on the actions of the Easter rebels. Bishop Fogarty, in a sermon given on 20 May 1916, said:

It is a long time since Ireland had such a great sorrow as she has now. The Dublin troubles have filled the country with grief. I am not going to trouble you with a denunciation of the unhappy young men who were responsible for that awful tragedy. There are enough and plenty in Ireland ready to do that. We bewail and lament their mad adventure; but whatever their faults or responsibility may be - and let God be their merciful judge in that - this much must be said to their credit that *they died bravely and unselfishly for what they believed -foolishly indeed - was the cause of Ireland.*

The Irish people would soon have to choose between rival claimants to political legitimacy. The Church of Ireland Bishop of Killaloe, Dr Sterling Berry, advised the 1916 annual diocesan synod that:

There are three courses open to us, members of the Church of Ireland, in the West and South to adopt. We can take up a hostile and unfriendly attitude, and thereby aggravate the difficulty of the situation, or we can hold coldly aloof as onlookers at a work in which we take no part. I earnestly hope that neither of these courses will commend themselves to any of our church members. Such action would be ungenerous; it would certainly be un-Christian. There is a third course which I take this opportunity to urge you most strongly to adopt. It is that we should heartily co-operate with the vast majority of

121

the representatives of our fellow-countrymen, who, at this critical period in our history have proved themselves to be loyal to the Empire to which they and we alike belong. We can never forget the stand taken by their leader (John Redmond) when at the start of the war he declared himself and his party to be heart and soul on the side of the Allies. We recall with deep appreciation that his brother, who is one of the Parliamentary representatives of this county, holds a commission as captain in the Army of our King. They and those who think with them have incurred some unpopularity by their attitude. I believe we owe it to them to give them in their coming task our sympathy and our support.[101]

Cumann Gaodhalach na h-Eaglaise, which represented Protestant Irish language enthusiasts passed a resolution deploring the Rising and affirming loyalty to the king. However, just after a year, this resolution was rescinded and Bishop Berry, as one of three vice-presidents of the Cumann, resigned his position in protest, fearing that the policy of the guild was becoming 'that of the extreme republican party in Ireland'. He helped to establish a new gaelic society, *Comhluadar Gaodhalach na Fiadhnuise*.[102]

The role of the Catholic Church in Clare in influencing the attitudes of the people of the county in the coming months will be assessed in chapter eight. Jenny Griffin, from Kildysart, a student in the Dominican Convent, Eccles Street, Dublin, wrote shortly after the Rising:

God grant the day is not far-distant when we will hear the rifle-crack for freedom once more in O'Connell Street. May God have mercy on the Irish heroes of '16 and be with the noble heroes in English dungeons. It was glorious to see the fight our boys put up against the English guns. Up the Republic! [103]

Canon O'Dea of Cranny was to state that the county ought to have been ashamed of itself for not having taken any part in the rebellion.[104] The cult of Easter 1916 was beginning.

CHAPTER SEVEN

SOLDIERS, PRIESTS AND EXILES

7.1 RECRUITMENT

The standards of literacy have been assessed to ascertain if there was possible differentiation between urban and rural dwellers in terms of education. This has been done in conjunction with examining the linguistic trends in both town and country, so as to help determine if there were differing socio-cultural levels between them. Staunton has alluded to the fact that not one of the Kilrush Munster Fusiliers was an Irish speaker.[1] This would give an indication of the background of the typical Clare recruit in World War I.

The literacy rates for the county as a whole stood at 81,487 (78%) of the county population. Those who could read only came to 2,896 (2% of the population) and those who were illiterate amounted to 7,354 (7%). Only those aged nine years and over were included in the illiteracy count. The two major districts of Clare showed percentages of 6% illiteracy in Ennis and 9% illiteracy in Kilrush. These results indicate that there was a shared standard of basic education in the county between both rural and urban elements.[2]

Of the Gaelic speaking population in the county prior to the War, 36,543 (35%) of the county could speak both Irish and English, whilst 161 (0.15%) people spoke Irish only. Of these tallies 126 of the Gaelic speaking only population were over sixty years. Of the 36,543 that spoke both Irish and English, just over half of those (19,470) were over forty years old. However, one finds that within the 10-18 years bracket, there is an upturn in the younger age group bilingual percentages when compared with older age brackets with 5,878 bilingual (5.5% of the county population in 1911). That only 1,159 juveniles from the same age bracket (1% of the county population in 1901) were speaking both Irish and English ten years previous, indicates that the Gaelic revival at the turn of the century was beginning to make itself felt in terms of statistics.[3]

Table 6:

Literacy Levels

	Total of County	Ennis UDC	Kilrush UDC
Total	104232	5472	3666
Read & Write	81487	4186	2779
Read Only	2896	129	104
Illiterate (9 yrs & over)	7354	361	355
Balance of Population	12495	796	428

Source: **Census of Ireland 1911**

In the urban districts of Kilrush and Ennis one finds that the process of anglicization was at a more advanced level in comparison with rural districts. In Ennis Urban District in 1901 nobody spoke Irish only, and 815 spoke both Irish and English; in 1911 while 750 spoke both Irish and English (13% of the town's population). In Kilrush, five people spoke Irish only in 1901, while 989 (23%) spoke both English and Irish that same year. In 1911, three people spoke Irish only while 847 (23%) spoke English and Irish in Kilrush. These figures are far behind the county average for bilingualism and even further behind some rural districts. For example, the Kilrush Rural District with a population of 21,981 had 12,816 bilingual speakers (58%) and 65 Irish only speakers. In Ennistymon Rural District there were forty-nine Irish only speakers and 9,476 bilingual speakers out of a population of 16,882; the bilingual speakers constituted 56% of the population.[4]

These statistics indicate that the urban areas were becoming English-speaking monoglot areas. The question is then posed; what was the correlation between anglicisation and recruitment? Bartlett has assessed that the inclination to enlist was primarily a function of economic and social context, rather than a religious or political choice.[5] MacNamara states that over half of Ennis' one thousand recruits were affiliated with the United Labourers Association.[6] Martin Staunton's thesis on the Royal Munster Fusiliers pointed to the urban bias with regard to recruitment into the British Army as the Munsters catchment area of Cork, Kerry, Limerick and Clare with a 25% urban population, provided 75% of its recruits from urban areas.[7] In Clare itself, the county had a distinctly rural population, yet wartime recruitment statistics for the Munsters showed that the two urban districts of Kilrush and Ennis with populations of 3,666 and 5,472 respectively (8.76% of the whole county) contributed 43.4% of the Claremen to the Regiment.[8] Of the Claremen who lost their lives fighting with the Royal Munster Fusiliers, it is claimed that forty of the dead were from Ennis, thirty seven from Kilrush, and the remaining ninety three from the rest of the county.[9] It must be pointed out that a sizeable proportion of the ninety three men would have come from towns such as Ennistymon, Killaloe, Corofin, Kilkee, Lisdoonvarna, Kildysart and Miltown-Malbay.

Prior to the Great War, there were amongst the persons engaged in the defence of the country, twenty three officers (effective or retired) living in Clare, along with nine soldiers or non-commissioned officers and fifty eight army pensioners living in the county. Of the pensioners twenty one lived in the two urban districts (36%), again indicating the sway that the urban districts held with regard to recruitment. However, one notes that apropos the location of army officers, of whom the majority belonged to the richer or landed classes, the ratio of location of residence was in proportion with the population indicators.[10] The 1911 census indicates that about two-thirds of the naval and military pensioners living in Ireland were Catholics.

Although the 1911 census provided an indication as to the location of military presence in the county and conveyed that there was a general if non-definitive indication of the trends of unskilled rural and urban recruitment, the military authorities did not compile comparable figures on the rural/urban recruitment ratios. Sample estimates have been made, which, along with statements made by contemporary recruiters, would seem to support a strong urban bias towards recruitment. The Central Council chairman of the Organisation of Recruitment in Ireland, Lord Wimborne, who had replaced Lord Aberdeen as Lord Lieutenant of Ireland, stated that the response from the rural areas had been disappointing, whilst the district inspector from Clare stated that the response from the towns 'have been good, surprisingly good'.[11] In a sample of five Irish Regiments taken by Patrick Callan from the regimental rolls of soldiers who died in the Great War, a few interesting statistics were revealed. In four regiments he examined, the urban proportion was higher, standing at 56%, with the Royal Munster Fusiliers, despite its high rural population catchment area, having the highest urban proportion. Yet in the fifth regiment, that of the Irish Guards, Callan reveals that this body yielded the highest proportion of rural recruits, with a total of 65%.[12] Staunton's statistics complemented Callan's findings with approximately two-thirds of rural recruits from Clare having enlisted with the Irish Guards Regiment.[13] The Irish Guards was the regiment which most RIC recruits enlisted into, and it was a more selective regiment; accordingly there could have been an element of snobbery held by rural recruits with regard to their choice of enlistment.

Stephen Glynn, a close friend of John Redmond, maintained that in Ireland prior to the war, "gone for a soldier"' was a word of disgrace for a farmer's son as it was in Great Britain.[14] The Irish Party, Glynn claimed, had been before the war, against recruitment into the British army to varying degrees. The findings of Chapter Five would seem to corroborate this view. According to Glynn:

> enlistment had been discouraged on the principle that from a military point of view, Ireland was regarded as a conquered country.

It is tempting here to examine the coloniser/colonised theory. Perhaps, from a republican standpoint, Bulmer Hobson best summarised: 'the battle is not with England but with the people of Ireland...'.[15] Recruitment was seen as a major factor in the process of the perceived anglicization of Ireland.

Yet once soldiers had taken the "saxon shilling" prior to the Great War, Willie Redmond like other IPP members did show a genuine concern for their welfare and the protection of their religious and national identity. His claim, contrary to some nationalists' allegations, that the troops were not becoming "Irish tommies" did raise a few eyebrows amongst the firebrands in the Party. Although he was openly in favour of the Boers in the Boer War, Redmond told the Commons:

> The Irishmen in South Africa are fighting as gallantly as Irishmen have always done.... These men we consider in the wrong but the Irish Party were as proud of their gallantry as any other people.[16]

On another occasion he told the Commons that the soldiers in the Irish Regiments of the British army:

> come mostly from the South of Ireland; they are Catholics by religion and in politics, they are nationalists and Home Rulers like we are. I have myself heard these gallant and brave men cheering members sitting upon these benches in the towns, which they have visited. You must not imagine because these men have entered your army that they are not in sympathy with us, because they are.[17]

126

It was Redmond's opinion that the Irish identity of these men was strengthened rather than weakened by service in the British army but he also accepted that there were 'those Irishmen who through lack of employment generally join the British army'.[18] Ironically, Redmond found himself asking in 1914 what he had been asking for in 1900; the right of the Irish to raise their own volunteer battalions, who could defend 'Ireland from invasion and would not be a threat to public order'.[19]

However, other MPs denounced recruitment. James Halpin, Redmond's fellow Clare MP between 1906 and 1909, told a UIL meeting in December 1907 that he was against Irishmen going into the British army.[20] Yet there was little proof of systematic attempts to disrupt enlisting by the main nationalist party although Sinn Féin were to rage a vociferous campaign against it, and this campaign was rekindled by the coming of the Great War. In spite of these campaigns and anti-recruitment journals such as the *Shan Van Vocht*, the March police report for Clare in 1900 noted that 'recruiting for the Militia (Special Reserves) and the regulators is just about normal, and the recruits are much better than average'.[21] The fact that James Halpin's predecessor was a major in the British army typified the indifference of much of the Clare electorate towards the Irish experience in the British army and all the attendant cultural baggage that went with it. This is what John Devoy referred to as the 'de-nationalisation of Ireland'.

World War One was to be the ultimate gauge of Irish recruitment into the British army. Jeffery has maintained that political factors were to influence the enlistment rates but he also observed that at first Ireland had responded nearly as willingly to the call to arms as Britain.[22] He has collated the imperial and national rates of recruitment during WW1 and found the following information;

England's percentage of manpower which enlisted - 24%
Scotland's percentage of manpower which enlisted - 24%
Wales' percentage of manpower which enlisted - 22%
Ireland's percentage of manpower which enlisted - 6%

Whilst Callan has argued that it would be more appropriate to examine Ireland's recruitment performance in the context of the Dominions, Jeffery indicated that even in that context, Ireland fares poorly. In stating that Ireland had a peculiar male population structure and that political events affected enlistment, Jeffery claimed that there were other forces at play, because 'the striking success of the1918 recruiting campaign casts some doubts as to whether there was any unequivocally direct correlation between recruitment and political opinion'.[23] It should be noted that the merging of the Royal Flying Corps and the Royal Naval Air Service into the Royal Air Force and its subsequent expansion in 1918 would also have contributed to such an upsurge in recruitment.

The statistics substantiate Jeffery's views. They show that it was the landlord and the labouring classes that were disproportionately represented with regard to enlistment and that a slight majority of the recruits from Ireland claimed no Volunteer connections whatsoever, with either of the 'green or orange hue'. Callan, in his reference to the improvement in recruitment rates in the last part of the war, stated that it was 'a confirmation of the opinions held by seasoned officials that the success of their operations depended more on social and economic factors than on political atmosphere'.

Table 7:

Irish recruits raised during the war, for each six-month period

Period	Total	Index
4 Aug 1914 to Feb 1915	50107	100
Feb 1915 to Aug 1915	25235	50
Aug 1915 to Feb 1916	19801	40
Feb 1916 to Aug 1916	9323	19
Aug 1916 to Feb 1917	8178	16
Feb 1917 to Aug 1917	5609	11
Aug 1917 to Feb 1918	6550	13
Feb 1918 to Aug 1918	5812	12
Aug 1918 to Nov 1918	9845	20
	140460	

Source: **Patrick Callan**, 'Recruiting by the British in Ireland during the First World War' in the *Irish Sword*, Vol.xviii, pp. 42-43.

The table above omits commissioned officers from Ireland but it is estimated that they come to 5,470 direct enlistments during the war.[25] It can be accepted that Callan's index figures bear much resemblance to the British experience of voluntary enlistment up to

February 1916, whernconscription was introduced there.

Yet it is the study of the urban bias in terms of recruitment that is of particular relevance for Clare, because it indicates a socio-cultural divide. Many of the peasantry in Clare saw the town recruits as being socially marginalised. These differences in attitudes were highlighted by incidents such as that which the Kilrush Petty Sessions heard on 12 July 1915 relating to Pte. Thomas O'Donnell, Munster Fusiliers, a native of Kilrush, who was at home on leave. During a row in a Kilrush public house, O'Donnell was accused by James McDonnell, a Kilmihil farmer, of being a 'mean man to fight the Germans' and 'that it was all the scruff and corner boys that were in the army and were they not rowdies, they would not be in it at all'. McDonnell then promptly struck O'Donnell on the head because he figured that O'Donnell 'did not get half enough from the Germans and he would give him more'.[26]

The existing British military authorities had a deeply held racial belief that the average Catholic Irish soldier was 'difficult to drive, but easy to lead', that he was fickle in his temperament and loyalty. Yet they also had a genuine patriarchal affection for the pugnacious qualities which they perceived and advertised the typical Irish recruit as possessing. Sir Lawrence Parsons, during the recruiting drive in World War One, informed T.P. O'Connor, the Liverpool Home Rule MP and F.L. Crilly, the general secretary of the U.K. Home Rule organisation, that the men he did want were the 'clean, fine, strong, temperate, hurley-playing fellows' and that one of his motives in refusing to accept the transfer of Irish in Britain to Irish regiments was that such transfers 'would mean filling us with Liverpool, Glasgow and Cardiff Irish who are slumbirds we don't want'.[27] This romantic image of the countrified soldier that permeated the ranks of the military authorities was just one aspect of the whole racial outlook and was misinformed when scrutinised against the process of Irish rural opinion on the war turning from apathy to general antipathy, with 'the hurley-playing fellows' for the most part standing on the ditch as a war they viewed as not of their own dragged on. A 1917 Ministry of Labour report on migratory labourers continues this theme. It stated that 'the labourers who are obtainable from the larger towns in Ireland have been of a very poor class and far inferior to the men from the country districts. The importation of men from these towns probably accounts for a great deal of the prejudice against Irish workmen. On the other hand the recruiting of men

129

from the country districts has an obvious effect in reducing the supply of labour for agriculture.'[28]

F.L. Crilly, referred to above, is a rare source source for the information on Irishmen enlisting in non-Irish regiments in Britain, during WWI. He estimates that 115,513 men joined up during WWI. This source however leaves out various regions in its estimate.[29] Edward Spiers has estimated that fewer than one in ten of the emigrant Irish recruits in Britain had a job at the time of enlistment in 1909.[30] These were usually men in their late teens for which the risks involved in fighting were outweighed by its benefits. Fitzpatrick having assessed the 'abstract' idealist motives, identifies two key guiding factors in the trends of Irish recruitment into the British army:

1. Family Precedent.
2. Peer group pressure which negated benefits of income and security.[31]

The 8th Royal Munsters under General Pereira undertook mine raids between 19 July 1916 and the end of that month so as to break the deadlock at the front. What made this 8th Battalion unique was that it had been reserved for Nationalist Volunteers and the make-up of this battalion differs to an extent from the make-up of the other battalions in the regiment. However, as politics did not, according to D.P. Moran, define nationality, neither could it, on its own, influence recruiting. There were socio-economic factors at play.

The economist, Professor C.H. Oldham, drew up a memorandum in October 1915 emphasising the problems inherent in rural recruitment in Ireland. He conveyed the differences of occupation of the recruiting reservoir in Ireland, compared to England and Scotland. To achieve this, he gave as an example the proportion of those from England, Scotland and Ireland working in :

(A) commerce and industry, compared to those in
(B) agriculture and fishing.

In England for every eighty eight in A, twelve were in B. In Scotland, for eighty six that were in A, there were fourteen in B, whilst Ireland has only forty three in A for every fifty seven in B. If Ireland therefore wanted to step up her contribution to the army, she would have to sacrifice her agricultural interests. Yet he also admitted that both branches of Irish exports had made remarkable progress during the war.[32] This economic scenario enticed the landowners from the Clare community of unionists to keep a grip on their lands and make peace with their neighbours. Prices for almost all agricultural produce, both crops and stock, rose consistently from 1915-1920 in response to the dislocation of the world trade. By 1920, the peak year, prices had roughly trebled since 1913.[33] However many farmers took advantage of Britain's difficulty to offload a high proportion of sub-standard goods and this was to jeopardise the reputation of Irish agriculture. War prices had created even further reluctance amongst the peasantry to lose out on their new found prosperity by enlisting. However the collapse of local industries, such as the liquidation of the Killaloe Slate company, led to an upsurge in recruitment from those who would have seen military service as a form of alternative employment.[34]

One area of recruitment that has escaped study, has been the role of the recruiting officer. It may have been possible that a recruiting officer, using his own initiatives and persuasions, could have had a considerable influence on the numbers enlisting. The *Sinn Féin* newspaper claimed that recruiters received 1s a day for three hours work, helping recruiting sergeants, and received a 10s bonus for each induction sanctioned by the Army Council.[35] Some have recounted how certain recruiting officers plied prospective recruits with alcohol prior to producing a signing-up form. In one instance in Kilkee, an intended target for the recruiting officer, wise to such tactics, availed of the free porter until he was approached to "join the colours". The gregarious man then asked the officer if the Kaiser and the King were relatives. When the officer answered back in the affirmative, the good civilian downed his pint and said it was not his style to get involved in family feuds![36] MacLysaght also refers to use of alcohol as a tactic by recruiting officers, and in his experience the use of such having its desired effect.[37]

There now follow two examples of recruiters who operated in Clare during the War period. The first case shows an individual who seemed to value both the prestige of wearing a uniform in his own locality and the British military tradition. One notes that he seemed to be operating on his own initiative and was seeking official recognition. He was also part of the administration establishment, being a clerk of the petty sessions for Tulla, Feakle and Tuamgraney.[38] He wrote to Colonel Caddell, Registrar of Petty Sessions Clerks, Dublin Castle:

Scariff,
Co. Clare.
28th Sept. 1915.

Sir,
    In obedience to a Circular passed last December, I interested myself in raising recruits for the Army and enlisted 10. [sic]
    I also during the period for Licensing dogs have out with each licence [sic] Capt. Redmond's letter. I had recruiting Bills posted over my Districts and exhibited in my Court houses.
    I am very much interested in recruiting being a Soldier's Son. (whose father served through the Crimean War and hold his medal and clasps, also Turkish medal and a brother served in the Connaught Rangers and was buried in Malta). [sic]
    I have made repeated applications for the post of Recruiting Officer with no effect. My applications were made to the Strand Barracks, Limerick in person and by letters and my letters (I was informed) was sent to the Commanding Officer-Tralee.
    There is no recruiting officer in my districts which reach on the Tulla side 15 miles and in the Feakle and Gort side about the same distance and on the Killaloe side about 4 miles and on the Mountshannon side about three miles.
    A Soldier's uniform is very rarely seen in my districts and I feel if it [sic] were regularly appointed with a uniform that I could raise more recruits. I also believe that my remarks would apply to a good many Petty Sessions Clerks. My duties take me over a large area and I could use my influence in the proper direction and I feel my energies are tied up for want of proper Authority and appointment as well as a Uniform.

Your obedient Servant,
John McAuliffe,
Clerk of Petty Sessions for Tulla, Feakle, & Tuamgraney which latter includes the town of Scariff where weekly Markets are held and two monthly fairs for cattle & pigs.

Colonel Caddell, in a communication with the under secretary, noted that the military authorities had already supplied McAuliffe with the necessary recruiting papers, notices and warrants as a recruiting officer and was not aware of any precedent for the appointment of a person employed under the crown as a recruiting officer with rank as such and the authority to wear uniform.[39] Caddell advised his appointment as a non-commissioned officer, provided the government permitted him to wear a uniform, and he sought clarification with regard to pay and travelling allowances or whether McAuliffe would be paid on a commission basis for each recruit he obtained.

Colonel Arthur Lynch, the much maligned West Clare MP, sought in late 1918 to turn his dream of an Irish Brigade, of which he spoke to the Lissycasey National Volunteers in 1914, into a reality. He had been granted permission from the British war cabinet to start up his own recruiting drive to establish such a brigade. However, his efforts were to prove in vain. The following excerpts show that not only had the vast majority of Irish turned against him but the highest echelons of British military were also disproving of both Lynch and his efforts:[40]

Exciting and at times, tumultuous and angry scenes were enacted on Tuesday night, August 27th at the Fountain, James's Street, Dublin, when Col. Lynch and Capt. O'Grady endeavoured to address a recruiting meeting. After repeated and fruitless attempts to speak to the enormous crowd which had gathered, Col. Lynch desisted, and he and Capt. O'Grady left hurriedly in a motor car to which they were pursued by an excited mob.

Col. Lynch, who stood at the time smiling on the crowd, was then subjected to a fire of questions, of which the following are samples: "Where were you when you were with McBride - who were you fighting for?": "Are you going to resign West Clare? Why misrepresent it?": "Is this your last meeting, Lynch?" "Have you a permit?": and such 'Voices' were heard as "Go up to Belfast, you will be heard there": "This is a German crowd".[41]

If this reaction in Dublin was not bad enough, the Viceroy, Sir John French, was totally dismissive of Lynch.[42] In a communication to Lloyd George he stated:

2nd September 1918.

The other matter is much more serious. It relates to Colonel Lynch & Captain O'Grady. They insist they must be allowed to issue an invitation to the Sinn Féiners throughout the country to come to public meetings, organised by them (Lynch & Co) and to hold a kind of general parley (I really don't know what to call it) in which the Sinn Féiners are to be allowed to express their views on every conceivable subject, and have them reported in every newspaper in the country. Now this is exactly what we have been doing our utmost to prevent. He saw me with the Chief Secretary this morning and our conference lasted about an hour. He is determined to appeal to you, the country and the House of Commons against my decision.

I much regret that he ever was allowed to come over here, for we have quite difficulties enough without men like that raising more for us.

This is only an outline of what has occurred, and it is quite possible you may

133

hear nothing more about it as I think it not unlikely that he may accept my decision and go on working as he has up to now with the recruiting council.......[43]

Such was the lot of an Irish recruiter. How some of the Claremen who were recruited or volunteered to join the military forces, fared in battle shall now be examined.

7.2 THE WAR FRONT

It did not take long for Claremen to meet their baptism of fire. The 2nd Royal Munster Fusiliers were amongst the regular regiments that contributed to the British Expeditionary Force. Landing in France, they were hurled into a horrendous situation of trying to bolster the Allied lines against the onslaught of the German forces whose flanking attack in an anti-clockwise movement through Belgium and northern France was intended to trap the Allies in a pincer fashion, as envisaged by Von Schliffen in a plan designed by him twenty years earlier. The Belgians had put up staunch resistance, buying valuable time for the Allies in the general retreat towards Paris. Probably the most heroic rearguard action in all of this campaign was the stance made by the 2nd Royal Munster Fusiliers at Etreux. Previously during the "Great Retreat" where the Germans outnumbered the Allies by four to one, three famous Irish regiments had held a ten mile line as part of Haig's 1st Army Corps. These were the 2nd Munsters in the 1st Division under General Lomax as part of the 1st Infantry Brigade under General Maxse; the 1st Irish Guards in the 2nd division under General Munro as part of the 4th Infantry Brigade under Brigadier-General Scott-Kerr and the 2nd Connaught Rangers in the 5th Brigade under Brigadier General Haking, which was also part of the 2nd division.[44]

This ten mile line was particularly attacked as the Germans sought a breakthrough. Generals Von Kluck and Von Bulow were pounding Binche and Bray to soften up the defences. Haig pushed his flank on which the Munsters were deployed back behind Bray and the 5th Cavalry brigade evacuated Binche. The Munsters were said to have fought tenaciously in these early engagements. By 10.00 p.m. on 24 August they had retreated to Landrecies-Marouilles. The enemy was still on their heels. Late at night a whole German army Corps coming through the forest suddenly flung themselves at Landrecies. Yet Haig with some help from the French managed to pull his troops out. The next day the retreat continued towards Messigny on the Oese. Incessant marching and fighting had the Munsters making an exhausting retreat southwards.

It was on that Tuesday morning at Etreux that the Munsters met disaster.[45] It is still not clear why they came to be cut off. It has been asserted that there was a delay in the orderly giving a dispatch for retreat. Captain Lebouef of the French army stated orders came that the Munsters were to hold their ground to cover the retreat of the main army and that subsequent counter-orders never reached them.[46] Cut off and surrounded and hopelessly outnumbered, they put up a fight which was to infuriate the German High Command in the delay the six hour fight caused them. Nine officers and a huge proportion of the rank and file were killed, with the remnant of the battalion surrendering at an orchard just outside the town, which they had held until their ammunition had given out. The war office posted 678 of the rank and file as missing.

The majority of the Claremen captured in the war were taken here at Etreux and this can explain why there was so much attention given to the war charities by the media on the plight of prisoners from an early stage in the war. The *Clare Journal* reported that there were 474 of the Munster Fusiliers taken as prisoners of war by early 1915 and that of these 'only eighty have great coats and the majority have only cotton shirts and no socks'. Colour Sergeant-Major John Browne of Turnpike, Ennis, who was a prisoner of war in Limburg wrote to his mother asking 'if there is any soldiers society formed in Ennis for the benefit of soldiers?'. There was in fact a Discharged and Disabled Soldiers and Sailors Federation charity established as well as a Prisoners Aid Organisation along with the Royal Munster Fusiliers Old Comrades Association.[47] In mid-1916, Mrs. F.N. Studdert of the Co. Clare Prisoners of War Aid Fund committee informed the *Clare Journal* that many Clare POWs had written to committee members, particularly those who 'god-mothered' certain prisoners, thanking them for parcels sent on to their camps, in particular to Limburg. There was an appeal for county support for the National Relief Fund under the auspices of Sir Michael O'Loughlin, Lord Lieutenant of Clare, residing in Drumconora. Other war-related services included the Red Cross unit in Clare and the Clare Needlework Guild.

The local press, especially the *Clare Journal*, frequently published letters sent home from the Front. In one such letter, Private Gormley of the Munsters described to Joseph Kennedy, Ennis, his experiences in the ill-fated Dardanelles campaign, as he lay in a military hospital in Port Said, Egypt:

> I happened to get wounded while up the Dardanelles. My wound is progressing favourably. We had a very warm time of it up in Gallipoli, most of my regret being knocked over. This hospital is situated down on the seashore, so we are in quite a healthy spot, with plenty of sea breezes, etc. We are getting well treated, so have no cause to complain. I have one consolation in knowing that I killed an opponent. I was coming from the firing line with a wounded comrade. I brought him to the first dressing station, about four miles from the Achi Baba. Returning again to the firing line, I had to pass a battery of howitzers on my right, when the Major of the battery called me and asked me if I was going back to the firing line. I told him I was, so he told me to look out for snipers. I went about 150 yards from the battery.
> I stood against a tree to have a drink when I heard noises. I got closer to the tree, from where I could see the bayonet and part of the rifle of a Turk protruding from behind the tree. Unfortunately, I did not have my rifle with me, having left it in the trenches. I made a grab for his rifle, and he fired, wounding me in my right hand. I made a grab with the left hand and caught hold of his rifle. I then forced the rifle upwards. He tried to wrench the rifle from me, but I still held on. I watched my opportunity and kicked him in the groin. He then dropped, letting go of the rifle. With his struggles, I gave him another kick, this time in the jaw. This knocked him unconscious for a time. I then pointed the bayonet at his stomach, and putting my weight on the butt, drove the point home. During the affair, the major of the battery heard the report, on which he came up with four men, and asked me if I were much hurt. He bandaged my hand up with my field dressing, there being a constant flow of blood. He congratulated me, and took my name, number and regiment. When I said it was the Munsters, he said he thought so. So that is the only one I can account for. I can tell you it is no picnic there. I regret to say Jack Regan was killed by my side on May 2 and Pat Frawley and young Burley. [48]

From a letter written by Sergeant James A. Campbell, L Company, 1st Munster Fusiliers, one can get an insight into the terrific slaughter and devastation that awaited those at the war front, especially for those who led the assault on Gallipoli:

> The forcing of the narrows by the combined British and French fleets proving a rather long and tedious operation, the British Government in conjunction with the French and Australian Governments decided to employ a sufficient land force to prevent Turkish troops from rebuilding numerous forts destroyed wholly, or partially by shellfire from the fleet.
> The 29th Division, consisting of troops that had been withdrawn from the regular garrisons of India and undoubtedly the last trained at that time in the army, were selected to attempt the disembarkation on the southern extremity of the Gallipoli peninsula. There, the shore close to the powerful fort of Sedd-el-Bahr, curved inwards in a shape of a cup, with Sedd-el-Bahr on the right and Fort Helles on the left, the latter fort being destroyed by naval

gunfire. The land rose in successive terraces inland til the highest peak, Achi Baba, about five miles distant was reached.

Owing to numerous defensive works erected by the Turks, the landing was considered an impossibility by both the Turks and their German Allies. The 29th was ordered to disembark from battleships and a party of 1st battalion Munsters, Hampshire Regiment, D Company of Dublin Fusiliers and some staff corps were selected to disembark from *SS River Clyde*, an old carrier converted temporarily into a troop ship which was intentionally run ashore between two Turkish forts. No sooner had the hull grounded when the Turks opened heavy shrapnel and machine gunfire. This damage was limited because of the bullet-proof plates.

The troops were ordered to disembark. The Munsters led the assault, running out and down specially prepared gangways connected with floats that were towed into position. On the troops emerged a perfect rain of fire and the losses were enormous but urged on by the officers, that attack was still pressed forward, with some gaining the shore and cover under the terraces. However, those who were wounded on the gangways were unable to maintain their hold and being thrust into the water, were for the greater part drowned.

The landing continued until such time as sufficient troops were ashore as to keep the Turks at bay. Then only, and owing to fearful loss of life, did the commanders stop the remainder until nightfall. An idea may be formed of the difficulty of the task from the casualty list of officers and non-commissioned officers of the company of Munsters who led. The losses were all five officers wounded (three seriously), company sergeant-major, company quarter-master sergeant, three sergeants and one corporal, all killed in action. The remaining two sergeants were wounded and two other corporals wounded. This being the case, how most of the ranks suffered.

One incident stood out prominently. In the evening, an officer from the *River Clyde* got a boat and under heavy fire rescued thirty or forty wounded from the rocks, who would have drowned as the tide came in. I was wounded in three places, yet still continued with the difficult and dangerous task. The general opinion following the disembarkment was that water is a very unpleasant factor in attack, especially when assisted by shellfire; however, "it's an ill wind that blows nobody any good". Here I am living the life of a country squire, having survived the disembarkation from *HMS River Clyde*.[49]

A number of Clare clergy members had volunteered their services to provide for the spiritual needs of the Irish troops fighting in the war. It was reported in the early stages of the war that there was 'evidence of dissatisfaction among the Irish soldiers in the field', in relation to the lack of chaplains. One chaplain had written from the Front:

I have seen the wounded Irish Rifles and others, and they have not met a priest since they left home, or heard mass on Sundays..... the arrangements are unsatisfactory and complaints are general. A succession of claims and counter-claims passed between the War Office and the Editor of the Irish Catholic, debating the controversy. On 13th October, 1914, at the Annual

Meeting of all the Irish Bishops, a resolution was passed that the supply of chaplains for the Irish Catholic soldier at the front is lamentably inadequate...... the spiritual wants of our people in the field must be duly safeguarded.[50]

Thereafter an influx of chaplains entered into service. Michael MacDonagh wrote about the influence of religous belief upon the typical Irish soldier:

The Irish are the most religious soldiers in the British Army; and it is because they are religious that they rank so high and brave.... In the average Irishman there is a blend of piety and militancy which makes him an effective soldier. For the reason that he is a praying man, the Irish Catholic soldier is a fine fighting man.[51]

The following were the Clare chaplains who served; Most Rev. Dr Patrick Joseph Clune, Fr. Francis Clune, Fr. Michael McKenna, Fr. Michael McMahon, Fr. Benedict Coffey, Rev. J.H. Thomas, Rev. Pierce Egan, Rev. J.A. Halpin, Fr. Michael Galvin, Fr. Michael Moran and Fr. O'Meehan. Fr. Benedict Coffey was the Guardian of the Irish Franciscan College at St. Isidore's, Rome in 1912 and was attached to the Royal Navy operating in the Adriatic sea.[52] According to the Royal Army Chaplains Department Depot (RAChD), Rev. Pierce Egan, M.A., applied to join their department on 17 June 1915, aged 56 years. He died of dysentery in Alexandria. Rev. J.H. Thomas, an ex-curate of Ennis, served as chaplain to the 77th Battalion of the Canadian Army and Rev. J.A. Halpin served the Australian forces, and was wounded in action in France.[53] Among the other chaplains who served at the Front was Fr. Michael Moran, B.A., a native of Tulassa, Inch. He was attached to the Royal Army Medical Corps (RAMC) and amongst his tasks were to give first aid on the battlefield, provide transport for the wounded and bury the dead.[50] Fr. Michael Galvin, who hailed from Kilnamona, served as an army chaplain at Mesopotamia during World War I. He died parish priest of Killimer on 27 February 1956.[54] Fr. O'Meehan, from Ennis, was attached to the RAChD and died at the end of 1919.

Most Rev. Dr Clune from Ruan was educated and ordained at the Missionary College of All Hallows. During the First World War, in 1916, he accepted the post of Chaplain General to the Australian Forces and he visited both the Egyptian and Western Fronts. He was present at the Battle of the Somme, and by coincidence he met his brother, Fr. Francis Clune who was also a chaplain to the Australian Forces. He visited troops in England and in Ypres, where he made an indelible impression. In March 1917 he returned to Western Australia where he took part in the appeal for Belgian patriotic funds and also assisted the families of Yugoslav internees. He expressed himself publicly to be mildly in favour of conscription.[55]

According to the Killaloe diocesan archives one of the other Clare chaplains who served during the war was Fr. Michael McKenna, Tulla. He was ordained at Maynooth in 1911. He had been serving in Glasgow prior to his appointment as a military chaplain.[56] He was commissioned on 29 February 1916, served in France and was mentioned once in dispatches. He relinquished his commission on 10 December 1917. In 1921, both Fr. McKenna and Fr. Gaynor were arrested by Black and Tans for having IRA sympathies. It was held locally that they owed their escape from "auxilary laws" to a Great War veteran who recognised Fr. Gaynor from the trenches.[57] Fr. McKenna died in February 1960. Fr. Michael McMahon, an Ennis curate and formerly of St. Joseph's, Lancashire, was chaplain to the RAMC in France. He was wounded in action and received the Military Cross.[58]

The Irish-American newspaper, the *Irish Advocate*, took very much a pro-war stance when its jingoistic tone is compared with that of the *Irish World*:

> We bid adieu to two of our boys from the Banner County, who are real fighting men, William O'Brien and Michael Maloney, both from Doolin, County Clare. The boys are only over from Ireland a short time, and have fought battles in and out of war. They said they were fighting landlords in Ireland for years, and have no doubt they will make good in battle with the good experience they have.
> Mickey Maloney says; "I am going into battle and I expect to come out also". William O'Brien says "I am going to see my birthplace when we have this war won - it is only across the Channel." [59]

Irish exile cultural organisations such as the GAA and Irish dancing groups rowed in behind "Uncle Sam" and the doughboys. Two of the 'best men' on the Clare hurling team, Thomas Sullivan and Michael Murphy, were called in the draft and got a rousing send-off from their fellow county men.[60] Danny McCarthy from Clohauninchy in the parish of Kilmurry-Ibrickane was also drafted, into the 78th Division of the US army. The Kilrush and Kilkee Dance Class held a reception for the 'young Clare boys' who were about to go to various training camps.[61] The recently married Clare exiles, Thomas Talty and Ellen Considine were to cut short their honeymoon as Mr. Talty was to join the U.S. army and Mrs. Talty was to serve under the Red

Cross.[62] The Clare Young Girls' Ball funds went to the Knights of Columbus War Fund,[63] and the Clare Young Men's Dance was advertised as follows:

> This Saturday night July 14, is the night chosen for the annual Summer night's festival and ball of the Co. Clare Young Men's Social Club which takes place at Donovan's Hall, 308W 59th St.. This is a night that will long be remembered in the heart of many a Clare exile and they will see many of the members of this social club dressed in khaki. These include President J. Murphy, Vice President J. Cuny, Treasurer J. Callinan and Floor Manager F. Callinan, all of who belong to the gallant 69th Regiment.[64]

The Claremen's Association held a solemn blessing of a service flag on St. Patrick's Day 1918 and called for Claremen:

> to stand behind the President and those who bravely left our ranks, ready to make the supreme sacrifice that liberty shall not perish from the earth..... We men of Clare, inspired by the glorious history made by our forefathers, are not found wanting by the present crisis.

'No greater fighting regiment has ever existed than the One Hundred and Sixty Fifth Infantry of the Rainbow Division formed by the old Sixty Ninth Regiment of New York', claimed General MacArthur of the very regiment he chose to represent New York state in a purpose built shock division that was formed from the cream of the U.S. National Guard. The 'Fighting' Sixty Ninth Irish Regiment was founded in 1851 by Irish citizens in New York City as a militia regiment known locally as the 2nd Regiment of Irish Volunteers. Regimental historian, Lieutenant Colonel Kenneth H. Powers related how the close identification of a regiment with a particular ethnic stock of the American population was quite rare in the U.S. army and made the Sixty Ninth unique. Called into active service in 1917, the regiment was engaged in some of the bitterest fighting of the war - Lorraine, Champagne-Marne, Aisne-Marne, St. Mihiel and the Meuse-Argonne.

The regiment was divided into three battalions with each battalion consisting of four companies. Each company numbered two hundred and fifty men and sixty officers. Two of these twelve companies were captained by Claremen. Company F of the 2nd battalion was led by Corofin native Captain Michael Kelly, a member of the New York Harbour Authority and ex-Boer War British army veteran. Company M of the 3rd "Shamrock" battalion was led by Captain Martin Meaney, a native of Cree, Co. Clare.[65] Meaney was to eventually lead the Shamrock Battalion in putting up one of the most heroic fights of the war at the Battle of the Ourcq.

Meaney's company and Company K had suffered a three day bombardment with mustard gas shells, resulting in the blinding of over 400 men who were just after celebrating St. Patrick's Day in the trenches in 1918.[66] A few months later, on 28 July 1918, the Irish-American regiment engaged the enemy on the river Ourcq, advancing without the normal preliminary artillery bombardment. They forced a crossing and fought alone with exposed flanks on the enemy's side of the river, against withering machinegun fire. The Shamrock battalion was in the eye of the storm, suffering heavy casualties, amongst them Sergeant Joyce Kilmer, renowned poet and author of the ballad *Trees* who was killed in action. It was at this juncture that the whole battalion came under the command of Captain Martin Meaney.[67] Meaney led them in the last attack that broke the German resistance which included the Fourth Prussian Guard Division under the Kaiser's son Prince Eithel Frederick. This victory was widely acclaimed as a great feat of arms. The newly promoted Colonel Martin Meaney was to go on to become a commander of the regiment itself. Later in 1940, he was alleged to have been one of the ring leaders of a counter-revolutionary right-wing plot to place a 'ring of steel' around Washington D.C. to combat an anticipated communist revolution, during the course of the Federal District Court trial of "The Sporting Club". Meaney denied any knowledge of the matter, was not called to trial and the case against "The Sporting Club", which was part of the Christian Front movement, was dismissed.[68]

Another Clareman to distinguish himself in combat was James J. Cullinan, a native of Kilnamona who emigrated to New York around 1900. He was decorated with high military honours and an American Legion Hall was named after him.[69] He lived for a while after the war at the New York State Soldiers and Sailors Home in Stueben County, and a *New York Times* article from 7 June 1929 reported: 'a silver star citation for gallantry was awarded by the War Department to James Cullinan of 1070 Park Avenue, New York City, formerly Sergeant in Company C 165th Infantry, 42nd Division for bravery during an attack at Laundreset-St. Georges, France on October 15, 1918'.[70]

Just as the Americans were joining the war, the 2nd army which included both the Irish nationalist 16th Division and the Irish unionist 36th Division prepared to attack the Messines Ridge. A fatally wounded Major Willie Redmond was to be carried away by Ulster Protestants from the field of battle. In his dying words to the Ulster chaplain that tended him, he said he always wanted to be friends with Ulster and spoke of the good feelings and confidence that existed between the two divisions before he gave his last message for his wife.[71] Major Willie Redmond died for a world that was rapidly fading away also. In a sign of the times, Kilrush UDC resolved that a fund be opened for subscription to both the Major Willie Redmond Memorial Committee, Wexford and the Tomás Aghas Memorial, Dublin.[72]

The following graphs have been compiled by the collation of the Clare dead/missing in the Royal Munster Fusiliers memorial rolls, Commonwealth War Graves listings and previous casualty lists prepared locally for other regimental and navy deaths by Gus O'Halloran, Peadar MacNamara and the Glynn family, Kilrush. I then in turn compared such an amalgamated list with the Registered Absent Voters List 1918 in East Clare and West Clare to ascertain the percentage breakdown of fatalities accounted for in these lists so as to gauge the overall accuracy of the tallies. These figures cannot be considered definite as approximate figures for Co. Clare deaths in the U.S. army are not included. MacNamara does assert that eighteen coffins carrying the remains of Clare born U.S. servicemen arrived at Ennis Railway Station during the Irish Civil War. Military honours were extended by the Irish Free State army in areas under their control. The Republican Irregular army extended military honours in their areas of control.[73]

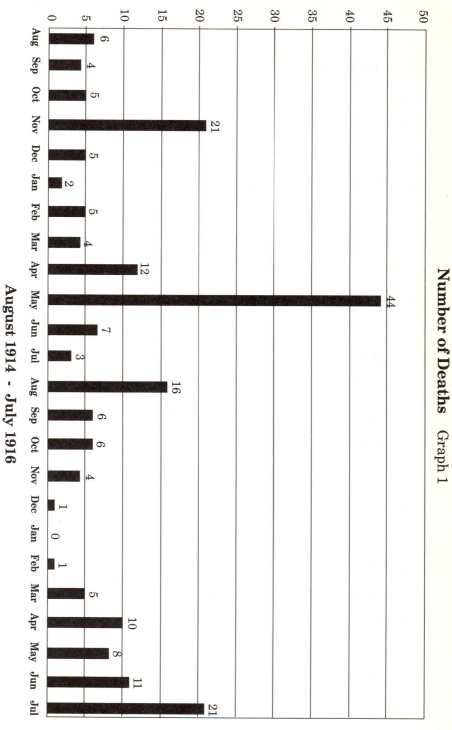

Number of Deaths   Graph 1

August 1914 - July 1916

Month	Deaths
Aug	6
Sep	4
Oct	5
Nov	21
Dec	5
Jan	2
Feb	5
Mar	4
Apr	12
May	44
Jun	7
Jul	3
Aug	16
Sep	6
Oct	6
Nov	4
Dec	1
Jan	0
Feb	1
Mar	5
Apr	10
May	8
Jun	11
Jul	21

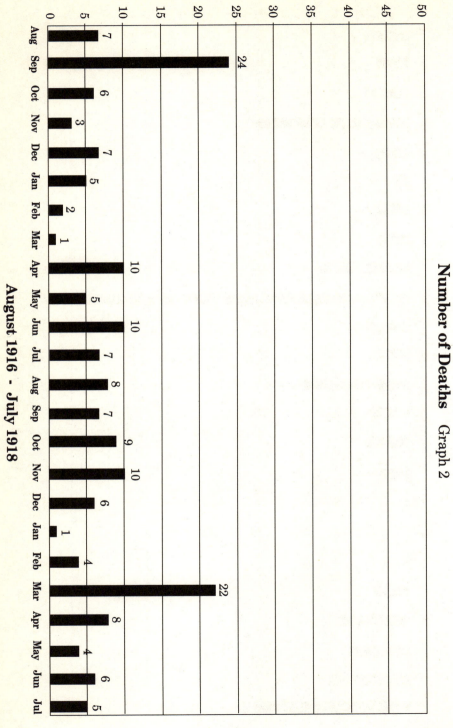

Number of Deaths Graph 2

August 1916 - July 1918

Aug 7
Sep 24
Oct 6
Nov 3
Dec 7
Jan 5
Feb 2
Mar 1
Apr 10
May 5
Jun 10
Jul 7
Aug 8
Sep 7
Oct 9
Nov 10
Dec 6
Jan 1
Feb 4
Mar 22
Apr 8
May 4
Jun 6
Jul 5

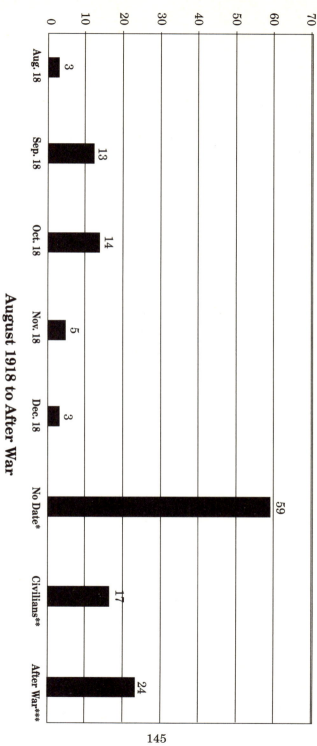

Number of Deaths   Graph 3

August 1918 to After War

* Dates not recorded for 59 casualties in Dysart O'Dea Exhibition on Great War.

** Drowned, *SS Leinster*, *Lusitania* etc.

*** Spanish Influenza, Died of Wounds, etc.

CHAPTER EIGHT

THE ADVENT OF REPUBLICANISM - A RISING TIDE

8.1 THE ELECTION OF DE VALERA

Cranny, Co. Clare   July 24, 1917

My Dear Brother,
I got your letter about ten days ago and as you hoped I was then free. We were released about a month ago. Needless to say were not sorry to get away from England's jails and jailers. Since my release I had a busy and exciting fortnight. We had an election East County Clare - a parliamentary election. There were two candidates a Sinn Féiner and an Irish Party man. Our man won by the magnificent majority of 2,975. He was in jail with me. His name is de Valera. For one year and two months England treated him as if he were one of the worst criminals and Ireland confers on him the highest dignity it is in her power to confer. Another comrade of mine was elected to represent South Longford while we were yet in jail. As the vacancies occur the same thing will happen everywhere throughout the country until we have wiped out the Redmondites who have betrayed Ireland.[1]

Peadar Clancy on the election of de Valera.

In the months after the rising, the attitude towards the rebels in Clare went from sympathy to adulation, if the public statements of representative bodies and later recollections of the period are held as a barometer of public opinion. Ennis RDC at their first meeting after the execution of Roger Casement, condemned 'in the strongest possible manner the action of the government in not extending to him (Casement) the same clemency as was afforded to the South African Rebel Leaders, General De Wet and Colonel Lynch MP, who were guilty of similar offence'.[2]

Corofin RDC also demanded the immediate release of the interned Clare prisoners in November 1916, forwarding a copy of their resolution to the chief secretary.[3] The same body had called for the IPP to oppose any settlement which would exclude any part of Ulster at a July 1916 conference at Omagh. Unknown to them, the coalition cabinet, after considering a draft bill for Home Rule in the same month, decided that 'Sir Edward Carson's claim for the definitive exclusion of Ulster was not to be resisted'.[4] Bishop Berry of Killaloe was one of three Church of Ireland bishops, together with seventeen Roman Catholic bishops, who signed a declaration against partition in May 1917. The *Church of Ireland Gazette* reported Bishop Berry telling his Synod in August 1917:

> We have heard much said by politicians as to the partition of Ireland. I believe every man who loves his country says from the depths of his heart, 'may no such partition ever take place,' but whatever politicians may decide let there be no partition in our Church of Ireland.[5]

The British cabinet ordered the authorities to prevent the organisation of a new Volunteer movement.[6] They also decided to carry out an estimation of how many men would be obtained for their army if in the end compulsion was found necessary and put in force.[7] Tulla RDC called for Claremen to be released who had been deported to Wakefield prison after the Rising while the Kildysart Board of Guardians condemned the inaction of the IPP, with Dillon and Ginnell excepted, and the 'reprobate deportations' from Clare in the aftermath of the Rising, as well as recording their 'profound admiration' for Bishop O'Dwyer.[8]

Bishop O'Dwyer had not openly committed himself to approval of the rebellion in his address on the Rising, but he had nevertheless put the Sinn Féin case with 'great ability and great courage', according to Bishop Fogarty.[9] Fogarty's own initial reaction to the speech was favourable, although not over enthusiastic. While he granted that O'Dwyer had nowhere in the address openly committed himself 'to an approval of rebellion', he thought that people might easily be led to form the opposite opinion. Although it might afford a certain satisfaction to know that his speech would 'shock the heroic Brittains (sic)', and would bring 'joy and consolation to many a troubled Irish conscience', he did not care too much for certain passages in which O'Dwyer seemed to show 'an implicit indifference to the moral aspect of rebellion'. He warned his Limerick colleague that for this reason he would be objected to by many of the other bishops. There was also the strong possibility that the British authorities would have his views 'dilated to Rome'. He wrote another letter to warn O'Dwyer that, although 'the real body of the people', especially the younger generation, were in 'boundless admiration' of him, he had

147

his critics among the 'sober brows' of the Hierarchy.[10]

In Bishop O'Dwyer's Lenten Pastoral for 1917, he spoke at length against the World War. He opined that the press coverage was uniformly in favour of the war and he thought it 'heartbreaking to see both the press and politicians calling for a continuance of the war and appealing to the worst passions of the ignorant people', and he questioned whether informed Irishmen would tolerate their 'flippant and irresponsible language' much longer. Bishop Fogarty wrote to his friend, O'Dwyer, to inform him of the 'furore of delight' with which O'Dwyer's published speech was greeted by most of the people. It struck a cord with them, he opined, particularly with the aspirations of the younger generation, who were sick of the 'falsehood, hypocrisy and cowardice with which the newspapers were drenching them'.[11]

Many commentators have alluded to the fact that political change was only effected in Ireland after the Easter Rebellion. However, the prolonged executions carried out after the Rising stirred a response that could only have been cultivated by the prevailing social and cultural influences of early twentieth century Ireland (as described in Chapter Four). Edward MacLysaght, an insightful and informed contemporary commentator, describes such idealism in the following terms:

> We realised that the republic was more than a dream and that home rule was a poor thing not worth striving, much less dying, for. Maybe we were asleep in that sense, but assuredly we had begun to stir in our sleep. I know that for my part, and I could name dozens of others like me, I had been captured by the ideals of the Gaelic League years before 1916. It seemed to me then that Home Rule politics were uninspiring, if not sordid, and in common with the other young men with whom I discussed things I felt that the one really vital desideratum was an Irish-speaking Ireland.[12]

The prisoners' issue was still very much a rallying point for republicans in 1917. Clare County Council again called on the government to grant a general amnesty to Irish political prisoners in June of that year and stressed the necessity of doing so before any settlement of the 'Irish question' could be reached. Yet Kilrush UDC was of the opinion that the prisoners were 'safe in the hands of the Irish Party' when a letter was received protesting against the treatment of the Irish prisoners from the Irish Workers Council in Dublin.[13] The same body was to later reject and burn a resolution received congratulating Count Plunkett (father of the executed rebel Joseph Mary) on his election victory. Kilrush had provided many men for the British war effort and the UDC's actions were prompted by this fact.

Being a republican prisoner in 1917 enhanced one's political credibility. Indeed to be a Sinn Féiner and avoid a jail sentence could lead to rumour, one Clareman discovered. The county inspector stated that this individual was regarded as an informer in his locality as he had not been arrested and interned and that this was the motive for gunshots fired at his house.[14] The *Evening Telegraph* asked the government to 'throw open the doors of the prison cells' and argued that:

> The prisoners and the deportees are a thousand times more dangerous to the Empire, a thousand times more injurious to the hopes of an Irish settlement, while kept in jail.[15]

A few weeks later, the doors of Lincoln prison were opened for Eamon de Valera, the sole surviving commandant of the Rising. The death of Willie Redmond at the Battle of Messines had left a vacancy for the East Clare seat. A meeting of Sinn Féin supporters from all over the constituency was held in Ennis and Michael Brennan, the Volunteer leader from east Clare, was asked to stand. He declined in favour of de Valera who was the recognised leader of the republican prisoners. Yet a strong majority favoured the nomination of Eoin Mac Neill. Austin Brennan (brother to Michael) secured an adjournment and stated that if Mac Neill were selected, the Volunteers wouldn't accept him because of his inertia in the Rising, but would run de Valera as the Volunteer candidate. This settled the question and eventually de Valera was agreed to unanimously.[16]

The Clare Volunteers had just recently formed a separate Volunteer brigade of their own, with Paddy Brennan (brother to Michael and Austin) as brigade commandant. There was a revamp of the battalion areas and within a few months companies doubled their strength.[17] During this reorganisation, the IRB ensured that its members were selected for key officer positions.[18] The by-election campaign in Clare saw the first public drilling and parading in Ireland since the Rising. The Clare Volunteers, on their own initiative, and independent of GHQ, embarked on a new, aggressive policy. The three phases of the new programme to come into force by the election were:

1. Volunteers unite to hold drill parades in public - preferably in the presence of the RIC.
2. When arrested and charged before a British court the men were to

formally refuse to recognise its authority to try them and they were not to plead nor to make any attempt to defend themselves.

3. When sentenced they were to go on hunger-strike for political prisoner status.[19]

The implications of this new departure will be examined later. Joe Barrett opined that the presence of released prisoners who had came to Clare to assist in the election, as well as the election meetings, gave a great boost to the morale of the Clare Volunteers, and that the by-election resulted in Clare becoming one of the best organised Volunteer counties in the country. Michael Brennan referred to the tensions between friends and relations of British soldiers and Sinn Féin supporters during the election with shots fired in two places.[20]

Arrests were made at Quilty, Cree and Cooraclare at election meetings.[21] Brennan and some of his volunteers had to patrol the roads which de Valera was to cover during his campaign in East Clare as rumours abounded that he was to be shot.[22] The *Clare Champion* had reported on 'disgraceful scenes' in Ennis in the run-up to the election as riots broke out between Sinn Féin supporters and Home Rulers after a National Aid Concert for republican prisoners was held where the tricolour flag was raised. A mob gathered outside, composed mainly of women, who threw stones at the republicans and sang loyal songs.[23] The newspaper noted that previous concerts held in aid of the prisoners of war in Germany had been generously supported and that a concert organised to bring relief to victims of the rebellion should have been 'subjected to such misguided opposition' was regrettable.[24] Incidentally it was Susan Killeen from Doonbeg, who was an avid Gaelic leaguer and close associate of Michael Collins, (indeed they were once lovers during their exile days in London) who helped to keep the Irish National Aid organisation alive.[25]

Kilrush UDC, again staunchly backing the IPP, called upon the East Clare electorate to show that they would not be led away by 'latter day politicians and factionists' and not to forget that the rights and freedom enjoyed by the tenant farmers were achieved 'through the loyal work of our dear Fenian and leader, Major Willie Redmond'.[26] The IPP put their candidate, Patrick Lynch, KC, forward as their standard bearer. He was a member of a popular East Clare political family and was held in very high esteem as he had defended many Claremen who were tried during the Land War days. Although John Redmond, mourning his brother, stayed detached from the election, the IPP very much invested its energy into getting Lynch elected.

De Valera's campaign was conducted with military precision and as a military campaign. He spoke in military uniform and Volunteer companies marched to and from his meetings, which ended with the singing of *The Soldier's Song*. He also demonstrated political sagacity in having Eoin MacNeill accompany him as speech-writer and chief supporting speaker, as MacNeill appealed to both moderate nationalists and the local clergy.[27] Not that de Valera was slow to court clerical favour himself. On his way through to east Clare de Valera had stopped off to visit Dr O'Dwyer and, in his own words, was accorded 'a reception of the warmest description'. O'Dwyer told de Valera that there would never be any improvement in the country until the old order was swept away. If Sinn Féin wanted to build from a 'decent foundation' it would first have to 'clean out the rubbish' and build anew.[28]

Edward MacLysaght recounted a humorous encounter between Fr. Scanlan of Tuamgraney and de Valera, during which a chair had been provided to carry the candidate shoulder high into the town. Fr. Scanlan decided to occupy the chair and to carry de Valera on his knee. Their combined weight caused the chair to collapse, hasty repairs were made and de Valera occupied it alone.[29] Josh Honan, whose father, T.V., was president of Sinn Féin, recalled how as a young six year old he travelled in the open motor which was to take his father and de Valera from the train station to the bishop's palace, and vividly described the slow, triumphant progress to meet Bishop Fogarty, who in full canonical, received de Valera in open arms.[30] Fogarty introduced the Sinn Féin candidate to the priests during the annual retreat a few days later in St. Flannan's College, Ennis.[31] Despite the accusation of being a harbinger of 'red ruin and revolution' by Fr. Slattery of Quin, de Valera was openly supported by almost as many parish priests as was Lynch, and by far more curates.[32]

The stalwart unionist, Colonel O'Callaghan Westropp, admired the integrity of the new political movement in Clare and its candidate:

> He (de Valera) stands for the purest nationality, unsullied by class hatred, uncorrupted by appeals to greed, while every word he utters is a cause of offence to the West Briton, may not we Irish hope that so great a fire may light us on the road to nobler things, rather than consume the land we all love in a senseless conflagration?[33]

In the course of his campaign de Valera made some provocative speeches, such as this one in Ennis:

Words are not what we want today. No protest in words is effective against John Bull. There is only one protest and I ask you all to be ready to make it when the time comes. That is the protest Tom Ashe made, a protest you can only make when ready to offer up your lives, to give your lives without grudge, as Tom Ashe gave his, for the honour and freedom of your country. When you are ready for such a protest, when every man in Ireland is ready for it, then as surely as Brian Boru drove the Norsemen into the sea at Clontarf, so surely will the united will and strength of Ireland drive that now tottering power of the English tyrant into the sea. We are dreamers, they tell us, but we are dreamers who are ready to sacrifice our lives for our dreams.[34]

He also spoke out against the World War and he also warned against the perils of conscription:

We do not know what the future - the immediate future - may hold. England is not satisfied to see the manhood of Ireland at liberty, instead of swelling her ranks to help as someone said, to drive the Germans beyond the Rhine. But by doing that you would be strengthening the power of your oppressor instead of fighting, as Irishmen can, the fight of small nations at home. Tis breaking John Bull's heart to see you here, but if he wishes to conscript Ireland, Redmond's or Dillon's or our words will not prevent it, but your determination to die at home can.[35]

De Valera was asked during one of the election meetings if he were in favour of votes for women. He replied that Irishmen have always regarded women as their equals and never as slaves.[36] Edward Carson had already stated that if the provisional government in Belfast became reality, women would be granted the vote. The Irish Women's Franchise League took a stance of non-involvement in the war effort, thereby somewhat aligning themselves with Sinn Féin's policy on the war.[37]

On 10 July, election day, some unsavoury incidents took place between rival supporters and the streets of Ennis were unsafe to walk.[38] The result was announced the next day: de Valera 5010; Lynch 2035. This was a stunning victory that electrified the country and alarmed the authorities in Britain. Lord Wimborne, the Lord Lieutenant of Ireland, wrote to the cabinet:

The Sinn Féin victory in East Clare is a fact of cardinal significance and has precipitated events. Following as it does on a course of extreme leniency and conciliation which culminated in the general amnesty of political prisoners and tacit tolerance of seditious and secessionist propaganda, it marks the definite failure of the policy to rehabilitate constitutional nationalism or disarm Sinn Féin defiance to English Rule. After making all deductions for local influence and the general revolt against the Redmondite party machine, the fact remains that in a remarkably well conducted political contest sustained by excellent candidates on both sides, the electors on a singularly frank issue of self-government within the Empire versus an Independent Irish Republic have overwhelmingly pronounced for the latter. [39]

When the news of de Valera's victory was announced O'Dwyer wrote to Fogarty, and describing de Valera's success as 'grand', stated that the entire course of the election had justified Fogarty's own belief that there was need for political change.[40] Kilrush RDC congratulated the electorate of East Clare on returning Eamon de Valera by a substantial majority.[41] Acting Sergeant Harrington of Killaloe was fined by Killaloe Petty Sessions Court for punching a civilian on the night of the East Clare result. When asked why he did so, Harrington replied that he hit the civilian for 'rubbing off me'.[42] Such displays of petulance by the authorities did not bode well for the immediate future.

8.2 THE RISING TIDE

England was proof against appeals; she does not understand them. The one thing she could be made to understand was a stand-up, unflinching fight, such as the men of Easter Week had fought, and such as had since been fought by those who were thrown into jail and branded as criminals. East Clare has given England her proper answer, and when the time comes I know that West Clare will add still further to the glory of the fighting county (cheers) ... ...Where was the Defence of the Realm Act this day? (A Voice - "Dead".) Aye, dead! And it is our business to see that it never comes to life again.
Eamon de Valera, 1917, in Kevin J. Browne, *De Valera and the Banner County.*

De Valera's stunning success gave a great impetus to Sinn Féin, not only in Clare but throughout the country and Sinn Féin clubs were formed in every parish and the Brennans' policy of public drilling was taken up again. The Sinn Féin clubs were closely bonded with the Irish Volunteers. Cumann na mBan groups and Fianna Sluagh (scout groups) proliferated especially in the big villages and towns.[43] Andy O'Donoghue claimed that the Volunteer movement grew stronger in the winter of 1917 and the spring of 1918 due to the threat of conscription into the British army.[44] Joe Barrett stated that the Clare volunteers had been already well organised during the 1917 election, and with most of the young men already joined

153

up, there was not, therefore, an influx of recruits as the spectre of conscription loomed.[45]

Even before the Military Service Act was passed in April 1918, which empowered the British government to extend conscription to Ireland, the Volunteers had became more active. There was full turn-out for drills, subscriptions and levies were promptly paid and anti-British feeling increased in intensity.[46] O'Donoghue and O'Keeffe alluded to these developments. Protest meetings were held throughout the county against conscription after Mass, which was the main congregating point for most of the people. Every Volunteer got orders from GHQ to provide himself with a pike for use against troops or police who would try to conscript him.[47] The pike remained as the poignant symbol of defiance in the consciousness of the generations since 1798. The blacksmiths forged pikes out of new rasps and they were fitted to handles six feet long. It must have been a new experience for the MI5 to document the pike-making going on around Doolough Lake.[48]

The British authorities also introduced tillage regulations in an attempt to increase food supply. Kilrush UDC had called for the Department of Agriculture to put into force immediately its compulsory powers and acquire the large numbers of grass ranches and divide them up amongst the uneconomic holders.[49] The regulations played into the hands of Sinn Féiners who decided to 'cash in' on agrarian discontent. In early 1918, Michael Brennan detected a new sense of urgency amongst people in Clare.[50] Cattle drives again became popular. Volunteers in east and north Clare took part in them as organised units, although Seán O'Keeffe praised the discipline of his own Crusheen company in 'seeing to it' that there were no land outrages. The inspector general stated that in the first four months of 1918 'a state of utter lawlessness existed amounting to anarchy'.[51] Cattle-driving was endemic. Large crowds numbering from 300 to 900 people assembled to execute pre-conceived raids.

With one eye on the influential Irish-American political lobby, Lloyd George attempted to improvise an Irish settlement 'to let the Irish people decide their own future'. The resultant Irish Convention was doomed from the outset due to Sinn Féin's refusal to participate in it and the fact that the Ulster unionists had received a prior pledge from Lloyd George that they would be excluded from any Irish parliament. Edward MacLysaght, though having no definite connection with Sinn Féin, was approved by its leaders to act as an unofficial liaison with the convention.[52] During what was considered by most of the convention members as an extreme speech, MacLysaght stated:

> It is true that Sinn Féin is demanding a republic - complete separation. Some men there are who would undoubtedly die for this. But the great bulk of Sinn Féin in the country wants only complete freedom for Ireland to work out her own destiny in her own way, without constant interference, benevolent or malign, by another nation.[53]

While the convention was procrastinating in January 1918, MacLysaght, acting upon Sinn Féin advice, resigned from the convention after Lloyd George refused to define for him the nature of the 'substantial agreement' that the British Prime Minister required from the convention if its recommendations were to be implemented. Reacting to this resignation, Bishop Fogarty wrote the following letter to MacLysaght:

> I have just read your letter on Irish Government in this day's paper. Taken with your resignation from the Convention it has already caused the greatest anxiety in many minds. Can it be possible that they are contemplating above the heads of the people another tragedy for Ireland in the hope of sham Home Rule? Any form of Irish Government short of the authority sketched in your letter will not satisfy Ireland, or bring peace to this country, and would only intensify our present confusion. A country without control of its own trade would be like the Irish farmer in the past, who could not get his daughter married without the consent of his landlord. If the great advocate of "Self-determination" for all the nationalities of the world has nothing for Ireland but feudal slavery of that kind, then he had better leave the Irish deputation at home. The country is sick of all this huxtering, where the path of national interest is so clear to every honest mind.[54]

Alice Stopford Green communicated to MacLysaght that the resignations of himself and AE (George Russell) from the convention 'were good moments to do it. With the Bishop's letter to you, the matter will be carried on and it will have its effect..... I think you started a movement and at the right time. All now justifies you.' [55]

Sinn Féin appeared to be a movement of solidarity in Clare. As Volunteer prisoners went on hunger strike, hostility was shown to the RIC, with boycotting widespread as police turf and potato supplies were destroyed.[56] Hundreds of Sinn Féin supporters converged on land for "potato digs" to aid Volunteer farmers who had been imprisoned. A Sinn Féin market was established in Ennis in January 1918 for the purpose of selling food at cut price to the people.[57] The Clare footballers who contested the All-Ireland football final in 1917 for the first and only time, against the great Wexford four-in-a row champions, marched behind a Sinn Féin banner held aloft by Harry Boland before the game to rapturous applause.[58]

The first Sinn Féin parish court was set up in Kilmacduane, west Clare, in November 1917, in response to a Sinn Féin Ard Fheis proposal for an alternative system of Irish justice. The court dealt with land and civil cases.[59] Patrick Green and James Connell, two Claremen, went on hunger-strike in Limerick prison, following an arrest in connection with an arms raid.[60] Hunger strikes were now widespread, and the police began to repeat the "cat and mouse" system they used against suffragettes pre-war to counter the new republican policy, as well as employing force feeding tactics which the Cooraclare Sinn Féin club denounced as 'brutal and disgusting'.

The Ennis and Kilrush Boards of Guardians were called upon by a Kilrush UDC motion to use their influence to stop the exportation of turf out of the county.[61] Michael Brennan and his Volunteer unit forcibly stopped a sawmill in O'Callaghan's Mills from cutting wood that was intended for the trenches in Europe, and trees that were sold for Government use were cut down also, with Volunteers openly stating that they would not allow timber from Ireland to be put to British use. Two Volunteers were later arrested for their part in this. Their following "prosecution" emphasises the declining powers of British authority in Clare:

> During the hearing of the charge of intimidation, a Constable in his evidence stated that two of the prisoners declared that they would not allow any Irish timber to be supplied to the English Government, and as their statement was received with loud cheering in Court and cries of 'Up Sinn Féin', the Magistrate ordered the court to be cleared, whereupon not alone did the sympathisers, but also the prisoners themselves, leave the court amid a scene of tumult and disorder. A scuffle ensued between police and prisoners but the spectators interfered and literally overwhelmed the police. Some of the prisoners who were too weak, as a result of hunger striking during their previous incarceration, were taken by willing hands, lifted over the benches and escorted triumphantly from the court amid loud cheering and cries of "Up the Rebels" and "Up Sinn Féin". The police in court appeared to be powerless to prevent the escape and an amusing part of the incident was that a large force of police outside in the hall of the Courthouse practically assisted the prisoners escape. One Constable told a number of prisoners "to clear out of that and don't be shouting".[62]

The Volunteers availed of arming themselves at every opportunity. Joe Barrett's brigade continued to pick up firearms at random.

He stated how in early 1918, the South Irish Horse were stationed at Edenvale outside Ennis. It was a yeomanry body, which had been mobilised for war service, and some arms were procured from them and others were bought. After a short time, the British military authorities became aware that these arms were missing and the South Irish Horse were transferred to another station.[63]

An RIC patrol of three men were rushed and deprived of their arms (carbines) at Knockerra Cross - three miles from Kilrush. The arms were dumped in a house only fifty yards off, while the police were still on the spot.[64] Such scenes also took place near Scariff, when clashes occurred between cattle-drivers and crown forces. Two police cyclists were met, and their rifles taken from them. An attempt was made to take a bayonet from a soldier but another soldier fired a shot, and the assailant ran away. The drive took place on the property of Dr Sampson, and the cattle were given to him. The telegraph wires were cut around Ennis, and a number of trees were felled across the roads to impede the police.[65]

The following extract of an intercepted letter from Clare to Rhode Island describes how the disruption of the annual exodus from Clare by the war lent itself towards giving greater impetus to the revolutionary fervour in the county:

> You know it is a glorious thing for one to fight for his country, as love of country comes next to love of God. You could apply this to me as an answer to your remark...... There is nothing I hate more than writing a letter and not able to put what you like in it or to explain the political state of the country. However, we must abide by John Bull as long as he holds the rope that is around our neck, or if not he gives us a chuck. Well, I hope to see that rope out of his hands some day...... You asked me to consider going out to you. Well, I think I can give you an answer just now. I would love to, but I am of the opinion there is work left for me to do in the liberation of my country from a foreign and unrelenting tyranny and in the advancement of the Irish nation as a whole.[66]

Further excerpts in a letter from Kilkee convey the open antagonism shown towards the British, in the country.

> I am sorry America entered the War, and I expected better from them. I hope you will never have to fight on the side of our ancient enemy, I mean under compulsion. England is still our enemy, our bitter enemy, and anyone who fights on their side is Ireland's enemy also.[67]

From Miltown, a correspondent wrote:

> When the English are blown out of the earth, Ireland will have her freedom. The Irish can't do much, when they haven't the guns, but the Old Kaiser might send us a few. Be ready to lend a hand to Sinn Féin, when needed, the

submarines won't touch you. Every Sinn Féiner in turn gets a trip in the German submarine.[68]

In February 1918, Clare was proclaimed a military area. The *Clare Champion* was banned, letters and telegrams censored and persons entering or leaving the country were issued with permits by the military. Bishop Fogarty of Killaloe wrote to Mr. Guinane of the Ennis Sinn Féin executive, this seething reaction to the introduction of martial law:[69]

> I must thank you and the Sinn Féin Executive for the resolutions you have sent me and which I highly value. Sinn Féin needs no vindication from me or anyone else. We had almost ceased to be Irish until Sinn Féin arose and struck the English rust from the Soul of Ireland.
> Unfortunately, that rust had eaten deep, and spoiled many a good Irish Heart. For one thing, I hope we are done forever with that mockery of a constitution of the English House of Commons. The self-control maintained by the young people of Ireland and especially of Clare, in spite of the callous provocation to which they are being subjected is beyond all praise. Everything truly Irish is being oppressed with a tyranny both brutal and scandalous. Young men, the flowers of the country, are being arrested wholesale, degraded, insulted, imprisoned, shot or bayoneted like poor Thomas Russell of Carrigaholt, the killing of whom is, in all its circumstances, one of the most horrid and atrocious things I have ever heard of. Were these things done in Belgium how the world be made to ring with the cry of German atrocities.
> But this policy of oppression and provocation will not succeed in its purpose, which is obvious enough, to clear the ground by extermination of national spirit for the English friends "of the Sanity" party, and, if possible prepare the way for conscription - which, by the way, no Government, in my opinion, has the moral right to inflict on any nation without that nations clearly expressed consent.
> Martial Law has not shaken the hand of Clare, which, still holds in a firm grasp the Sinn Féin banner of Irish Independence. No scheme of federalism which leaves Ireland as a morsel swallowed in the British stomach will be accepted here. I enclose, with my good wishes, a cheque for the support of the Clare prisoners.

A correspondent of the *Manchester Guardian* reporting on Clare said the trouble 'is an economic one', that 'scanty plots, which cannot nourish a family,' are side by side with farms consisting of thousands of acres, which are only used for feeding cattle. Yet he hastened to add that 'bolshevism had not taken root in Clare'. Fogarty agreed with this correspondent's sentiments on bolshevism, in an interview with the *Cork Examiner*.[70] However the establishment of workers councils or soviets in Broadford and in Kilfenora soon after, made it clear that the message of bolshevism was being heard in Clare.[71]

The anti-conscription movement further boosted Sinn Féin, as the people felt that it was they who were preventing conscription. Then in May 1918 Joseph Dowling (of Casement's former Irish Brigade) was put ashore on Crab Island just off Doolin from a German submarine, and was immediately arrested. Lord French disingenuously proclaimed that there was a "German Plot" and proceeded to crack down on the Sinn Féin leadership.[72] Bishop Fogarty highlighted the dubious nature of the government accusations. Speaking at Moneygall in June 1918, the bishop said that he wished he could assure the people that the menace of conscription had passed forever. The published evidence of the German Plot only confirmed:

> suspicions as to the bogus character of it, and showed that the Government thought the Irish were fools. The action of the Government has created a great peril for Ireland. The leaders having been taken from us, the best thing to do is to carry out Mr. de Valera's parting advice - "be calm and confident". Any departure from this would be ruinous and would give the Government an opportunity of justifying arrests, and of conscripting the country.

Conscription was never realised and Sinn Féin's dominance in both Clare and Irish politics was confirmed in the general election of December 1918. "Faugh a Ballagh", the *Freeman's Journal* columnist, wrote to the Clare County Court Judge, Bodkin, asking him to encourage the Irish Party to step up the urgency in their constituency prior to the election:

> The Sinn Féiners have distributed leaflets wholesale, and I am surprised at the lack of energy of those working for the party both in canvassing and in sending through the constituencies some telling literature..... however it is not too late yet if it is done between now and polling day. Do not hesitate, those who do get lost. With best wishes to you and the Irish Party for a glorious victory for poor old Ireland...[74]

Such apparent lethargy, symptomatic of a tired Party contrasted with Sinn Féin's sense of purpose. Brian O'Higgins, a poet and the principal of the Gaelic College in Carrigaholt, won the West Clare Sinn Féin convention nomination, (he was selected ahead of Patrick Brennan of the Volunteer family in Meelick and Seán Ó Muirthuile, the Gaelic League organiser for West Clare - although it was later reported that Peadar Clancy had never replied to letters originally nominating him for the seat)[75] and was returned unopposed as was the outgoing East Clare member, Eamon deValera, now the president of the political and military wings of the republican movement. The circle was near complete.

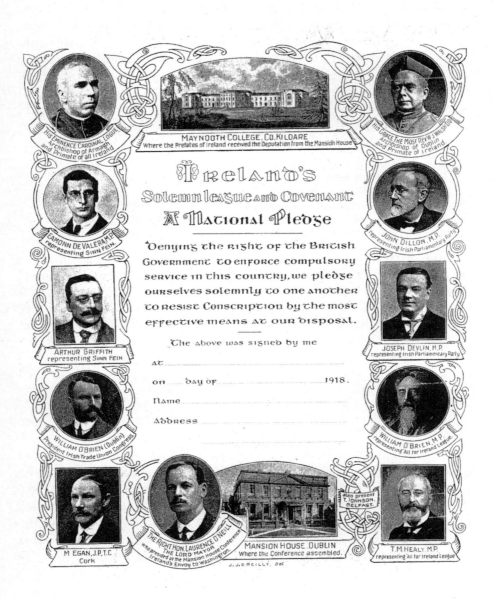

Anti-Conscription Pledge 1918

EPILOGUE

RINGING OUT THE OLD?

So it came to pass that on the eleventh hour, of the eleventh day in the eleventh month of 1918 the guns fell silent upon the killing fields of Europe. Over five hundred Clare natives perished as a result of the four years of conflict, with many more wounded and traumatised. In 1998 a sixty year old resolution prohibiting the inscription of regimental badges on the gravestones of men who fought in the war was replaced by an adopted motion to allow the insignia of regimental badges be placed on the gravestones of former soldiers irrespective of regimental attachment.[1] Such prior legislation typified the political and social amnesia regarding participation in the Great War that enveloped Clare and much of Irish society post 1918.

It is interesting to assess some of the experiences of Great War veterans in Clare to gauge the mood of the environment to which they had returned. Jane Leonard, curator of History in Ulster Museum, has detailed the nature of the disdain with which 'green redcoats' were held by the majority of Sinn Fein supporters in Ireland.[2] She addressed the motives for IRA antagonism towards the ex-soldiers, among which was included republican envy of their military skills and experience and the rewards that this had brought - not just military honours but pensions, housing and land schemes and government sponsored employment such as auxiliary postmen.[3] Such an example in a Clare context was Martin Clune from Quin who served in the Mesopotamian campaign and after the war took up a position as a postman.[4] Indeed it is legitimate to argue that the fact employers were inclined to favour veterans after demobilisation, when additional thousands came on to the job market, led to favourable conditions for the growth of trade unions which offered protection to workers. That trade unions could camouflage more covert republican activities also helped to foster the growth of twenty two branches of the Irish Transport and General Workers' Union in Clare by 1920.[5]

However, Tadhg Moloney, Secretary of the Royal Munster Fusiliers Association, in his postgraduate research on Co. Limerick and the Great War, refers to a very different scenario encountered by a Limerick Corporation employee who upon returning from the War was denied the resumption of his position despite previous assurances to the contrary by his employers at the time of recruitment. Sonny Enright, a cattle dealer from Ballynacally, Co. Clare described the pitiful conditions under which Great War veterans who worked as drovers lived:

> They were great men 1914-18, ex-soldiers and their pension that time was sixteen shillings a week. They had tattered clothes, bad boots and were lucky if they had a bag over their shoulders on a wet day. They knew how to dress cattle, hold them up and would stay with you until 10p.m. at night if you needed them..... My principal drover was Dan Moore and if you asked Dan where he slept last night, he would tell you that he slept with the widow green, that was the side of the road or the green field.[6]

Martin Morrissey, in his depiction of a west Clare parish in the aftermath of the Great War, described the experiences of a returned native who had worked in a navy dockyard in Southampton.[7] He resented his state of poverty and longed for the navy again. Many of his fellow parishioners had served in the Great War with several suffering serious injuries, especially those who had served in the army. These had come home amputated or partially blinded, or suffered respiratory problems as a result of being exposed to mustard gas. The war-wounded were in receipt of a British army or navy disability pension, which helped to provide for their families and gave the security of a guaranteed monthly cheque. Some of these recipients were still able to engage in light work on the strand in Quilty to supplement their small income.[8]

Martin Staunton also referred to cases of former soldiers from Clare suffering from respiratory ailments, such as Patrick McSparron from Kilrush, who died in 1929 from bronchitis and physical debility that was brought on by four years spent as a prisoner of war, having been captured at Etreux where the Munsters were cut off by the early German advances in 1914.[9] Dr McClancy of the Clare Infirmary informed the *Clare Champion* that there were numerous ex-servicemen being treated in the institution, on average three or four continually for the twelve months prior to October 1918.[10] The War Office paid at the rate of £1.8s per ex- military patient per week.[11]

First World War veterans were to make significant contributions to the republican cause in the 1919-21 period. Their combat experience was valued by local volunteer units. Brennan, O'Keeffe and O'Donoghue have already highlighted that the volunteer drill instructors pre-war were all ex-British soldiers. Joost Augusteijn outlined the importance of experience in accounting for the high number of ex-soldiers among the IRA forces, with officers preferring to repeatedly rely on men already seasoned in battle.[12] After the Mid-Clare IRA brigade council decided to establish a flying column (active service unit) in late 1920, training was led by Ignatius O'Neill and Martin Slattery who were ex-Allied soldiers. This involved lectures on the care and mechanism of Lee Enfield service rifles, aiming exercises and judging distances.[13] Patrick O'Mahony, Ennis, enlisted in the British Army, because he had 'became unhappy during his apprenticeship and was hoping to satisfy some of his adventurous desires'.[14] After demobilisation he returned to his native Ennis where he became a member of the Ennis Company, 1st Battalion, Mid-Clare IRA and was soon active as a drill instructor. During the Civil War, he was imprisoned by the Free State army and later executed in Ennis.

There were similar examples across the nation of the contributions made by these veterans to the IRA, with the most renowned being that of Tom Barry, the leader of the West Cork Flying Column, who had previously served in the British army. Yet even for some of those who had apparently fallen in behind the republican banner, there was the issue of confronting the niggling doubts harboured by a section of their new comrades - highlighted by the case of former British soldier, Thomas Kirby of south Tipperary.[15] This was because the majority of returned ex-servicemen were no longer seen as being part of the community but were perceived by republicans as being outsiders, dupes of an alien authority. Consisting mainly of Anglo-Irish locals, some nationalist politicians, clergy and ex-servicemen, many of the Great War charities and bodies were to later amalgamate to form the British Legion. Many Clare veterans also communicated with the Royal Munster Fusiliers Old Comrades Association. Such groupings became bastardized in the outlook of the new status quo, notwithstanding the strong polling of war veteran candidates who represented either the Comrades of the Great War or the Labour party in the urban areas of Ennis, Kilrush and Kilkee during the local elections of 1920. Those who remained in contact with former comrades from the Great War became legitimate targets for many republicans. The ex-serviceman John O'Reilly, assassinated in Newmarket-on-Fergus, had marked on his body:

'Getting them at last - Beware'.[16]

This unfurling scenario goes some way towards contextualizing the tensions and ambiguities involved in the official memorialising of those Clare natives who had contributed to the Great War struggle. The slow death of Asquithean Britain had rendered the Irish Parliamentary Party irrelevant as the arbitrary policies of the British government swept the middle ground from underneath them. The aim of the Home Rulers had been to remove the British political presence in Ireland through their parlance, whereas Sinn Féin sought to sever the link through its actions. The Irish Party was to be systematically dismantled by an advanced nationalism that had at its core, the cult of redemption, and this left the Home Rule ship floundering in the revolutionary tide. The emergent State was too embittered to engage in goodwill overtures towards a nation and those in its service which 'Irish-Ireland' had been taught to defy.

However in the era of the Good Friday agreement, almost a century on from the end of the war that was to end all wars, there appears now to be a sympathetic attitude towards those who had been near obliterated from the public memory. In November 1998, President Mary McAleese dedicated the Island of Ireland Peace Park in Messines, Belgium, near to where William Redmond had fallen, to the Irish who had fought in the Great War, standing alongside the King and Queen of Belgium and Queen Elizabeth II. Kilrushman, Colonel Michael Shannon was a trustee of the Journey of Reconciliation Trust Fund which financed the building of the peace park. There was also a large gathering for the Armistice Day commemoration at the war memorial in the Old Shanakyle cemetery in Kilrush. The North Clare War Memorial committee was also set up. The editorial of the *Clare Champion* under the headline, 'Lest We Forget', concluded:

> If nothing else, these tributes should ensure that the rest of us never again forget the heroes and heroines of the Great War.

These tributes do not gainsay the fact that the representations of the public remembrance of the war does not remain as an emotive issue for many. Yet there is no doubt that there is now a greater public appreciation of the nuances of our past than previously held. For this reason alone, society is enhanced.

APPENDIX I

Fatality List of Clare Casualties in Great War.

Note: b = born, e = enlisted, d = died, DOW = died of wounds,
KIA = killed in action F & F = France and Flanders

(1)   Allingham, Pte. Edward V., b. Kilfarboy, e. Dublin, F & F.
      Irish Guards, 27/9/18.
(2)   Armstrong, Lieut. Charles Martin, Age 23. KIA France, 18/2/17.
(3)   Adams, Herbert George, Royal Air Force, 26/10/19, Bristol.
(4)   Baird, Pte. Robert, 2nd Batt. Royal Irish Rgt., 1/6/18, Killaloe.
(5)   Baker, Capt. T., RGA formerly Indian Service, KIA.
(6)   Barren, Pat, 1st Garrison, Royal Irish Regt. 1/1/17, Lisdoonvarna.
(7)   Barrett, John, accountant, e. 10/9/14 Durkirk, KIA F & F 20/4/17, when
      advancing at head of his squad of riflemen on assault of heavily defended
      trench, Croix de Guerre.
(8)   Bayliss, Driver, Herbert Gerald, 7th Bde., Royal Horse Artillery, 12/3/19,
      Clare.
(9)   Baxter, Gunner, John, 206th Siege Bty, RGA, 24/4/12, Killaloe.
(10) Beakey, Pte. Martin, 2nd Bn., Royal Irish Regt., 22/10/20, Ennistymon.
(11) Behan, Stoker, John, Monmouth Royal Navy, 1/11/14, Kilkee.
(12) Bentley, Pte. William, 1st Bn. RMF 22/11/18, Cratloe.
(13) Blake, Pte. Frank, Corbally, RDF, Died of Wounds, Quin.
(14) Blake, Pte. Martin, 1st/7th Bn (King's Liverpool Reg.), 22/9/17, Killaloe.
(15) Blake, Pte. F., 2nd/1st Batt. RDF, 20/7/16, Quin.
(16) Blood, Patrick, Ennistymon & Limerick, 8th RMF, 4/9/16.
(17) Bothwell, Pte. 2nd Class, George Alfred, Wireless School Royal Air Force,
      4/10/18, Chippentiann, b, Kilkee.
(18) Brazil, Pte. James, 2nd Bn. Canadian Inf, Hector St., Kilrush, 4/5/15.
(19) Breen, Pte. Michael, 2nd Bn. RMF, 25/9/15, Kilrush.
(20) Breen, Pte. Michael, 2nd/1st Bn. RMF, 9/5/15, Knock, Ennis.
(21) Breen, Pte., John, b. Stratford, enlisted. Kilrush, Mesopotamia,15/4/17,
      Conn Rngs.
(22) Breen, Pte., Pat, b. Kilrush, e. Ennis, F&F, 3/9/16, 2nd Bn. RIR.
(23) Brennan, Joseph, 1st Bn. RMF, 21/8/15, Grace St., Kilrush.
(24) Brennan, James, Bunratty, enlisted. Limerick, RMF, 1st, 27/7/16.
(25) Breslin, Pte., Thomas, 59th Batt. Aust. Infantry, 19/7/16, Edinburgh, Scotland.
(26) Brogan, John, Drumcliffe, e. Wigan, Lancs. 6th RMF, 21/3/18, KIA. Palestine.
(27) Browne, Thomas, Clareabbey, e. Ennis, 8th RMF, 22/6/16.
(28) Browne, John, S.I.M., 29/3/17, Ballynacally.
(29) Browne, Pte. Michael, b. Kilmacduane, e. Manchester Lancs.
(30) Buckley, James, Kilrush, e Kilkee, 2nd RMF, 9/5/15.
(31) Burley, Pte., RMF, KIA, Dardanelles, 3/8/15, Ennis.
(32) Burley, Pte., Michael, 1st Bn., RMF, 25/4/15, Cornmarket, Ennis,
      KIA. Gallipoli.
(33) Burke, Pat Joseph, 4th Batt., Aust. Inf., 15/4/17, Rock Cottage, Clonlara.
(34) Burke, William, St. John's Limerick, e. Limerick, 2nd RMF, 17/4/16, Ennis.
(35) Burke, Michael, Drumcliffe e. Limerick, RMF, 1" 12/1/17.
(36) Burke, Pte., John, b. Foynes, e. Ennis Limerick F&F, 7/6/17.
(37) Butler, Pte., Michael, Drumcliffe, e. Ennis RMF 1st KIA, Gallipoli, 25/4/15.
(38) Butler, Sgt. RMF, KIA, DCM, Ennis.
(39) Byrne, John Francis, 58th Batt. Aust. Infantry, 5/1/18, Killaloe.
(40) Cahill, L/Cpl Thomas, Steele's Terrace, DOW France, Ennis.
(41) Calahane, Gunner W, RGA, KIA, Kildysart.

(42) Carey, Pte.,Daniel, b. Kilmacduane, Clare, e. Dublin, F&F, Irish Guards, KIA Gallipoli, 15/9/16.
(43) Carpenter, Pte., Patrick, Drumcliffe, e. Nenagh 1st RMF, KIA Gallipoli 26/4/15.
(44) Carmody, Daniel, 1st Bn. Leinster Reg., 9/5/15, e. Ennis.
(45) Carroll, Lance Corporal, William, 5th Royal Irish Lancers, 2/5/15, Edenvale, Ennis.
(46) Cagey, Peter, Miltown, 9th RMF, 28/5/16, e. Ennis.
(47) Casey, Thomas, 16th Batt. Aust. Inf. 8/8/18, Tubber, Clare.
(48) Casey, Ginger, Sniper, KIA.
(49) Casserly, L/Cpl, Tom, Cornmarket, RE, KIA France 1/4/18.
(50) Chambers, James Francis, 2nd Batt. Wellington Regt., 15/9/16, Cooraclare.
(51) Clancy, Thomas, 4th Batt. Guards Machine Gun Regt., transferred to Royal Air Force 9/10/17, Kildysart.
(52) Clancy, 2nd Lt. William Joseph, Army Service Corps, 16/10/18, Kilrush.
(53) Cleary, Daniel, Fireman Glasgow, Merchantile Marine, 18/12/17, Clare.
(54) Cleary, Pte., Stephen, Drumcliffe, e. Limerick, 1st RMF, KIA Gallipoli, 2/9/18.
(55) Clohessy, Pte., John, 8th Batt, RMF, 21/8/15, Ennistymon, KIA Gallipoli.
(56) Coalpoise, Pte. Frank, b. Ennistymon, e. Cork, F&F, 17/11/14, Irish Guards.
(57) Coffey, Pte. John, b. Kilkishen, e. Ennis, F&F, 8/5/18, Irish Guards.
(58) Coffey, Lieut. F. W., RIR, KIA France, Kilkee.
(59) Coughlan, Thomas, 2nd Batt., Leinster Regt., 5/4/16, Ennis.
(60) Cole, Fireman R. Limerick, Mercantile Marine, 10/6/17, Ennis.
(61) Colgan, Edmond, Tralee e. Limerick, 1st RMF, 30/6/15, Ennis.
(62) Collins, Thomas, Sixmilebridge, e. Limerick, 31/3/16.
(63) Coleman, Michael, 6th Bn. Conn. Rangers, 1/8/16, Sixmilebridge.
(64) Comber, Edward, 2nd Bn. Royal Irish Regt., 7/9/14, Ennistymon.
(65) Conway, Bombadier, KIA.
(66) Conway, Pat, Drumcliffe, 8th RMF, 20/7/16, e. Ennis.
(67) Conway, Martin, 2nd Bn., Irish Guards, 30/9/15, Ennis.
(68) Conway, Patrick, Monmouth, Royal Navy, 1/11/14, Kilrush.
(69) Considine, William, 13th Bn. Aust. Inf. AIF, 1/5/19, Cooraclare.
(70) Considine, Peter, Canterbury Regt., 6/5/18, Clare.
(71) Considine, Arthur, *S.S. Keeper*, Clare Civilian, Clarecastle.
(72) Cooney, Michael, 1st Coy, Australia Gun Corps., 24/9/17, Broadford, Clare.
(73) Coonan, Thomas, 4th Bn. Guards Machine Gun Regt., 7/5/18, Ogonnelloe, Killaloe.
(74) Cooney, Patrick, 1st Garrison Bn. Royal Irish Fus., 26/6/16, Kilrush.
(75) Copley, Joseph, Ennis, 2nd Bn. RMF, 22/3/18, e. Ennis.
(76) Corbette, Michael, Kilrush, 8th Bn., 20/7/16 RMF, e. Ennis.
(77) Corbett, John Patrick 1st Bn. East Lancashire Regt., 2/11/14, Tulla.
(78) Corry, T., 75th Bn. Canadian Inf., 30/9/18, Miltown.
(79) Corry, Joseph, 1st Bn. RDF, 5/10/17, Miltown.
(80) Corry, R., North Lancs., KIA.
(81) Cosgrove, John, Castlebank, Clare, e Limerick, 2nd RMF, 17/8/16.
(82) Costelloe, Cornelius, 2nd RMF, Kilkee, e Kilrush, 13/5/15.
(83) Costelloe, Corporal John, 1st Bn., RMF, 30/9/18, Kilkee.
(84) Costello, J., b. Mullagh, 7th Bn. RMF, d. Greek Macedonia,13/11/15.
(85) Crawford, Sapper, William Robert, Engineer, 4/5/17, Miltown.
(86) Crowe, Pte. M., 8th Bn. Canadian Inf., 29/3/18, Querrin.
(87) Creagh, Lt. O'Moore Charles, 108th Army Bde., RFA, 23/3/18, Cahirbye.
(88) Crowe, T. H., St. Anthony's Terrace, KIA, 10/10/16, Ennis.
(89) Crowe, Col. H. Thomas, 16th Batt. Canadian Scottish, KIA France, 9/9/17.
(90) Crowe, Pte. M., 8th Bn. Canadian Inf., 29/3/18, Querrin.
(91) Coughlan, J., 1st Bn. RMF, 9/9/16, Ennis.
(92) Coughlan, Michael Joseph, 8th Bn. RMF, 14/5/16, Kilrush.
(93) Courtney, Pte. Patrick, b. Corofin, e. Limerick. F&F, 12/4/18, Irish Guards.

(94)   Courtney, Paul James, Royal Army Service Corps, 26/7/20, Killaloe.
(95)   Coyne, John, RDF, Labour Corps 10/10/18, Tuamgraney, Clare.
(96)   Cullinan, Capt. P. B., 3rd Batt. Lein. Reg., wounded and gassed 23/3/18, N.-on-Fergus.
(97)   Cullinan, Charles, 1st Bn. Leinster Reg, 7/5/15, Ennis.
(98)   Cullinan, Lt. Robert Horridge, 7th Bn. RMF, 8/8/15, Bindon St., Ennis.
(99)   Cullinan, John, 2nd Bn. RMF, 18/5/15, Ennis.
(100)   Cunneen, John, N.-on-Fergus, e. Ennis, 27/8/14, RMF.
(101)   Cunningham, John, 2nd Bn. RMF, 9/5/15, Turnpike, Ennis.
(102)   Cunningham, William, 2nd Bn. Leins. Regt., 20/10/14, Turnpike.
(103)   Curtin, Laurence, 1st Bn. RMF, Kilrush, 12/5/15 DOW. Gallipoli.
(104)   Cuny, Pte. Michael, D.,Cratloe, e. Ennis, F&F, 6/11/14, Irish Guards.
(105)   Cusack, Sapper Oliver, 11th Field Coy. Royal Engineers, age 20, DOW, Edmonton Hospital, Clarecastle.
(106)   Cusack, Thomas. 2nd Bn. RMF, 24/10/16, Kilrush.
(107)   Cusack, James, 1st Regt. South African Infantry, 18/7/16, Sixmilebridge.
(108)   Daly, Trimmer Michael Francis HM (Trawler) R. Naval Reserve, 10/2/18, Kilrush.
(109)   Danaher, Sgt. Patrick, 2nd Bn. Royal Irish Regt., 5/7/16, Killaloe.
(110)   Davis, F. Buried Ennistymon 8/11/18, 5th RMF.
(111)   Davis, Pte. Thomas, 1st RMF, executed Dardenelles, 2/7/1915.
(112)   Davoren, Nurse Delia, Claureen, Ennis, drowned *SS Leinster*, Clare civilian.
(113)   Davoren, Nurse Nora, Claureen, Ennis, drowned *SS Leinster*, Clare civilian.
(114)   Deenihan, Thomas, Kilrush, 6th RMF, 11/8/15, e. Ennis, DOW. Gallipoli.
(115)   Delohery, Pte. Michael, 3rd Bn. Royal Irish Regt., 30/12/16.
(116)   Dicks, Bombardier Thomas, 121st Heavy Bty RGA, 24/4/17, O'Callaghan's Mills.
(117)   Dillon, Patrick, 8th Bn. RMF, 8/6/16, Kilnaboy, Clare.
(118)   Doherty, Cornelius, Miltown, 14/4/16, enlisted, Ennis.
(119)   Doherty, Pte. Michael, 2nd Bt. KIA, France, 12/4/17.
(120)   Doherty, 2nd Lt. Patrick, 1st Bn. Royal Irish Rifles, 1/8/17, Kilshanny.
(121)   Dolaghty, Gunner W. L., RGA, 12/3/21, Quin.
(122)   Donaghue, Thomas, buried Kilrush, 11/2/20, RMF.
(123)   Donnelly, John, 6th Bn. RMF, 19/10/15, Lisdeen, Clare.
(124)   Dooley, L/Cpl John, b. Starell e. Dublin, F&F, 31/7/17.
(125)   Doyle, Pte. J., KIA, Ennis.
(126)   Dowling, Captain J., South African Medical Corps, 19/10/18, Ballynacally.
(127)   Droney, Pat, Ballymagh, Clare, 2nd RMF, 22/9/16, e. Ennis.
(128)   Duffy, Michael, 13th Bn. King's Liverpool Regt., 16/7/16, Quin.
(129)   Duggan, John, died of heart failure, Sept. 1915.
(130)   Earls, Martin, Miltown, e. Limerick, 1st RMF, 25/4/15 KIA Gallipoli.
(131)   Edwards, Patrick, Ennistymon, 2nd RMF, 21/12/14, e. Limerick.
(132)   Egan, Rifleman Francis, 2nd/6th Bn. London Regt., 16/4/18, Corofin.
(133)   Egan, Pte. Michael, b. Kilkishen e. Ennis, F&F, 1/11/14.
(134)   Egan, Rev. Pierce, MA, died of dysentery, Alexandria, 6/4/16.
(135)   Ensko, John, Drumcliffe, e. Ennis, 1st RMF, 21/8/15, KIA Gallipoli.
(136)   Fahy, John, Irish Guards, KIA, Ennis.
(137)   Falvey, Private D., 1st Bn. RMF, 10/8/17, Inchbeg, Ennis, DOW, F & F.
(138)   Fennell, James, Kilkee 6th Bn. RMF, 31/7/16, e. Ennis, d. Greek 'Macedonia'.
(139)   Fitzgerald, Pte. Patrick, 1st/7th Bn. Worcestershire Regt. 26/8/17, Dromleigh.
(140)   Fitzpatrick, Pte. John, 1st Bn. RMF, 21/8/15, Ennistymon, KIA Gallipoli.
(141)   Flaherty, Patrick, Ennis, lst Bn. 30/9/14, e. Ennis.
(142)   Flannagan, John, Ennistymon, Ist Bn., 8/3/16, e. Ennis.
(143)   Flynn, Arthur, Adare, Limerick, 1st RMF, 27/9/18, e. Limerick, Killaloe.
(144)   Fogarty, 1st Bn. RMF, 27/12/18, Corbally, Quin.
(145)   Fogarty Pte. John, 1st Bn. RMF, 27/12/18, Quin, DOW Home.
(146)   Fogarty, Lt. John Frederick Cullinan, 227th, Field Coy, Royal Engineers, b. Limerick, 25/9/17, Bank Place, Ennis.

(147) Fogarty, Lt. William Perrott, 57th Wilde's Rifles, 19/10/19, Bank Place, Ennis.

(148) Foley, Lance Sergeant Timothy, 2nd Bn. Irish Guards 13/4/18, Ennistymon.

(149) Foran, Michael, Kilkee, e. Kilkee 1st RMF, 27/12/16, KIA F & F.

(150) Forde, Rifleman John, 8th Bn. London Regt., 15/9/16, N.-on-Fergus.

(151) Frazer, Cpl. Robert, Lancs, legs amputated DOW, Ennis.

(152) Frazer, Pte. Thomas, e. Ennis, F&F, 15/10/18

(153) Frawley, Pte. Patrick, I3th Bn. RMF, 25/4/15, Turnpike, Ennis, KIA Gallipoli.

(154) Friel, George, Liscannor, Ennistymon, 2nd RMF, 10/11/17, e. Limerick.

(155) Gallagher, Rifleman Thomas, 1st Bn. Royal Irish Rifles, 24/4/17, Ennis.

(156) Galvin, Michael, Kilmurry McMahon, drowned on *Lusitania*, 3/5/15.

(157) Gardiner, Pte. Thomas, b. Ennis, e. Dublin, F&F, 12/7/16, Irish Guards.

(158) Garrahy, Pte. John Joseph, b. Lahinch, e. Ennis, F&F, 3/9/16, Leinster Reg.

(159) Garry, Dr Joseph, Kildysart, drowned on *Lusitania*, 3/5/15.

(160) Gissane, Sapper James, Royal Engineers, 5/7/18, Killaloe.

(161) Gleeson, Pte. Pat, shot on wires KIA.

(162) Gleeson, Pte. Thomas, 2nd Bn. RMF, 24/8/16, Clarecastle.

(163) Glynn, Pte. T, 2nd Bn. RMF, 26/9/16, Ballyvaughan.

(164) Gordon, Frank, 103rd Field Artillery NM US army, KIA rescuing another, Croix de Guerre, Clarecastle.

(165) Grogan, Gunner P, 2nd Reserve-Bde., RFA, 18/6/18, Clare.

(166) Gorman, Pte. Martin, 2nd Bn. RMF, 4/10/18, Kilrush.

(167) Griffin, Able Seaman John, Bulwark, Royal Navy, 26/11/14, Kilrush.

(168) Griffin, Pte. John, 1st Bn. RMF, 25/4/15, Ballyvaughan, KIA Gallipoli.

(169) Griffin, Pte. Joseph, 1st Bn. RMF, 22/3/18, Miltown Malbay, KIA F & F.

(170) Griffey, Pte. Matthew, 2nd Bn. Leinster Regt., 20/10/14, Jail St.,Ennis.

(171) Griffin, Michael, 2nd Bn. O'Brien's Bridge, 6/10/15, e. Limerick.

(172) Griffin, Thomas, 1st Bn. O'Brien's Bridge, Clare 21/12/14, e. Limerick.

(173) Griffin, Pte. Patrick, 2nd Bn, RMF, 27/3/15, Kilkee

(174) Griffin, Pte. Patrick, 2nd Bn. Irish Regt. 24/11/18, Kilrush.

(175) Griffin, 2nd Lt. Stephen, 88th Sq. Dr., Royal Air Force, 18/5/18, Kilmaley

(176) Hallinan, Pte. J., Railway Station, 2nd Leinster KIA, Ennis.

(177) Hallinan, Pte. Michael, 7th Bn. RMF, 15/8/15 O'Callaghan's Mills, KIA Gallipoli.

(178) Halloran, Michael, b. Tulla, e. Galway, d. Mesopotamia, 17/8/17, Conn. Rngs.

(179) Halloran, Pte. Patrick, b. Ennistymon, e. Gort, F&F, 29/4/15, Conn. Rngs.

(180) Hanrahan, John, Barefield, 1st Bn/2nd Bn, 9/5/15, e. Ennis.

(181) Hanrahan, Pte. James, 2nd Bn. RMF, 27/8/14, Ennis.

(182) Harding, Capt. James Golding, 213th Trench Mortar Bty RFA, 30/10/17, Ennistymon.

(183) Hartigan, Pte. P., 2nd Bn. Sherwood Foresters (Notts & Derby Rgt.) 26/4/18, Ennistymon.

(184) Hartigan, Patrick, St. John's Limerick, 1st Bn. RMF, 21/12/14, e. Limerick,

(185) Hartigan, Pioneer M. RE, RMF, died.

(186) Harvey, Sgt. May William E., Aust. Light Horse, twice WIA South Africa, KIA Dardanelles.

(187) Haugh, Pte. F, Royal Irish Regt., 27/2/20, Ennis.

(188) Hayes, Pte. Michael, 4 Fergus Row, A Company 8th Bn. RMF, KIA 19/6/16.

(189) Hayes, Pte. James, 1st Bn. Irish Guards, 7/7/17, Quin, Clare.

(190) Heavy, Pte, Thomas, Royal Army Service Corps, 8/4/19.

(191) Heenan, Timothy, b. Limerick, e. Limerick (Clareen) Cpl. 10/10/18, S.I. Horse.

(192) Hegarty Lee, Sgt. Patrick, 3rd Bn. Irish Guards, 23/2/20.

(193) Hickey, Pte. John, b. Kilrush e. Limerick, F&F, 28/10/18, S.I.Horse.

(194) Hickey, Pte. J. J., 60th Bn. Aust. Infantry, 27/1/18.

(195) Hickman, Capt. Poole Henry, age 35, 7th Batt, D Company, RMF, KIA Dardanelles, 15/8/15, Kilmurry McMahon.

(196) Higgins, Cpl. Michael, Irish Guards, KIA France, 15/9/18, Liscannor.

(197) Hill, Cpl. Tom, 8th Bn. RDF, 7/9/16, Miltown.
(198) Hoare, Driver John Joseph, RFA, 26/10/18, Clare Rd., Ennis.
(199) Hogan, Gunner F., 4th Canadian Field Artillery, 1/11/18, Killaloe.
(200) Hogan, Nurse Nellie, N. on Fergus, drowned on *SS Leinster*, Clare Civilian.
(201) Hogan, Lance Cpl. Patrick, 11th Bn. Lancashire Fusiliers, 16/15/16, Killaloe.
(202) Honan, Cpl. John, 2nd Bn. RMF, 9/5/15, Kilrush.
(203) Hough, Able Seaman John, Glasgow, Mercantile Marine, 11/4/17, Clare.
(204) Houlihan, Pte. M., 2nd Bn. Irish Guards, 18/9/16, Kilrush.
(205) Hourigan, Patrick, Corofin, Clare, 1st/2nd Bn., 21/3/18, e. Ennis.
(206) Howley, Thomas, Clare, 1st/2nd Bn., 19/4/17, e. Cashel.
(207) Howe, Daniel, KIA France, Clarecastle.
(208) Howard, John, Ennistymon, 1st RMF, 19/10/15, e. Ennis, KIA Gallipoli.
(209) Howard, Thomas, Miltown, 1st/2nd Bn. 4/2/15, e. Limerick.
(210) Hussey, Pte. James, 1st Bn. Royal Welsh Fus., 16/5/15, Feakle.
(211) Hynes, Pte. Michael, 8th Bn. RMF, 20/6/16, Ennis.
(212) Hynes, Mr., Tulla, drowned on *SS Leinster*.
(213) Hynes Claire, Tulla, drowned on *SS Leinster*.
(214) Ives, Pte. Joe, RAMC, disease in Egypt, died in London.
(215) Jones, Andrew, 12th Labour Batt. Royal Engineers, 24/6/16.
(216) Kane, Robert Romney Godfred, RMF, KIA, 1/10/18, Tulla.
(217) Keane, Beltard, KIA France, Doonbeg.
(218) Keane, Pte. J., Burton, St., 1st Bn. RMF, Military Medal, KIA. F & F, 9/9/16, Kilrush.
(219) Keane, John, Ballyvaughan, 13th RMF, 27/8/22, d. India.
(220) Keane, Pte. Michael, 1st Batt. RMF, 26/4/15, Kilrush, KIA Gallipoli.
(221) Keane, Pte. John, 1st Batt. RMF, 9/9/16, Kilrush.
(222) Keane, Pte. Thomas, Conn. Rangers, 23/11/14, Clarecastle.
(223) Kearney, Pte. Michael, 1st Batt. RMF, V5/15, Ennis, KIA Gallipoli.
(224) Keehan, James, Irish Guards, KIA, 9/9/17.
(225) Keating, Pte. Patrick, 51st Batt. Aust. Infantry 27/9/17, Tulla.
(226) Kelly, Blake, John, 13th Batt. Manchester Regt. 9/1/18, Kilkee.
(227) Kelly, Pte. Patrick, 2nd Batt. Leinster Regt. 20/10/14, Lifford.
(228) Kelly, Lieut. R. J., RFA, Caher, KIA .
(229) Kelly, Thomas, Tulla, Ennis, e. Ennis, 1st RMF, 9/9/16, KIA F & F.
(230) Kenneally, John, b. Tulla e. Limerick, 26/9/16, Irish Guards.
(231) Kenneally, Pte. Pat, 1st Batt. North Staffordshire Reg., 5/1/15, Lisdeen.
(232) Kenneally, P. E., KIA 14/12/17, Ennis.
(233) Kenny, Lieut. C. S., Moymore 9th Shropshire, drowned 11/11/15, Lahinch.
(234) Keogh, Lieut., 2nd Leinster Regt., 22/3/18, Killaloe.
(235) Keogh, Capt. Bertram, Birchfield MC Tanks Corps ex. Conn. Rngs. KIA, Liscannor.
(236) Kerr, Col. Samuel, age 24, Highland Light Infantry, KIA, 8/11/17.
(237) Kiely, Pte. Christopher, St. John's Limerick, e. Limerick, F&F, 4/12/17.
(238) Kildea, Pte. Michael, 4483, 1st Batt. RMF, 19/10/16, Miltown, KIA. F & F..
(239) Killeen, Pte. Timothy, Irish Guards, 31/7/19.
(240) Killeen, Thomas, Doonbeg, 1st/2n Bn., 4/10/18, e. Cork.
(241) Killon, P., RMF, KIA, Corofin.
(242) King Pte. P., 2nd Batt. South Lancashire Reg., 2/2/15, Turnpike.
(243) Kingsley, Michael, Fothera, 9/5/15, e. Ennis.
(244) Kingsley, Able Seaman Francis, Royal Navy, 1/11/14, Seafield.
(245) Lahiffe, Pte. Michael, 2nd Batt. RMF, 9/5/15, Islandavanna, Tiermaclane.
(246) Larkin, Pte. John, b. Killaloe e. Wexford, F&F, 24/5/15, RIR.
(247) Leahy, Pte. John, 1st Batt. RMF, 1/5/15, Causeway, Ennis, KIA Gallipoli.
(248) Leahy, Pte. William, 1st Batt. Irish Guards, 6/11/14, Ennis.
(249) Lefroy, 2nd Lieut. Gerard, Killaloe, 1st/2nd Bn., 24/8/16.
(250) Leggatt, Edward, Royal Navy, 1/11/14, Kilrush.
(251) Lenane, James, Lisdoonvarna, 1st/2nd Bn., 2/11/14, e. Tralee.

(252) Lennon, Pte. Thomas, 1st Batt. Conn. Rangers, 12/11/14, Kildysart.
(253) Leyden, Lance Corporal Martin, 2nd Batt. Royal Irish Regt., 19/12/16, O'Callaghan's Mills.
(254) Leman, Pte. Ronald, b. Newtown Forbes, Longford, e. Liverpool Lancs. F&F, 27/8/18, Irish Guards.
(255) Loftus, Peter, Ennistymon, 1st RMF, 19/5/15, e. Ennis, DOW Gallipoli.
(256) Looney, Pte. James,1st Batt. Irish Guards, 2/6/18, Miltown.
(257) Lyden, Martin, b. Killuran, e. Ennis, O'Callaghan's Mills, 19/12/16, R.I.R.
(258) Lynch, Pte. Patrick, Aust. Infantry, Gallipoli, Salvia Bay, KIA France, 6/8/16.
(259) Lynch, Sapper Thomas Joseph, 11th Field Coy Royal Engineers, 16/5/15, Quin.
(260) Lynch, Pte. James, 7th/8th Batt. Royal Irish Fus., 7/6/17, Sixmilebridge.
(261) Lynch, Michael, Kilrush, e. Tralee, 1st RMF, 1/5/15, KIA Gallipoli.
(262) Lynch, Pte. Martin, 19th Batt. Manchester Regt., 23/7/16, Miltown Malbay.
(263) Lynch, Able Seaman T., Royal Navy, 28/6/17, Carrigaholt.
(264) Lyons, Patrick, N.-on-Fergus, 1st RMF, 3/5/15, e. Ennis, KIA Gallipoli.
(265) Lysaght, Lieut, Scariff, died France
(266) Lucitt, John, b. Labasheeda, e. Tralee, F&F, 1/12/17, Irish Guards.
(267) Madigan, Pte. John, 2nd Batt. RMF, 10/7/17, Kilbaha.
(268) Magee, Pte. Michael, Scariff, e. Limerick, KIA Gallipoli 26/4/15.
(269) Mahoney, Myles, R.N.H.M.S., 23/5/16, London.
(270) Mahoney, John, Kilrush, 1st Bn., 18/7/15.
(271) Mahony, John, Drumcliffe, 8th Bn., 29/7/16, e. Limerick.
(272) Mahony, Pte. John, Mill St., RMF, KIA, Ennis.
(273) Mahony, 2nd Lieut. T. S., King's Liverpool Regt., KIA, Tulla.
(274) Mahony, Pte. T., 8th RMF KIA, honoured, Ennis.
(275) Manning, Driver Patrick, 76th Bn. RFA, 10/9/16, Kilrush.
(276) Mannix, Patrick, Auckland Mounted Rifles, NZEF, 5/11/17, Ballyvaughan.
(277) Markham, Pte. Thomas, 2nd Bn. RMF, 21/3/18, Cratloe.
(278) Maunsell, 2nd Lieut. George Lyndham, age 28, Indian Army.
(279) Meade, Michael, Kilrush, 8th RMF, 21/8/15, KIA Gallipoli.
(280) Meaney, Pte. James, 1st Bn. RMF, 2/4/18, Kilkee, KIA F & F.
(281) Meehan, Pte. Daniel, b. Clonlara, e. Limerick, F&F, 17/10/18, RIR.
(282) Mescal, Mark, J., b. Kilrush, e. Dublin, F&F, 1/12/17, Irish Guards.
(283) Minogue, John, Feakle, 7th Bn. RMF. 17/8/15, e. Yorks, DOW Gallipoli.
(284) Mitchell, 2nd Lieut. James, Royal Flying Corps and 5th Canadian Inf., Kilrush, 26/4/16.
(285) Moloney, Patrick, Kilrush, lst Bn., 24/8/16, e. Limerick.
(286) Moloney, Michael, O'Brien's Bridge, 5th Bn., 13/8/14, e. Limerick.
(287) Moloney, Michael, 7th Bn. of Royal Inniskilling Fus., 27/4/16, Miltown.
(288) Moloney, P., Machine Gun Corps. 12/3/16, Ennis.
(289) Moloney, Company Sergeant Major Tom, 7th Bn. Royal Irish Reg., 2/9/18, Killaloe.
(290) Moloney, P., 2nd Bn. Royal Irish Reg., 26/10/15, Kildysart.
(291) Moloney, Corporal, 2nd Bn. Leinster Reg., 14/3/15, Flagmount.
(292) Moloney, Pte. John, 1st Bn. RMF, 21/3/18, Kildysart, KIA F & F.
(293) Moloney, John, 23rd Bn. Rifle Brigade, 4 Feb. 1917, Ennis.
(294) Moloney, James, Edward, Auckland Mounted Rifles, 5/8/15, Market St. Ennis.
(295) Moloney, John, 1st Bn. RMF, 1/5/15, Kilrush.
(296) Moloney, Seaman Martin, Royal Naval Reserve, 25/1/17, Miltown.
(297) Moloney, Thomas, b. Ogonnelloe, e. Dublin, F&F, 2/9/18, RIR.
(298) Moody, Cpl. Thomas, age 23, Waterpark, Irish Guards, ex. RIC, WIA 9/10/17, DOW, Warrington, 29/11/17.
(299) Moody, Lt-Col. Thomas, 2nd Bn. Irish Guards, 27/11/17, Ennis.
(300) Moran, Able Seaman William, Royal Navy 6/10/14, Scattery Island, Kilrush.
(301) Morgan, Pte. Martin, b. Ennis, e. Ennis (Sixmilebridge) F&F, 23/11/14, Conn. Rngs.
(302) Moroney, Sgt. M., KIA, France, 8/1/17, Miltown.
(303) Moroney, Sgt. Martin, 99th Coy Machine Gun Corps, 27/7/16, Miltown.

(304) Morris, Lance Sgt. John, 8th Bn. RMF, 4/5/16, Kilmihil.
(305) Morrissey, Patrick, Teacher in Bronx, 165th Inf. US Army, KIA Marne, 18/7/18.
(306) Morrissey, Sgt. Walter George, Conn. Rngs., b. Ennis, e. Sheffield d. India 6/5/16.
(307) Mulcahy, Pat, RAMC, DOW, Ennis.
(308) Muldoon, Thomas, Feakle, e. Feakle, 1st RMF, 9/9/16, KIA F & F.
(309) Muir, Pte. William, A., b. Ballycoyney, Clare, e. Roscrea, 6th Batt., RIR, 12/4/17.
(310) Mullins, Gunner, Michael, RGA, 1/7/18, Sixmilebridge.
(311) Mulqueen, Pte. Jack, b. Kilfenora, e. Ennistymon, F&F, 15/9/16, Irish Guards.
(312) Mungovan, Pat, 46th Batt. Canadian Inf., 27/9/18, Ennis.
(313) Murchie, Private William, 1st Batt. Black Watch (Royal Highlanders), 15/9/14, e. Glasgow, Sixmilebridge.
(314) Murphy, W. J., Irish Guards, KIA.
(315) Murphy, Pte., Irish Guards, ex RIC, Clarecastle.
(316) Murphy, Pte, Joseph, RMF, KIA.
(317) Murphy, James, 1st Batt. Leinster Reg., 14/5/15, Ordnance House, Ennis.
(318) Murray, Rifleman Michael, age 17, father - organist at Friary, F. Company, RIR, killed by blow of broom handle, Dublin, e. Ennis.
(319) Mylne, Capt. C. G., Irish Guards ex. RIC District Inspector, DOW, Ypres, Sixmilebridge.
(320) MacNamara, Major George, 2nd Batt. Wiltshire & Staffordshire Regt., 27/5/17, Ennistymon.
(321) MacNamara, Francis, Joseph, 2nd King's African Rifles, 8/7/17, Kilrush.
(322) MacNamara, Pte. Patrick, Francis, 42nd Batt. Canadian Inf., 4/3/19, Limerick.
(323) McAuley, John, Drumbiggle, 6th Batt., 3/10/16, e. Ennis, KIA Greek Macedonia.
(324) McCarthy, John, Drumcliffe, 1st/2nd Batt., 9/5/15, e. Ennis.
(325) McCarthy, Pte. Michael, 2nd Batt. RMF, 21/12/14, Kilrush.
(326) McCormack, Pte., RMF, KIA.
(327) McCormack, Stoker, 1st Class, Alfred, Royal Navy, 19/1/17, O'Brien's Bridge, Clare.
(328) McCormack, Pat, b. Ennis, e. Ennis, F&F, 19/6/15, Conn. Rngs.
(329) McCready, Master, William, Mercantile Marine, 20/6/17, Antrim (Clarecastle).
(330) McDonald, Pte. Michael, b. Drumcliffe, e. Ennis (Kilmaley), 24/5/15, RIR.
(331) McDonnell, John, Kilrush, 8th Batt. RMF, 14/10/16, e. Ennis.
(332) McEvoy, Pte. Michael, Army Service Corps, 4/7/16, Killaloe.
(333) McGann, Pte. Thomas, b. Ennistymon, e. Ennis, F&F, 6/11/14, Irish Guards.
(334) McGee, Michael, 1st Batt. RMF, 26/4/15, Killaloe.
(335) McGee, Patrick, Killaloe, 9th Batt., 28/4/16, e. Nenagh.
(336) McGrath, Pte. Martin, b. Drumcliffe, e. Ennis, 17/8/18, 5th Bn RIR.
(337) McGrath, John, Kilrush, 1st/2nd Batt., 9/5/15, e. Ennis.
(338) McGrath, Martin, RMF, 15/9/16, Kilrush.
(339) McGrath, Pte., M., RMF, e. Limerick, DOW, Home 15/9/16, Kilrush.
(340) McGravin, Pte. P., RMF, DOW Kilkee.
(341) McGreen, Patrick, Kilkee, 8th Batt., 30/6/16, e. Limerick.
(342) McInerney, John, 2nd Batt. RMF, 10/11/17, Killaloe.
(343) McInerney, Pte. T., 2nd Batt. Leinster Reg., 16/5/15, Broadford.
(344) McInerney, Michael, 2nd Batt. RMF, 22/3/18, Meelick.
(345) McInerney, 1st Reserve Bde. RFA, 22/12/16, Quilty.
(346) McInerney, Pte., b. Meelick, Co. Clare. e. Limerick, (Derrymeelick, Clare), 15/4/16, Irish Guards.
(347) McKeogh, Lieut. J., KIA, Killaloe.
(348) McKnight, Pte. Stephen, 1st Batt. RMF, 22/3/18, Kilrush, KIA F & F.
(349) McLaurin, Cadet, John Henry, RAF, 29/9/18.
(350) McMahon, Pte. Michael, KIA - stray shell at H.Q. C. Cast.
(351) McMahon, F., RIF, DOW, Ennis.
(352) McMahon, Thomas, drowned on *Arabic*, Liverpool to New York, 18/8/15.

171

(353) McMahon, Charles, Kilrush, 1st/2nd Batt. 9/5/15, e. Kilrush.
(354) McMahon, John, Kilrush, 1st/2nd Batt. 2/6/17, e. Kilrush.
(355) McMahon, Patrick, Drumcliffe, 1st/2nd Batt. 9/5/15, e. Ennis.
(356) McMahon, James, Ennis, 9th Batt., 15/6/16, e. Ennis.
(357) McMahon, Pte. Michael, 1st Batt. RDF, 20/8/17, Clarecastle.
(358) McMahon, 2nd Lieut. Pat Senan, 8th RMF, 29/12/15, Clarecastle.
(359) McMahon, Pte. J., 2nd Batt. Irish Guards, 17/9/15, Tuamgraney
(360) McMahon, Lance Col. M., 2nd Batt. RMF, 10/10/15, Kilrush.
(361) McMahon, Pte. F, 1st Batt. RDF, 22/10/16, Lifford.
(362) McMahon, Pte. P., 1st Batt. RMF, 22/3/18, Shanahea, Ennis, KIA F & F.
(363) McMahon, Thomas, 2nd Batt. Aust. Inf., 20/5/15, Kilmaley.
(364) McMahon, J., *SS Keeper*, Mercantile Marine, 10/6/17, Clarecastle.
(365) McMahon, Dmr. John, 2nd/5th Batt. K.O. Scottish Borderers, 7/7/17.
(366) McMahon, Pte. Martin, b. Kilmurry McMahon, e. Ennis, F&F, 10/10/17,
      Irish Guards.
(367) McNamara, Gnr. Rody, RFA, 27/3/16, Scariff.
(368) McNamara, Chief Stoker Pat, Royal Navy, 15/5/17, Ennistymon.
(369) McNamara, Pte. Patrick, 2nd Batt. RMF, 10/11/17, Corofin.
(370) McNamara, Pte. J., 8th Batt. RMF, 27/7/16, Crusheen,
(371) McNamara, Francis, 7th South Irish Horse, 27/9/18, Ennis.
(372) McNamara, Joseph, 2nd Batt. Irish Guards, 15/9/16, Knockalough.
(373) McNamara, Francis, Joseph, Wellington Reg. NZEF, 8/10/20, Clare.
(374) McNamara, Pte., John, Drumcliffe, 1st RMF, 1/5/15, e. Ennis, DOW Gallipoli.
(375) McNamara, William, Whitegate, 8th Batt. 18/6/16, e. Tuamgraney
(376) Naylon, Thomas, 25th Bn. Aust. Infantry, 29 July 1916, Kilshanny.
(377) Nevin, Pat, Kilkee, 9th Bn. RMF, 28/4/16, e. Limerick.
(378) Neylon, Michael, Royal Army Medical Corps, 2/11/14, Inagh.
(379) Neylon, Simon, Ennistymon, 22/7/16, 5th RMF , e. Ennis.
(380) Niall, Corporal, P. J., 1st Bn., Kings Own Royal Lancs., 21/3/18, Birkenhead.
(381) Nolan, John, Michael, 9th Bn. Aust. Inf., 3/6/18, Killimer.
(382) Noonan, Francis, 2nd Bn. RMF, 9/5/15, Killaloe.
(383) Noonan, Pte. Joseph, b. Killaloe e. Dublin, F&F, 17/6/15.
(384) O'Brien, Flight Lieut, D., Royal Naval Air Service, 16/2/15, Inchiquin.
(385) O'Brien, Lieut. D. J., 2nd RMF, 10/11/17, Clarecastle.
(386) O'Brien, George, Drumcliff, 25/4/15, 1st RMF, e. Ennis, DOW Gallipoli.
(387) O'Brien, Hugh, Ballyalla, 8th Bn. RMF.
(388) O'Brien, John, Doonbeg, 25/6/15, 1st RMF, e. Kilrush.
(389) O'Brien, Michael, Joseph, lst/8th Bn. Liver. Reg. 18/7/1917, Rhode Island, Clare,
      d. Gallipoli.
(390) O'Brien, M., 2nd Bn. RMF, 9/5/15, Kilkee.
(391) O'Brien, Gnr. Michael, Royal Garrison Art., 4/9/14.
(392) O'Brien, Martin, Ball Alley Lane, KIA France, Kildysart.
(393) O'Brien, Martin, St.. Michael's, Limerick, 28/6/15, 1st RMF, e. Ennis, Kildysart.
(394) O'Brien, Sgt. Patrick, b. Killaloe, e. Chelsea. F&F, 21/3/18, Conn. Rangers,
(395) O'Brien, Thomas, Royal Naval Res. 15/9/18, Doonbeg.
(396) O'Connor, Chief Steward Michael, Merc. Marine, 15/7/17, Music Hill, Clare.
(397) O'Connor, John, Liscannor, Clare, 27/8/14, 2nd RMF, e. Ennistymon.
(398) O'Connor, Michael, 2nd Bn. RMF, 24/9/16, Ennistymon.
(399) O'Dea, Lance Corp. Jim, 2nd Bn. Irish Guards, 27/11/17, Cooraclare.
(400) O'Dea, Daniel, 1st Bn. Royal Dub. Fus., South Irish Horse, 3/4/18, Kilmihil.
(401) O'Dea, Daniel, Joseph, 7th South Irish Horse, 12/12/17, Ballynacally
(402) O'DonnelI, Philip, 3rd Bn. RMF, 5/11/18, Kilrush.
(403) O'Donoghue, Private C., 2nd Bn. RMF, 12/11/14, Clarecastle.
(404) O'Flynn, Capt. M. C., RAMC, DOW Sixmilebridge.
(405) O'Gorman, John, Mercantile Marine, 2/11/17, Carrigaholt.
(406) O'Grady, Lieut. Delmege, KIA.
(407) O'Grady, Nurse Mary, Newmarket on Ferg., drowned on *SS Leinster*.

(408) O'Halloran, Pte. Thomas, b. Kilkee, e. Kilrush, 30/11/15, Conn. Rangers.
(409) O'Leary, Pte. Michael, e. Galway, d. Salonika, 5/7/16, Conn. Rangers.
(410) O'Loughlin, Pat, Joseph, 3rd Bn. Aust. Inf. 18/9/17, Ballyvaughan.
(411) O'Louglin, Sapper J., Royal Engineers, 14/1/15, Ennistymon.
(412) O'Loughlin, Thomas, Miltown Malbay, 9/5/15, e. Ennis.
(413) O'Meehan, Chaplain, 4th Class James Royal Army Chap. Dept. 19/12/19, Ennis.
(414) O'Neill, Michael, Ist Bn. Irish Guards, 6/11/1914, Labasheeda.
(415) O'Neill, Michael, 21st Bn. Aust. Inf., 18/5/17, Lisdeen, Clare.
(416) O'Neill, Pat, Ennis, 9/9/16, 8th Bn. RMF, e. Feakle.
(417) O'Shea, J., 2nd Bn. Royal Dublin Fus. 13 March 20, Turnpike.
(418) O'Shea, Sgt. Thomas, age 28, 9th Infantry, US Army, 18/7/18, Ruan.
(419) O'Shea, Gnr. T., Royal Garrison Artillery, 3/1/19.
(420) O'Sheen, Pte. Pat, 2nd Irish Guards, KIA France, Miltown.
(421) O'Sullivan, John, 2nd RMF, 3/6/15, Ennistymon.
(422) O'Sullivan, Gunn. John, RFA, KIA, Kilrush.
(423) Parker, Lieut. R. E,, Ballyvalley, Royal Horse Artillery KIA France, Killaloe.
(424) Peacocke, 2nd Lieut. Herbert Parker, Lancs. Reg., 3/7/16, Kilrush.
(425) Perry, George, Tulla, 19/8/15, 6th Bn. RMF, e. Ennis, DOW Gallipoli.
(426) Persse, Capt. Dudley Eyre, 4th Bn. Royal Dublin Fus., Corofin.
(427) Pierce, Michael, Drumcliffe, 7th Bn. RMF, 16/8/15, e. Limerick.
(428) Power, John, 10th Royal Dublin Fus., 13/11/16, Clarecastle.
(429) Power, Pte. John, 'Pals Batt', RDF, KIA France, 13/11/16, Clarecastle.
(430) Purtill, H., 6th RMF, b. Kilrush, e. Limerick, KIA Greek Macedonia.
(431) Quaile, Francis, b. Killaloe, e. Carrick-on-Suir, d. India, 11/11/14, RIR.
(432) Quin, Pte. John, Lahinch, e. Ennis, DOW F&F, 23/2/18.
(433) Quinn, John, Kilrush, 3/5/15, 1st RMF, e. Ennis.
(434) Quinlivan, Alfred, 1st Bn. RMF, 15/8/17, Corofin, KIA F & F.
(435) Redmond, Major W., MP, RIR, KlA Ypres, 7/6/17.
(436) Regan, John, Kilrush, 3/5/15, RMF, e. Ennis, KIA Gallipoli.
(437) Reidy, Pte. J., Royal Inniskilling Fus., 5/7/19.
(438) Reidy, Pte. Michael, b. Leitrim, Kilrush, 19/7/18, RIR.
(439) Reilly, Pte. John, b. Drumcliffe, e. Lancaster, 31/7/17, Irish Guards.
(440) Reybault, William, Drumcliffe, 3/9/16, 8th RMF, e. Ennis.
(441) Reynolds, James, 2nd RMF, 9/5/15, Corrovorin, Ennis.
(442) Rochford, Pte. William, 8th RMF, 4/9/16, Drumbiggle.
(443) Riordan, Pte. Pat., 25th Bn. Aust. Infantry, 20/5/16, Ennistymon.
(444) Roy, Jr. Royal Army Medical Corps, 2/10/18, Ennis, (Itchen).
(445) Rowan, Thomas, 21/1/15, Royal Navy, Kilrush, Portsmouth.
(446) Russell, James, Cork, 22/3/18, 2nd RMF, e. Cork.
(447) Russell, Lance Corporal Thomas, 1st Bn. RMF, 15/8/17, Kilmaley, KIA F & F.
(448) Russell, P., 2nd Bn. RMF, 9/5/15, Corrovorin, Ennis.
(449) Ryan, Austin, Ballyvaughan, 9/6/16, 3rd RMF.
(450) Ryan, Pte. James, 8th Bn. RMF, 28/7/16, Clarecastle.
(451) Ryan, Pte. James, RMF, WIA, drowned at Ballsbridge, Clarecastle.
(452) Ryan, John Pat, 1st RMF, 1 July 1918, Kildysart, DOW F & F.
(453) Ryan, Pte. William, 1st Bn. Irish Guards, 9/10/17, Killaloe.
(454) Ryan, Thomas Joseph, 2nd RMF, 19/5/16, N.-on-Fergus.
(455) Saunders, Pte. Francis, b. Clareabbey, e. Ennis, 19/6/18, RIR.
(456) Savage, Pte. F, KIA, Ennis.
(457) Scanlan, Bmr. M., Royal Field Artillery, 9/2/16, Mother - Kilrush.
(458) Scanlan, Patrick, Kilrush, 1st RMF, 20/11/17, e. Limerick, KIA F & F.
(459) Seaman, Pte. T., Labour Corps formerly RMF, 19/3/20, Mother - Kilrush.
(460) Scully, Pte. Michael, 1st Bn. Irish Guards, 1/11/14, Tiermaclane.
(461) Scully, Martin, South Africa, RIA.
(462) Sexton, Sgt. Michael, Army Service Corps, 26/1/19, London, Miltown Malbay.
(463) Shannon, Seaman Edward, Royal Naval Reserve, 16/6/18, Quilty.
(464) Shannon, Pte. Edward, 2nd Bn. RMF, 20/12/16, Kilkee.

(465) Sharry, Rifleman Thomas, 1st Bn. RIR, 9/5/15, Burren, Clare.
(466) Shaughnessy, Pte. Michael, b. Drumcliffe, e. Ennis, 21/3/18, RIR.
(467) Shipley, J. P., 1st/7th Bn. Manchester Reg., 16/10/15, Claureen, Ennis.
(468) Slattery, Capt. Francis, James, 8th Field Coy Royal Engineers, 9/1/19, Darragh.
(469) Smith, Simon, Lisgreen, Clare, Ist RMF, 21/8/15, e. Limerick, DOW Gallipoli.
(470) Somers, 2nd Lieut. 1st Bn. Royal Inniskilling Fus., 20/5/17, Mountshannon.
(471) Sparrow, 2nd Lieut. F. E., KIA, 3/8/16.
(472) Spillane, Christopher, Athlone, 1st/2nd Bn., 27/8/14.
(473) Stinchcombe, Pte. John, William, Welson, b. Miskin, Mountain Ash,
      Glamorgan, e. Ennis, F&F, 27/9/18, RIR.
(474) Stokes, John, Gort, 1st RMF, 28/6/15, e. Ennis.
(475) Studdert, Lance Corp. Theodore, 52nd Bn. Canadian Infantry, 30/11/15, Kilkee.
(476) Sullivan, John, Mercantile Marine, 7/10/17, Carrigaholt.
(477) Sullivan, John, Killaloe, 8th Bn. 29/5/16, e. Nenagh.
(478) Sullivan, Thomas, Kilrush, 1st/2nd Bn., 21/12/14, e. Limerick.
(479) Talty, Pte. John, Royal Army Service Corps. 2/11/18.
(480) Taylor, Goff, Kilrush, 2nd Bn. RMF, 9/5/15, e. Kilrush, KIA F & F.
(481) Taylor, 2nd Lieut. John, Arthur, Harold, 1st RDF, Dardanelles, 24/9/15.
(482) Thynne, Pte. John, b. Ennistymon, e. Ennis, F&F, 6/12/16, RIR.
(483) Thynne, Michael, 1st Bn. RMF, 4/5/15, Ennistymon, DOW Gallipoli.
(484) Thynne, Patrick, b. Ennistymon, e. Ennis, F&F, 17/5/15, Irish Guards.
(485) Tierney, John, 8th RMF, 3 Nov. 1916, Lisdoonvarna.
(486) Tierney, Pat, Drumcliffe, 6/7/15, 1st Bn. RMF, e. Ennis, DOW Gallipoli.
(487) Toomey, Patrick, Kilkee, 10/4/16, e. Limerick.
(488) Tuohy, Pte. Edward, b. Clare e. Galway, 26/4/15, Conn. Rang.
(489) Tuohy, Pte. Michael, b. Scariff, e. Scariff, F&F, 30/4/18, Irish Guards.
(490) Tuttle, John, 2nd RMF, 25/9/15, Ennis, KIA F & F.
(491) Twyford, Thomas, Mere. Marine, 13/5/18, b. Kilrush.
(492) Vandeleur, Lt. Alexander Moore, 2nd Life Guards, 30/10/14, Kildysart.
(493) Walsh, Lance Corp. J., 1st Bn. RMF, 7/6/17, Miltown Malbay, KIA F & F.
(494) Walsh, Pte. Michael, 9th Bn. Northumberland Fus., 22/3/18, Ennis.
(495) Walsh, Pte. Robert, I81 Bn. RMF, 12/8/17, Kilrush, KIA F & F.
(496) Walsh, Gnr. Michael Joseph, RN HMS, 3/10/17, wife of Kilrush Ward, Const.
      Ennis, drowned on *SS Leinster*.
(497) Ward, Pte., Michael, 1st Bn. RMF, 3/10/18, Scariff, DOW F & F.
(498) Watt, Pte. Eugene, Canadian Motor Machine Gun Bde., 24/3/18.
(499) Whelan, M. 2nd Bn. Connaught Rangers, 7/11/14, Kilnaboy
(500) White, Lt., Army Vet Corps, 16/3/16, Tulla.
(501) Williams, James, Drumcliffe, 1st/2nd Bn., 27/8/14, KIA F & F.
(502) Williams, Gunner Michael, 159th Heavy Bty Royal Garrison Artillery, 27/10/17,
      Ennis.
(503) Woods, John, Innishehir, Galway, 4/9/16, e. Lisdoonvarna.
(504) Woulfe, Pte. Patrick, 13th Bn. The King's Own Liverpool Regt., 28/3/18,
      Lahinch.
(505) Wynne, Pte. Christopher, 1st Bn. Irish Guards, 30/3/18, Ennis.

APPENDICE II

POEM ON CLARE'S FOREIGN BRIGADE
by Emily Lawless

Before the Battle; night.

I

Oh! Bad the march, the weary march, beneath these alien skies,
But good the night, the friendly night, that soothes our tired eyes.
And bad the war, the tedious war, that keeps us sweltering here,
But good the hour, the friendly hour, that brings the battle near.
That brings us on the battle that summons to their share
The homeless troops, the banished men, the exiled sons of Clare.

II

Oh! Little Corca Baiscinn, (old name for Clare) the wild, the bleak,
the fair!
Oh! Little stony pastures, whose flowers are sweet, if rare!
Oh, rough the rude Atlantic, the thunderous, the wild,
Whose kiss is like a soldier's kiss which will not be denied!
The whole night long we dream of you, and waking, think we're
there,
Vain dream, and foolish waking, we never shall see Clare.

III

The wind is wild tonight, there is battle in the air;
The wind is from the west, and it seems to blow from Clare.
Have you nothing, nothing for us, loud brawler of the night?
No news to warm our heart-strings, to speed us through the fight?
In this hollow, star pricked darkness, as in the sun's hot glare,
In sun-tide, in star-tide, we thirst, we starve for Clare!
Hark! Yonder through the darkness one distant rat! tat! tat!
The old foe stirs out there. God bless his soul for that!
The old foe musters strongly, he's coming on at last,
And Clare's Brigade may claim its own wherever blows fall fast.
Send us, ye western breezes, our full, our rightful share,
For Faith and Fame and Honour, and the ruined hearts of Clare.

After the Battle; early dawn, Clare coast.

'Mary Mother, shield us! Say, what men are ye,
Sweeping past so swiftly on this morning sea?
'Without sails or rowlocks merrily we glide
Home to Corca Bascinn on the brimming tide'.

'Jesus save you, gentry! Why are you so white,
Sitting all so straight and still in this misty light?'
'Nothing ails us, brother, on the morning sea.'

'Cousins, friends, and kinsfolk, children of the land,
Here we come together, a merry, rousing band;
Sailing home together from the last great fight,
Home to Clare from Fontenoy, in the morning light.

Men of Corca Bascinn, men of Clare's Brigade,
Harken stony hills of Clare, hear the charge we made;
See us come together, singing from the fight,
Home to Corca Bascinn, in the morning light.'

Source: *Sinn Féin*, 20 December 1913.

ELECTION 1917

Men of the Banner county you are closely watched today,
So vote like your ancestors in an independent way,
The seat by two is contested, their names you all did hear,
One is a Castle servant and Eamon de Valer'

His mother she was Irish, his father came from Spain,
He was born 'neath the stars and stripes, and a child to Ireland
came,
He fought in the rebellion, and the soldiers did not fear,
So on the tenth of July, be sure to vote for our hero de Valer'

You stupid headstrong parents, take heed of what I say,
But for those gallant heroes your sons they'd force away,
To fight the noble German who no power on earth could fear,
Remember Dan O'Connell and vote for de Valer'

For a week they held our capital and England did defy,
And when they did surrender he was sentenced for to die,
The sentence was commuted and banished him away,
To an English jail for sixteen months was the length of his stay.

Again he is in the fighting ranks my boys you needn't fear,
That on Tuesday next we'll head the poll with Eamon de Valer'
And come what may, though times be tough, to him we will prove
true,
And rise the flag of freedom from Ennis to Killaloe.

Source: Seán P. Ó Cillín, *Ballads of Co. Clare*, 1976, p. 27.

GOD SAVE IRELAND FROM CONSCRIPTION

Hear the news that fills the land,
Spreading forth from each strong band,
Joined together in one common cause today,
To Lloyd George's man's bill.
We'll oppose a nation's will,
And with earnest hearts together here we say.

Chorus
God save Ireland from conscription,
God save Ireland say we all,
Whether on the scaffold high,
Or the battlefield we die,
Oh! What matter when for Erin dear we fall,
We will jog Lynch later on,
But tomorrow Pat be gone,
Your plamás won't do a Clareman when you call.

If North and South were gathered here,
From the Causeway to Cape Clear,
From Dublin city across to Galway Bay,
Oh! Conscription we defy,
Let the chorus reach the sky,
And let England hear United Ireland say.

Lynch uneasy seems to be,
He longs to sit beside T.P.
Sailing o'er the main across to Pat and Mike
Bolstering, bloodhound Balfour's side,
Battering ram and Clifford pride,
Claremen remember, Micheltown and brave Bodyke.

Every vote that's cast for Lynch,
Means conscription to the trench,
On a foreign soil to languish and to die,
Give your vote to de Valer',
Keep your men at home in Clare
Do not fight at England's side is our cry.

Source: Seán P. Ó Cillín, *Ballads of Co. Clare*, (1850-1976), p. 27-28.

REFERENCES

Preface

1. *The Irish Times,* 9 June 1992.
2. *Clare Journal*, 12 July 1917.
3. Kevin J. Browne, *Eamon de Valera and the Banner County,* Dublin 1982, p. 9, in foreword by Thomas P. O'Neill.
4. *Irisleabhar Mhá Nuad*, 1985, p. 44.
5. The practical eclipse of the Home Rulers at the 1918 General Elections would seem to confirm this, although in three consecutive by-elections in early 1918, Sinn Féin suffered defeats in South Armagh, in Waterford (Captain William Archer Redmond retained his late father John's seat) and in East Tyrone; Liz Curtis, *The Cause of Ireland,* Dublin 1994, p. 299.

Chapter One

1. Trans. Regis Durand, reprinted from *The Post-modern Condition: A Report on Knowledge*, trans. G. Bennington and B. Massumi, Manchester 1984, p.71.
2. D. George Boyce, "Ireland and the First World War", *History Ireland.* Autumn 1994, pp. 48-53; Ciaran Brady (ed.). *Interpreting Irish History,* Dublin 1994, pp. 1-11.
3. Terence Denman, *Ireland's Unknown Soldiers.* Dublin 1992, p. 146. Willie Redmond was quite despondent in this conversation with his fellow Nationalist MP and comrade Stephen Gwynn. See also Stephen Gwynn, *John Redmond's Last Years*, Dublin 1919.
4. *Census of Ireland, 1911.* Province of Munster, County of Clare; Summary Tables (1912/13, CXV, Cd6050).
5. Brendan Clifford (ed.), *Ireland in the Great War,* Belfast 1992, p. 86.
6. Patrick Callan, "Recruiting for the British Army in Ireland during the First World War", *The Irish Sword*, Vols. 16-17, pp. 42-56.
7. Brian P. Murphy, *Patrick Pearse and the Lost Republican Ideal,* Dublin 1991, p. 18. Murphy recounts how in 1912 Pearse appeared on a platform for Home Rule, at a massive demonstration in O'Connell Street, Dublin and spoke in support of the constitutional policy of John Redmond.
8. Due to the carnage of both the War of Independence and the Civil War, the following list had been unavailable in a collective body for the study of Local Government in Co. Clare from 1914-18:
Poor Law Union Records, Co. Clare.
Ballyvaughan Union.
Kildysart Union.
Scariff Union (incorporating the Tulla Union which it had been amalgamated with in 1908).
Rural District Council Records, Co. Clare.
1. Scariff Rural District Council.
2. Kildysart Rural District Council.
3. Limerick No. 2 Rural District Council (including Clare Divisions).

At the time of research, the surviving Rural District Council records, along with the Poor Law Unions records, for Co. Clare were maintained at the Co. Clare Local Studies Centre, Manse House, Ennis. The Clare County Council records for 1914-18 were stored away at Ennis Courthouse but are now housed in the Co. Archives.

The Kilkee Town Commissioners Minute Books are kept at their offices in Kilkee.

Both the Ennis and Kilrush Urban Council records were available at their respective offices.

9. There was another contemporary "newspaper" in print, the *Kilrush Herald and Kilkee Gazette*, but was more akin to a newsletter. With regard to the copies I have in my possession of Republican statements, it is unfortunate that, due to bureaucratic constraints, they cannot be augmented by the Bureau of Military History's centralised collection, which was still sealed from public viewing at the time of writing.

10. These listed British administration records are available in the National Archives with the Cabinet Reports available in the NUI Galway Special Collections Library, along with the British Control Administration Records of Intercepted Letters in the 1914-18 period.

11. Keith Jeffery (ed.), *An Irish Empire?*, Manchester 1996, p.1.

12. Ibid. p. 98. Also see "WWI in Modern Irish Memory" in Fraser & Jeffery (eds.), *Men, Women & War*, Dublin 1993.

13. Keith Jeffery, "Irish Artists and the First World War", *History Ireland.* Summer 1993, pp. 42-45.

14. H. E. D. Harris, *The Other Half Million - the Irish Regiments in the First World War*, Dublin 1993, p. 32.

15. Curtis, *Cause of Ireland*, p. 260. John Redmond told the House of Commons: 'For the first time - certainly for over one hundred years - Ireland in this war feels her interests are precisely the same as yours... I say the manhood of Ireland will spring to your aid in this war... it is their duty, and should be their honour, to take their place in the firing line in this contest.' F.S.L. Lyons, 'The Passing of the Parliamentary Party', pp. 95-106, in Desmond Williams (ed.), *The Irish Struggle, 1916-1926.* London 1966; Emmet O'Connor, *A Labour History of Ireland*, Dublin 1992, pp. 30-33.

16. David Fitzpatrick, *Politics and Irish Life*, Aldershot 1977, p. 101; Brian Farrell, *The Irish Parliamentary Tradition*, Dublin 1973, pp. 203-205.

17. However, one may make general assumptions, e.g. almost half of the members of Dáil Eireann in 1932 had been members of the Gaelic League.

18. Edna Longley, *Culture in Ireland - Division or Diversity*, Belfast 1991, p. 83.

19. E. Rumpf and A. C. Hepburn, *Nationalism and Socialism in 20th Century Ireland*, Liverpool 1977.

20. John Horgan, *Parnell to Pearse*, Dublin 1948, p. 27.

21. Peter Childs and Patrick Williams, *An Introduction to Post-Colonial Theory*, London 1997, p. 73.

22. Thomas Bartlett and Keith Jeffery, 'An Irish Military Tradition?' in Bartlett and Jeffery (eds.), *A Military History of Ireland*, Dublin 1996, p. 22.

Chapter Two

1. Noel J. Mulqueen, *The Vandeleur Evictions in Kilrush, 1888,* p. 77.
2. Fr. Patrick White, *History of Clare and the Dalcassian Clans,* Dublin 1893, p. 371.
3. Terence Denman, *Willie Redmond - A Lonely Grave,* pp. 51-52.
4. National Archives. *CO 904/78.* f.681.
5. Numerous *Monthly Police Reports* for Ireland in the 1914-18 period testify to this. Chapters Seven and Eight will recount these.
6. Denman, *Lonely Grave,* p. 78.
7. *Clare Champion,* 26 September 1908.
8. T. P. O'Neill, 'Clare and Irish Poverty, 1815 to 1851', *Studia Hibernica,* 1974.
9. Ibid.
10. Timothy W. Guinnane, 'The Vanishing Irish', *History Ireland,* Summer 1997.
11. Michael Turner, *After the Famine: Irish Agriculture 1850 - 1914,* pp. 34-39.
12. *Clare Journal,* 14 April 1902. Willie Redmond, in his speeches, heaped vitriolic abuse on the landlords and grabbers and, for his trouble, was arrested in November 1902, as was P.J. Linnane, who was among a group that was sentenced to three months imprisonment for making inflammatory speeches in Corofin. Willie Redmond was released two months later, as a new wave of violence hit Clare.
13. *Irish Country Towns,* Thomas Davis Lecture Series, Dublin and Cork 1994, p. 27.
14. Kieran Sheedy, *The Clare Elections,* pp. 306-307.
15. Ibid.
16. Ibid.
17. Ibid.
18. National Archives, *CO/904 166.*
19. Ibid.
20. *Report of the Departmental Committee of Agricultural Credit in Ireland, 1914,* Command Paper [CD.7375], Co. Clare 8059 to 8133.
21. Ibid.
22. Ibid.
23. *Clare Champion,* 7 November 1914.
24. Fitzpatrick, *Politics,* p. 48.
25. Ibid.
26. *Report of the Land Commission, 1951,* p. 29, stated that 63% of the total acreage of the County was purchased by tenants under the Land Acts of 1881-1909.
27. K. Theodore Hoppen, *Ireland Since 1800, Conflict and Conformity,* London 1999. Samuel Clark and James S. Donnelly, Jr. (Eds.), *Irish Peasants, Violence and Political Unrest 1780-1914,* Dublin, p. 380.
28. E.R. Hooker, *Re-Adjustments of Agricultural Tenure in Ireland,* N. Carolina 1938, p. 146; Tom Garvin, *Nationalist Revolutionaries in Ireland, 1858-1928,* Oxford 1987, p. 3.
29. Hooker, *Agricultural Tenure,* p. 155.
30. Rumpf and Hepburn, *Nationalism and Socialism,* p.225; Fitzpatrick, *Politics,* p. 48.

31. *Census, 1911,* Province of Munster, Table XXI.
32. Ibid.
33. W.M. Williams, *A West Country Village,* London 1963, *passim.*
34. Conrad Arensburg, *The Irish Countryman.* Massachusetts 1937.
35. Siobhan Griffin-McCarthy, *The Changing Face of Clare Rural Farm Families,* B.Ed Thesis (unpublished), St. Angela's College, Lough Gill, Sligo 1997, p. 9.
36. Ibid.
37. Rita M. Rhodes, *Women and the Family in Post-Famine Ireland.* New York 1992, pp. 108-109.
38. Ibid.
39. H. Hammond, *Readings in Sociology of Community,* The Clarendon Press 1968, pp. 70-76.
40. Donald Akenson, *Small Differences,* Quebec 1988, *passim.*
41. Griffin-McCarthy, op. cit, pp. 9-13.
42. D. F. Hannan, L. Katsiaouni, *Traditional Families: From Culturally Prescribed to Negotiated Roles in Farm Families,* Dublin 1977, p. 33.
43. Guinnane, op. cit. Children who grow up in a society where there are many single people, are more likely to remain unmarried themselves.
44. Ibid; Cormac Ó Gráda, *A New Economic History, 1780-1930,* Oxford 1994, p. 341.
45. Arensberg and Kimball, op. cit., pp. 31-37.
46. Rita M. Rhodes, *Women and the Family in Post-Famine Ireland,* New York 1992, pp. 109-111.
47. Brian Merriman, *Cúirt an Meán Oíche. The Midnight Court;* Trans. by David Marcus. Dublin 1966, p.25.
48. *Census, 1911;* Clare Journal, 8 December, 1913.
49. *Census, 1911;* R. Kennedy, *The Irish - Emigration. Marriage and Fertility,* University of California Press 1973, p. 76.
50. Ibid; W.E. Vaughan and A. J. Fitzpatrick, *Irish Historical Statistics: Population, 1821-1971,* Dublin 1978, p. 105.
51. Fitzpatrick, *Politics,* p. 241.
52. Jacqueline Genet, *Rural Ireland, Real Ireland,* Irish Library Studies, Gerrards Cross 1996, pp. 41-43.
53. R. Kennedy, op. cit., p. 76.
54. R. Crotty, *Irish Agricultural Productions,* Cork 1966, p. 185.
55. Rita Rhodes, op. cit, pp. 86-109.
56. R. Kennedy, op. cit, pp. 86-109.
57. Fitzpatrick, *Politics,* p. 239.
58. Ibid. p. 241.
59. Boyle, 'Irish Rural Labourer' in Clark and Donnelly (eds.) *Irish Peasants,* Manchester 1983, p. 334.
60. Ibid.
61. *Report of the Departmental Committee on Agricultural Credit in Ireland, 1914.* Command Paper [CD 7375].
62. *Ibid.,* In 1900, Clare was only one of seven counties not to have an Agricultural Society; see Patrick Bolger, *The Irish Co-operative Movement: Its History and Development.* IPA, Dublin 1977, p. 251.
63. J. J. Lee, *Ireland, 1912 - 1985, Politics and Society,* Cambridge University Press 1989.
64. H. Hammond, op. cit., p. 74.

Chapter Three

1. Tim Kelly, *The History of Ennis*. MA (unpublished), UCG, 1971; Ciarán Ó Murchadha, *Sable Wings Over the Land*, CLASP 1999. Curtin and Wilson, *Ireland from Below;* Arensberg and Kimball, op. cit., 1968. The urban dimension to Arensberg and Kimball's study, that is their work on the town of Ennis - has received much less attention, even though it was based on a more reliable footing than their work in rural areas.
2. Curtin and Ryan, "Clubs, Pubs and Private Houses in a Clare Town" in Curtin and Wilson, op. cit., pp. 128-141.
3. C. Ó Gráda, op. cit., p. 200.
4. Curtin and Ryan, op. cit., p. 131.
5. Ibid. p. 131.
6. Ibid. p. 133.
7. Arensberg and Kimball, op. cit., p. 317.
8. Silverman and Gulliver, *In the Valley of the Nore: a Social History of Thomastown. County Kilkenny, 1840 - 1983,* Dublin, 1986.
9. Ibid.
10. However, gross statistics at national level in 1961 indicate that employers and managers (mainly small shopkeepers, publicans, owners of family businesses and contractors) comprised 3.2% of the population in 1961 but 31% of the county council members, 34% of Dáil Éireann deputies and 20% of cabinet ministers at about that time. Thom's Directory for 1915, pp. 136-8, 224 *et seq.*
11. *Report of Agricultural Credit in Ireland*, op. cit.
12. Gulliver, op. cit., p. 196.
13. *Report on Agricultural Credit in Ireland*, op. cit.
14. B. MacGiolla Choille, *Intelligence Notes, 1913 - 1916,* Dublin 1966.
15. Arensberg and Kimball, op. cit., p. 313.
16. Tony McMahon, 'The Evolution of Local Government', *Old Limerick Journal*, pp. 18-21.
17. Virginia Crossman, *Local Government in 19th Century Ireland*, Queen's University Belfast 1994, p. 93.
18. Dick Roche, *Local Government in Ireland*, IPA 1992, p. 47.
19. Ibid. p. 48.
20. *Report of the Royal Commission appointed to inquire into the financial relations of Great Britain and Ireland.* [C 8262], HC, 1896, XXXIII.
21. Andrew Gailey, *Ireland and the Death of Kindness,* pp. 45-46.
22. *Clare Journal*. 5 January 1899; so spoke Fr. Halpin at Scariff meeting.
23. *Clare Champion* Jubilee Edition, 1966; Arthur Lynch, *My Life Story,* London 1924, *passim*.
24. Arthur Lynch, op. cit..
25. *In Memoriam Major Willie Redmond*, Dublin 1918; T. Denman, *Lonely Grave,* op. cit.
26. Fitzpatrick, *Politics*, p. 86.
27. *Clare County Council Minute Book*, 1913.
28. W. Feingold, *The Revolt of the Tenantry: The transformation of Local Government in Ireland, 1872-1886,* Boston 1984, p. 181.
29. Mary E. Daly, *The Buffer State; the Historical Roots of the Department of the Environment,* Dublin 1997. p. 21.

30. Ibid. p. 21.
31. Tony Farmer, *Ordinary Lives,* Dublin 1991, p.ll.
32. Brian Ó Dálaigh, *The Stranger's Gaze,* p. 309.
33. Kieran Sheedy, *Clare Elections,* p. 285.
34. *Clare Journal,* 23 October 1890.
35. J. J. Lee, *The Modernisation of Irish Society, 1848 - 1918*, Dublin 1984, p. 115.
36. *Clare Journal*, 8 December 1890.
37. Ibid. 1 December 1890.
38. John S. Kelly, *The Bodyke Evictions,* Clare 1987.
39. Ibid. pp. 122-123.
40. Kieran Sheedy, *Clare Elections*, p. 289.
41. Ibid. p. 290.
42. *Irish Studies Review*, Volume 6, 1998, p. 43.
43. Arthur Lynch, *Ireland - Vital Hour,* London 1915, *passim*; Tom Garvin, *Nationalist Revolutionaries in Ireland 1858 - 1928*, Oxford 1987, p. 10. Terence P. McCaughey, *Memory and Redemption,* Dublin 1993, p. 32.
44. Maurice Goldring, *Pleasant the Scholar's Life,* London 1993, pp. 72-85.
45. Ibid.
46. Garvin, op. cit., p. 11.
47. J. J. Lee, *The Modernisation of Irish Society*, op. cit.,p.63.
48. Arensberg and Kimball, op. cit., *passim.*
49. Ignatius Murphy, *The Diocese of Killaloe*, 1850-1904
50. Arensberg and Kimball, op. cit, *passim.*
51. Mícheál Ó hAodha, *'The Iceman Cometh'* in St. Flannan 's. 1881 - 1981. Ennis 1981.
52. W. P. Ryan, *The Pope's Green Island*, 1912, p. 41.
53. Sheedy, *Clare Elections*, p.294.
54. J. J. Lee, *The Modernisation of Irish Society*, Dublin 1973.
55. *Freeman's Journal*, 14 July 1892.
56. John S. Kelly in *The Bodyke Evictions*, pp. 122-123 touches on this theme.
57. Sheedy, *Clare Elections*, p. 291.
58. Maura Cronin, *Country, Class or Craft?* Cork University Press 1994, p. 9.
59. Fitzpatrick, *Politics*, p. 236.
60. Mary Linehan and Vincent Tucker (eds.), W*orkers Co-operatives*, UCC Bank of Ireland Centre for Co-operative Studies 1983, p.29. See also Margaret Morse; 'Ralahine: A New Dimension to the Irish Owenite Community 1831-1833', in *The Other Clare.* Vol.23, 1999; Emmet O'Connor, *A Labour History of Ireland.* Dublin 1992, p. 24.
61. F S L. Lyons, *The Irish Parliamentary Party 1890-1910.* Faber & Faber 1951, p.190.
62. Sheedy, *Clare Elections*, p. 299.
63. M A G Ó Tuathaigh, 'De Valera and Sovereignty' in J.Murphy, and J.P. O'Carroll, *De Valera & His Times*, Cork 1983, p. 65.
64. *First Report of the Royal Commissioners appointed to enquire into the Financial Relations of Great Britain and Ireland*, (c.8262), H.C. 1896 xxxiii.
65. Sheedy, *Clare Elections*, p. 299.
66. Patricia Jalland, "Irish Home Rule Finance 1910-14", in W.F. Mandle, *Reactions to Irish Nationalism*, London 1987, p. 297
67. Sheedy, *Clare Elections*, p. 299.

68. Tom Garvin, *The Evolution of Irish Nationalist Politics*, New York, pp. 92-93.
69. Ibid. pp. 92-93. Garvin quoted James Lynan, an experienced veteran of INL campaigns, as claiming that west Clare was the only area in the country where priests had not been hostile to his organising efforts.
70. Conor F. Clune, *The Clunes from the Dalcassians to Modern Times*, Cork 1997, p. 69.
71. Denman, *A Lonely Grave*, p. 84.
72. *Clare Journal*, 30 September 1901.
73. Sheedy, *Clare Elections*, p.294.
74. Denman, op. cit., p. 53.
75. Ibid.
76. Ibid.
77. Father Harry Bohan, 'Economic and Social Trends 1881-1981' in *St. Flannan's 1881-1981,* Ennis 1981.
78. *The Leader*, 25 July 1914.
79. Ibid.
80. PRO *C0 904 89.*
81. Edward P. O'Callaghan, *Bishop O'Dwyer and the Course of Irish Politics 1870-1917*, MA (unpublished) 1976, NUIG Special Studies Library.
82. Ibid.
83. Ibid.
84. Garvin, *Irish Nationalist Politics.*
85. Donal P. McCracken, *Irish Commandoes in the Boer War*, London, 1999.
86. *Clare Journal*, 9 August 1909.
87. Sheedy, *Clare Elections*, p.314.
88. *Sinn Féin*, 21 February 1914.
89. Ibid.
90. *Clare Champion*, March 1914.
91. *Clare Journal*, 27 April 1914.
92. Ibid. 2 April 1914.

Chapter Four

1. *Clare Journal*, 6 December 1894.
2. National Archives, *Crime Branch Special Dics.*, (hereafter *CBS*) Carton 1, January 1898
3. Tom Garvin, *Nationalist Revolutionaries*, p. 7.
4. Unpublished memoirs of Joseph Barrett. (copy in possession of author).
5. Ibid.
6. *Statement of Andrew O'Donoghue*, Mid-Clare IRA brigade, Clare Local Studies Centre.
7. Ibid.
8. *Statement of Lieutenant General Michael Brennan* (made in 1966), Cathal Brugha Barracks, Archives Section, Dublin.
9. Ibid.
10. Memoirs of Sean O'Keeffe cited in Thomas Coffey, *The Parish of Inchicronan*, Whitegate, Co. Clare 1993, p. 217
11. *Gaelic American*, August 1918. See also *Clare Champion,* 3 February 2000.

12. *Gaelic American*, August 1918.
13. *Clare Journal*, 18 January, 1915.
14. Pat Sweeney, "John Holland - Father of the Submarine" in the *Irish Maritime Journal*, pp. 9-12, quoting from paper by James Gallagher, chairman of the Ancient Order of Hibernians of America on *Holland and the Fenian Connection*.
15. The Royal Navy Submarine Museum, *HM Submarine Torpedo Boat No. 1 (Holland 1), booklet, unpublished, n.d.*.
16. Father Martin Coen, "John Philip Holland", in Thomas Dillon, *The Banner,* New York 1967, pp.300-301.
17. Sweeney, op. cit..
18. Tim Pat Coogan, *Wherever Green Is Worn*, London 2000, p.654
19. Dr Richard K. Morris, *John P. Holland, Inventor of the Modern Submarine,* New York 1980.
20. National Archives, *CBS* 2400 5.
21. O'Callaghan, *Bishop O'Dwyer,* op. cit.
22. National Archives, *CBS* 1905, 1565/44451.
23. Ibid. *CBS* 1905, 1815/44280.
24. Letter to the author from Donal P. McCracken, Dean of Arts, University of Durban-Westville. Fahey's remains were recently transferred to Caesar's Camp overlooking Ladysmith.
25. National Archives, *CBS* 1906, 3145/46545.
26. Ibid. 1815/46754.
27. Ibid. 1595/4700.
28. Ibid. 1595/47054.
29. Diarmuid Lynch (ed. Florence O'Donoghue), *The IRB and the 1916 Insurrection*, Cork 1957, p.36.
30. National Archives, *CBS* Miscellaneous, 29 September 1907.
31. Fitzpatrick, *Politics*, p. 135. For an unflattering account of another staunch fenian, Michael Considine, see Brian Ó Dálaigh (ed.) *The Stranger's Gaze*, Ennis 1988, p.285.
32. *Seán O'Keeffe memoirs*, op. cit.
33. Ibid.
34. Cathal Brugha Military Barracks, Archives Section. Commandant Liam Haugh, *History of the West Clare Brigade*, 9 July 1934.
35. *Andy O'Donoghue memoirs,* Clare Local Studies Centre.
36. National Archives, *MCR* and *IG* reports between 1900 and 1918 continuously refer to Clare and Galway's notoriety for land agitation.
37. Cathal Brugha Barracks, Archives Section, *Michael Collins Papers*. A/0263; *Joe Barrett memoirs*, op. cit.
38. *Joe Barrett memoirs*.
39. Ibid.
40. Ibid.
41. *Andy O'Donoghue memoirs*, op. cit.
42. Ibid.
43. Bulmer Hobson, *The History of the Irish Volunteers*, Vol. I, Dublin 1918.
44. Cathal Brugha Barracks, Archives Section, *Statement of Lieutenant General Michael Brennan*. Cathal Brugha Barracks, Archives Section, *Michael Collins papers*.
45. Ibid.

46. *Andy O'Donoghue memoirs.*
47. *Seán O'Keeffe memoirs; Andy O'Donoghue memoirs.*
48. *Joe Barrett memoirs.*
49. *Andy O'Donoghue memoirs.*
50. *Celtic Times,* 21 May 1887.
51. For more information on this theory see Margaret O'Callaghan "Denis Patrick Moran and the Irish Colonial Condition" in D. George Boyce, Robert Eccleshall and Vincent Geoghegan (eds.) *Political Thought In Ireland since the Seventeenth Century,* London and New York 1993, pp. 146-160.
52. M.A.G. Ó Tuathaigh, "De Valera and Sovereignty" in J. Murphy & J.P. O'Carroll, *De Valera and His Times,* Cork 1983. p.66.
53. Tom Garvin, *Nationalist Revolutionaries in Ireland,* p. 11.
54. Earnán de Blaghd, "Hyde in Conflict", Seán Ó Tuama (ed.), *The Gaelic League Idea,* pp.19 - 36.
55. Mark Tierney, *Ireland Since 1870,* Dublin 1988, pp. 110-111. See also Brother Sean McNamara, *Micheál ón gCarn,* 1997 and his article on Cusack in the *Clare County Express,* July 1999.
56. Clare Museum caption for the hurley of Michael Cusack, Ennis, Co. Clare, 2000, sourced by the author from Pat Brennan, Clonroadmore, Ennis.
57. Oilie Byrnes, *Memories of Clare Hurling,* Cork 1996, p. 14.
58. Marcus de Búrca, *The GAA:* see also *Clare Champion,* 29 September 1972; Joost Augusteijn, *From Public Defiance to Guerrilla Warfare,* Dublin 1996, pp. 38-42.
59. "Clár Cuimhneacháin, Faithche Phadraic, Cinn Mhara. Oscailt Oifigiuil, 2 April 1963", in Liam Ó Caithnia, *Micheál Cíosóg,* An Clóchomhar Tta 1982, p.45.
60. National Archives, *CBS,* March 1887.
61. W. F. Mandle, "The IRB and the Beginnings of the GAA" in *Reactions to Irish Nationalism, 1865-1914,* London 1987, p. 108.
62. Ibid. See also Noel O'Driscoll "Growth of GAA in Clare" in Jimmy Smyth's *Ballads of the Banner,* Dublin 1998, p. 34.
63. *Joe Barrett memoirs.*
64. National Archives, *CBS* 4985/451381906.
65. *Seán O'Keeffe memoirs.*
66. *Andy O'Donoghue memoirs.*
67. National Archives, *CBS* 1595/46975 1906.
68. Ibid.
69. Proinsias Mac Aonghusa; *Ar Son na Gaeilge. Connradh na Gaeilge 1893-1993.* An Chéad Chló, Dublin 1993, Ith. 34. The screeen was a system of punishment devised by both teacher and parent where the child was the recipient of corporal punishment if a certain number of notches was made on a piece of wood which they had to wear around the neck. A notch was accrued each time the child spoke Gaelic.
70. Fitzpatrick, *Politics.* p. 57.
71. *Joe Barrett memoirs.*
72. Brian P. Murphy, *Patrick Pearse and the Lost Republican Ideal,* Dublin 1991, p.18.
73. Denman, *A Lonely Grave,* op. cit.
74. Sheedy, op. cit., p753; Brian Ó Dálaigh *The Stranger's Gaze,* p. 319; *History of Kilmihil,* p. 95; *The Parish of Cranny / Coolmeen - Kilfidane*

Parish, Ennis 1980; *Sinn Féin,* 28 June 1913.
75. John Hutchinson, *The Dynamics of Cultural Nationalism: The Gaelic Revival and the Creation of the Irish Nation State,* Dublin 1987.
76. Patrick O'Farrell, *Ireland's English Question,* London 1971, p.225.
77. Fitzpatrick, op. cit. Appendix, Table A: 3, p.289.
78. M. E. Collins, *History in the Making 1868-1966,* p. 120.
79. Hachey and McCaffrey, *Perspectives on Irish Nationalism,* p. 79.
80. Edward MacLysaght, *Changing Times,* Gerrards Cross 1978, p.43; Sr. Pius O'Brien, *The Sisters of Mercy of Ennis, Clare* 1992, p.66; *St. Flannan's 1881-1981,* p.63.
81. Ó Dálaigh, *The Stranger's Gaze,* p. 319.
82. An tAthair Seoirse Mac Cluin, *Cáint an Chláir,* 1940.
83. Thomas Murray, *The Story of the Irish in Argentina,* NY 1919, p. 78.
84. Ó Dálaigh, *The Stranger's Gaze,* p. 307.

Chapter Five

1. *Anon, Poems by a County Clare West Briton,* Limerick, 1907, p. 7.
2. *Census of Ireland, 1911.*
3. Ian D'Alton, "Southern Irish Unionism" in O'Flanagan and Buttimer (eds.) *Cork History and Society,* Dublin 1973, pp. 755 - 793.
4. "Southern Irish Unionists, 1906 - 1914" in W. F. Mandle, *Reactions to Irish Nationalism, 1865 - 1914,* London 1987, p. 372.
5. Ibid. p. 373.
6. Ibid.
7. Irish Unionist Association, Annual Report 1912-13, Appendix A; minute book of the Joint Committee of the Unionist Associations of Ireland, PRO Northern Ireland.
8. *Clare Journal,* May 1899.
9. Edward MacLysaght, *Changing Times,* p. 51.
10. Ibid.
11. *Clare Journal,* 3 February 1911.
12. Ibid.
13. Ibid.
14. *Clare Journal,* 22 June 1911.
15. Kieran Sheedy, *Clare Elections,* p. 316.
16. Ibid. Fitzpatrick, *Politics,* p. 58.
17. *Clare Journal,* 25 January 1912.
18. R. McDowell, "The Broadening of the Church" in R. McDowell (ed.) *The Church of Ireland,* London 1975.
19. Ibid.
20. MacLysaght, *Changing Times.*
21. Conor F. Clune, op. cit., p. 41; see also Michael McConville, *Ascendancy to Oblivion,* London 1986, p. 1.
22. John S. Kelly, op. cit., pp. 122-123.
23. Fitzpatrick, op. cit., p. 47; Desmond Bowen, *History and the Shaping of Irish Protestantism,* New York 1995, pp. 603-612.
24. *Andy O'Donoghue memoirs.*
25. Ibid. Richard Hawkins, "The Irish Model and Empire" in R.Hawkins, *Policing the Empire,* Manchester 1991, pp. 18-32.

26. P. Ó Snódaigh, *Hidden Ulster: Protestants and the Irish Language*, p. 75.
27. Michael Hurley (ed.), *Irish Anglicanism*, Dublin 1970, p. 117.
28. Ibid. p. 117.
29. Ibid. pp. 106, 118, Kit and Cyril Ó Ceirín, *Women of Ireland: A Biographic Dictionary,* Galway 1996, pp. 170-171.
30. R. McDowell, *The Church of Ireland*, London 1975, p. 103.
31. Mark Bence-Jones, *Twilight of the Ascendancy*, London 1987, p. 138.
32. *Clare Champion*, 30 July 1999. See also Patrick Buckland, *Irish Unionism, 1885 - 1923*, Dublin 1972, p. 34.
33. *Clare Advertiser*, August 1999.
34. *Clare Champion,* 7 January 2000.
35. National Archives, *CBS* 1900, 208695.
36. Ibid.
37. Ibid.
38. Ibid.
39. E.A Muenger, "A National Reserve for Ireland" in the *Irish Sword*. Vol. XIII, pp. 134-151. See also Con Costelloe, *The British Army on the Curragh of Kildare, Ireland, 1855-1922* in Cathal Brugha Military Barracks, Archives Section. See also E.A. Muenger, *British Military Dilemma in Ireland, 1886-1914*, Dublin 1991, pp. 146-147.
40. Farrell, (ed.) *The Irish Parliamentary Tradition*, Dublin 1973. p. 204. Also see "From a Hermitage" in *Patrick Pearse: Political Writings and Speeches*, p.155.
41. Stephen Gwynn, *John Redmond's Last Years*, London 1919.
42. Ruth Dudley Edwards, *Patrick Pearse, The Triumph of failure,* London 1977.
43. *Clare Journal*, 27 October 1913.
44. National Archives, *Chief Secretary's Office, Registered Papers (CSORP) 1914,* No. 12820.
45. *Irish Historical Documents,* Dublin 1995, Table 9.2.
46. F.S.L. Lyons, "The Meaning of Independence" in Brian Farrell (ed.) *The Irish Parliamentary Tradition*, p. 227.
47. *Joe Barrett memoirs.*
48. *Andy O'Donoghue memoirs.*
49. National Archives, *CBS,* synopsis of Clare Co. Inspector's Report, April 1914.
50. Ibid.
51. Ibid. June 1914.
52. Ibid.
53. Cathal Brugha Barracks, Archives Section, AO/363/1.
54. NLI, MSS Dept, *Col. Maurice Moore Papers*, Mss 10547, No. 5.
55. *Clare Journal*, 11 June 1914.
56. *Barrett memoirs.*
57. National Archives, *CBS,* synopsis of Clare Co. Inspector's Report, June 1914.
58. *Clare Journal*, 8 June 1914.
59. National Archives, *CSORP 12735 / 1914*
60. *Clare Journal*, 30 July 1914.
61. *Sinn Féin*, 1 August 1914.
62. Ibid.
63. *Clare Champion*, 8 August 1914.
64. Ibid.

65. Republican statements and contemporary newspaper accounts refer to this aspect.

66. Charles Townshend, *Political Violence in Ireland*, Oxford 1983, *passim*; R. J. Sawyer, *The Failure of the IPP 1910 - 1918,* Ph.D., Columbia 1966 [66-9374]; P. Snoddy, *Irish Volunteers 1913 - 1916*, MA, UCD 1963 *passim*; John P. Duggan, *A History of the Irish Army*, Dublin 1991, p. 3.

67. George Dangerfield, *The Damnable Question*, London 1977, *passim*; Liz Curtis, *The Cause of Ireland*, Dublin 1994, pp. 295-299; Grenfell Morton, *Home Rule and the Irish Question*, Longman 1986, pp. 47-51.

68. *Clare Champion*, 8 August 1914.

69. Ibid.

70. J. J. Lee, *Politics and Society,* p. 22.

71. *Clare Journal*, 10 August 1914.

72. PRO Kew, *CO/904,* CI Report, August 1914.

73. MacLysaght, *Changing Times.*

74. *The Leader*, 6 August 1914.

75. *The Clare Champion*, 8 August 1914.

76. Elizabeth Muenger, op. cit., in *Irish Sword*, Vol. XIII, pp. 134-151.

77. Jimmy Smith, *Ballads of the Banner*, Dublin 1998, p. 52.

78. *Clare Journal*, 8 August 1914.

79. Ibid.

80. Ibid.

81. *Clare Journal*, 7 September 1914.

82. Ibid.

83. *Clare Journal*, 29 August 1914.

84. Ibid.

85. *Kilrush UDC Minute Book*, 1914.

86. *Ennistymon RDC Minute Book*, September 1914.

87. *Kilrush RDC Minute Book*, October 1914.

88. NLI, *Moore Mss.*, Ms 10547, No. 5.

89. Ibid.

90. Ibid.

91. Ibid.

92. Ibid.

93. *Kilrush RDC Minute Book*, 19 September 1914.

94. *Kilrush UDC Minute Book*, 21 September 1914.

95. *Clare Journal*, 26 September 1914.

96. James McGuinn, *Sligo Men in the Great War*, Sligo 1996.

97. *Sinn Féin*, 26 September 1914.

98. Deirdre McMahon, *Ireland and the Empire during the First World War,* Unpublished lecture, Mary Immaculate College, Limerick, March 2000.

Chapter 6

1. *Clare Journal*, 26 September 1914.

2. *Moore Mss.* 10545 no.7.

3. Ibid.

4. Ibid.

5. Ibid.

6.   Ibid.
7.   *Clare Journal*, 25 October 1914.
8.   *Moore Mss.* 10547 No.5.
9.   *Moore Mss.* 10544.
10. National Archives, *CBS* 1913-17, 5 Nov 1914 report by DMP.
11. Ibid.
12. *Moore Mss.* 10547 No. 5.
13. *Clare Journal*, 14 January 1915. The innovative MacLysaght was also part of an initiative to establish a Nua-Ghaeltacht, or an Irish speaking community in Raheen.
14. *NLI. MacLysaght Mss.*, Ms. 2649.
15. *Clare Journal*, 5 September 1914.
16. Peadar MacNamara "The Great War" in *The Other Clare,* Vol. XII, 1989.
17. *The Leader,* 22 January 1916.
18. Fitzpatrick, *Politics*.
19. Mark Bence-Jones, op. cit..
20. Ibid.
21. *Moore Mss.* 10547 No. 5.
22. Ibid.
23. Ibid.
24. Ibid.
25. Ibid.
26. *Clare Journal*, 19 August 1914.
27. Representative Church Library, Braemor Park, Churchtown, Dublin, *Church of Ireland Gazette*, 28 July 1916.
28. Patrick Buckland, *Irish Unionism I: 1885-1922*, Dublin 1972, p. 38.
29. Ibid. p. 41.
30. PRONI, D 939/A/G/7, *Wilson's Tour of Clare, 1916*.
31. *Clare Journal*, 4 February 1915.
32. Fitzpatrick, *Politics*.
33. *Clare Journal*, 25 February 1915.
34. Ibid.
35. *Clare Champion*, January 1915.
36. *Clare Journal*, 25 February 1915.
37. Terence Brown, *Ireland - A Social and Cultural History*, London 1989, pp. 183-184.
38. Brian M. Walker, Art Ó Bróin and Sean McMahon, *Faces of Ireland*, Appletree Press Ltd., 1980, p. 16.
39. Letter to the author from Peter J. Power-Hynes, Researcher of the Connaught Rangers, Islington, London.
40. *Clare Journal*, 11 January 1915.
41. Ibid. 4 February 1915.
42. *Clare Journal*, 11 September 1915.
43. *Irish World.* 23 October 1915. Ms. Nellie Mulcahy, Co. Clare suffered a similar fate, being interned in Breslau for ten weeks at the beginning of the war and was only released on the intervention of the American Consul by whom she was accorded a safe passage.
44. *Clare Journal*, 25 January 1915.
45. National Archives, *CSORP 21639 / 1915*
46. Kieran Sheedy, *Clare Elections*, p. 322.

47.   Terence Denman, *A Lonely Grave.*
48.   Ibid.
49.   MacNamara, *"The Great War".*
50.   *Irish World,* 19 June 1915.
51.   *Clare Journal,* June 1915.
52.   *Irish Times,* 4 November 1915.
53.   National Archives, *CSORP 18210/1915*
54.   *Clare Champion,* 22 April 1915.
55.   *1915 Minute Books of Clare Co. Council, Kilrush RDC and Ennis RDC.*
56.   *Clare Journal,* 31 May 1915.
57.   *Clare Champion,* Jubilee edition, 1966.
58.   Ibid.
59.   Ibid.
60.   *Clare Champion,* 12 February 1916.
61.   Ibid.
62.   Ibid.
63.   *Clare Champion,* 15 January 1916.
64.   *Haugh memoirs.*
65.   *Barrett memoirs,* op. cit..
66.   Ibid.
67.   *Peadar Clancy letters*, courtesy of Shannon Family, Cranny, Co. Clare.
68.   *Barrett memoirs.*
69.   *Michael Brennan memoirs,* op. cit..
70.   Ibid.
71.   National Archives, *CBS* 1915.
72.   *Barrett memoirs.*
73.   *O'Donoghue memoirs,* op.cit..
74.   *Haugh memoirs,* op. cit..
75.   *Clare Champion*, 29 August 1914.
76.   Fitzpatrick, *Politics.*
77.   *Moore Mss.* 10547 No. 5.
78.   O'Callaghan, *Bishop O'Dwyer.* op. cit..
79.   National Archives, *CBS* 1913 -17, list of clergymen under notice.
80.   *Moore Mss.* 10547 No. 5.
81.   Thomas Coffey, *The Parish of Inchicronan*, p. 163.
82.   *The Leader*, 19 February 1916.
83.   *The Irish World,* 3 July 1915.
84.   Ibid. 5 June 1915.
85.   Ibid. 25 November 1916.
86.   *Ennis RDC Minute Book*, 3 December 1915.
87.   *Irish World*, 4 December 1914.
88.   National Archives, *CSORP 9365/1914*
89.   Ibid. *CSORP 22567/1914*
90.   *Barrett memoirs.*
91.   *Haugh memoirs.*
92.   *O'Donoghue memoirs.*
93.   *Barrett memoirs.*
94.   *Brennan memoirs.*
95.   *O'Keeffe memoirs.*
96.   PRO Kew, *CO 903/19 CI Co. Clare Report*, 1916.

97. *Clare Champion*, 29 April 1916.
98. Ibid. 6 May 1916.
99. P. J. Cleary, N.T., Gallow's Hill, Ennis, kindly furnished the author with family papers on General Lynch. See also Bridie Cleary, "GPO Easter Week" in *Kilfidane Parish*, Ennis 1980
100. *Clare Co. Council Minute Book,* May 1916.
101. *Church of Ireland Gazette*, 28 July 1916.
102. R. McDowell, *The Church of Ireland,* p. 103.
103. Extract from the *Diary of Jenny Griffin*, courtesy of Mrs. Veronica Reynolds, Hertshire, United Kingdom.
104. PRO Kew, *CO 903 / 19 CI Co. Clare Report,* 1916.

Chapter Seven

1.   Martin Staunton, *Royal Munster Fusiliers,* p. 101.
2   *Census of Ireland,* 1911, Province of Munster, Table XX, p. 75.
3.   Ibid.
4.   Ibid.
5.   Bartlett and Jeffery, "An Irish Military Tradition?" in Bartlett and Jeffery (eds.) *A Military History of Ireland*, Dublin 1996.
6.   Peadar MacNamara, "County Clare and WWI" in *The Other Clare*, Vol. X, 1987.
7.   Staunton, op. cit. The county was within the Cork or South-Western military district and in conjunction with the Counties Cork, Kerry and Limerick formed the No. 70 Regimental District.
8.   Ibid.
9.   *Clare Champion*, 14 February 1997.
10. *Census*, 1911.
11. Staunton, *Royal Munster Fusiliers.*
12. Patrick Callan, "Recruiting by the British Army in Ireland during the First World War" in the *Irish Sword*, Vol. XVIII.
13. Staunton, *Royal Munster Fusiliers.*
14. Terence Denman, "The Red Livery of Shame" in *Irish Historical Studies*, Vol. XXIX, 1994.
15. *The Republic*, 20 December 1906.
16. Denman, "The Red Livery of Shame", op.cit..
17. *Hansard, IXXIX*, 406, 19 February 1900.
18. *Hansard, IXXX*, 136, 16 March 1900.
19. *Hansard, IXXX*, 135, 16 March 1900.
20. Irish Facts, December 1907, pp. 319-320.
21. National Archives, *CO 904 / 70*, Police Intelligence Reports, March 1900.
22. Keith Jeffery, *An Irish Empire?* p. 97.
23. Ibid. p. 100.
24. Philip Orr, *Irish Historical Studies*, 1993.
25. Patrick Callan, op. cit., pp. 42-43.
26. Martin Staunton, *Royal Munster Fusiliers.*
27. L.W. Brady, *T. P. O'Connor and the Liverpool Irish*, p. 221. For more on the racial environment which the Irish soldier in the British army

encountered, see T. Denman, "The Racial Environment" in *Irish Historical Studies,* 1990-1991.

28. National Archives, *CSORP 92176/1917.*
    See NLI Manuscripts Library, John Redmond Mss., Ms. 1525 8 for percentages of Irishmen in Irish units raised out of Ireland, e.g.:

24th Battalion, Northumberland Fusiliers	20%
25th Battalion, Northumberland Fusiliers	18%
26th Battalion, Northumberland Fusiliers	10%
27th Battalion, Northumberland Fusiliers	4%
1/8th Liverpool Regiments	18%
2/18th London Regiments	25%

29. See also Patrick Callan, op. cit., for a geographic breakdown of regional recruitment.
30. David Fitzpatrick, "Militarism in Ireland, 1900-22" in Bartlett and Jeffery (eds.) *A Military History of Ireland*.
31. Ibid.
32. C.H. Oldham, "The economic interests involved in the War" in *Studies*, 1915.
33. Fitzpatrick, *Politics*.
34. National Archives, *CSORP 10144/1917*. The collapse came about despite the chief secretary's office considering the Killaloe Slate company as possibly 'being the means of saving much cross channel shipping in the rebuilding of the destroyed area of Dublin.' See also Gordon Daly, 'Killaloe Slate' in Sliabh Aughty. 2000, pp. 43-48.
35. *Sinn Féin*, 25 October 1918.
36. An interview with Mr. Falvey, Kilkee, whose father survived the war.
37. MacLysaght, *Changing Times*, p. 58.
38. National Archives, *RP*, 1915.
39. Ibid.
40. *Sinn Féin*, 3 September.
41. Ibid.
42. Imperial War Museum, Sir John French papers.
43. Ibid.
44. Parnell Kerr, *What the Irish Regiments have done*, London 1916.
45. Mrs. Victor Rickard, *The Story of the Munsters*, London 1921.
46. Parnell Kerr, op.cit.
47. *Clare Journal*, 28 June, 1915; Peadar MacNamara, "The Great War", op. cit..
48. *Letter of Sgt. James A. Campbell, L Company, Royal Munster Fusiliers* in the Liddle Library Collection, Leeds University.
49. "Catholic Army Chaplains - a Diary" in *The Catholic Bulletin*, 1919.
50. Michael MacDonagh, "Irish Catholic Chaplains in the War" in the *Irish Ecclesiastical*, December 1915.
51. Franciscan Library, Killiney, *Benedict Coffey Papers*.
52. Royal Army Chaplains Department, DS/184/A.
53. *Kilmaley Parish Magazine*, 1988, p. 39.
54. *History of Kilmurry Ibrickane*, 1982, p. 34.
55. Conor F. Clune, op. cit. pp. 83-88.
56. Killaloe Diocesan Records, Westbourne, Ennis.
57. Ibid.
58. Irish Advocate, 16 April 1918.

59. Ibid. 30 May 1918.
60. Ibid. 22 September 1917.
61. Ibid. 18 April 1918.
62. Ibid. 17 July 1917.
63. Ibid. 24 November 1917.
64. In an interview with Lieutenant Colonel Kenneth H. Powers, regimental historian of the Sixty Ninth regiment of New York, March 1998.
65. Frank Forde, *They called themselves Irish -The Seventh Cavalry Regiment of the US Army*; Copy in Cathal Brugha Military Barracks, Archives Section.
66. Interview with Powers, op.cit..
67. Frank Forde, op. cit.; see also Brigadier A.E.C Bredin, *A History of the Irish Soldier*, Belfast 1987.
68. Charles Higham, *American Swastika,* pp 88 - 93, Doubleday & Co., 1985.
69. WWW.Geocities. com/The Cullinane Family Genealogy Project Website.
70. Ibid.
71. *Irish Times article,* 14 March 1966, courtesy of the Somme Heritage Centre.
72. *Kilrush UDC minute book*, 19 November 1917.
73. In an interview with Peadar McNamara.

Chapter 8

1. Peadar Clancy to his brother M. J. in Chicago, *Peadar Clancy Letters,* op. cit..
2. *Ennis RDC Minute Book*, 30 August 1916.
3. *Corofin RDC Minute Book*, 1 November 1916.
4. *Cabinet reports to George V,* 19 July 1916, R/294, NUIG Special Collections Library.
5. *Church of Ireland Gazette*, 3 August 1917.
6. *Cabinet Reports to George V,* 13 November 1916, R/308, NUIG Special Collections Library.
7. Ibid. R/302, October 1916.
8. *Clare Champion*, 10 June 1916 and *Irish World,* July 1916.
9. O'Callaghan, *Bishop O'Dwyer,* op. cit..
10. Ibid.
11. Ibid.
12. NLI, article by Edward MacLysaght, *East Clare 1916-1921.*
13. *Kilrush UDC minute book*, March 1917.
14. PRO, *C0904 MR, CI*, February 1917.
15. National Archives, *RP 1917*, No 14934.
16. *Michael Brennan memoirs*; Also see *Irish Times*, 9 June 1992.
17. *Barrett memoirs; O'Donoghue memoirs.*
18. *O'Donoghue memoirs.*
19. *Brennan memoirs*, op.cit.
20. Ibid.
21. PRO, *CO / 904 Prosecutions arising out of elections*, (Reel 100 Box 32)
22. *Brennan memoirs.*
23. *Clare Champion,* 12 May 1917.
24. Ibid.
25. Meda Ryan, *Michael Collins and the women in his life*, Dublin 1996 pp.23-26.

26. *Kilrush UDC Minute Book*, 18 June 1917.
    Saturday Record, 14 July 1917.
27. Oliver Snoddy, "Three by-elections of 1917" in *Capuchin Annual*, 1967, pp. 341-346.
28. O'Callaghan, *Bishop O'Dwyer*, op. cit..
29. *Irish Times*, 28 November 1966.
30. In an interview conducted by the author with Josh Honan, Co Clare, 1998.
31. Ibid.
32. *Capuchin Annual*, op. cit., p. 344; David Fitzpatrick, 'The undoing of the Easter Rising" in J. Murphy, and J.P. O'Carroll, *De Valera & his Times*. Cork 1983
33. MacLysaght, *Changing Times*, op. cit., p. 68.
34. Kevin J Browne, *Eamon De Valera and the Banner County*, Dublin 1982, p. 8.
35. Ibid.
36. *Irish World,* 4 August 1917.
37. *Irish Citizen*, 19 September 1914.
38. Brian Dinan, *Clare and its people*, op. cit., p. 102.
39. *Irish Times*, 28 November 1966.
40. O'Callaghan, *Bishop O'Dwyer*, op. cit..
41. *Kilrush RDC minute book*, July 1917.
42. *Irish Advocate*, September 1917.
43. O'Donoghue, op. cit..
44. Ibid. Some republicans are still dismissive of Volunteers who joined during this period.
45. *Barrett memoirs*; Sean O'Keeffe also concurred with Barrett's claim. (see *O'Keeffe memoirs*, op.cit.)
46. Ibid.
47. *O'Keeffe memoirs: O'Donoghue memoirs*.
48. PRO, C0904 Intercepted Letters, 27690, MI5.
49. *Kilrush UDC minute book*, 15 February. 1918.
50. *Michael Brennan memoirs*.
51. PRO *CO 903 / 19*; *IG Report*, Co. Clare 1918
52. Edward MacLysaght, "Some Memories of the Irish Convention 1917-1918" in *The Capuchin Annual, 1966.*
53. Ibid.
54. PRO *CO/904*: Letter from Reverend Dr Fogarty, Bishop ofKillaloe to Mr E.E. Lysaght.
55. NLI, Mss. MacLysaght,
56. PRO *CO 903 / 19, IG Report,* Co. Clare 1918. See also David Fitzpatrick, *Revolution?*, op. cit., p.38.
57. *Nationality*, 28 January 1918.
58. In an interview with John Keane, Chairman, Comhar Conradh na Boirne.
59. Tom Queally, *A History of the Republican Courts Of Justice in the parish of Kilmacduane* 1917-22, p. 3, Clare Local Studies Centre.
60. *Irish World,* 9 March 1918.
61. *Limerick Leader,* 16 December 1972; *PRO MR CO / 904 / 164.*
62. Ibid.
63. *Barrett memoirs.*
64. *Haugh memoirs.*
65. PRO, *CO / 904 / 162*

66. PRO, *CO/ 904/* MI5G Intercepted Letters 23608.
67. Ibid.
68. Ibid. No.28109
69. Extract from the *Diary of Jenny Griffin*, op.cit..
70. *Irish World*, 6 April, 1918.
71. Michael McCarthy, "Parteen- to organise or not?" in *The Old Limerick Journal,* pp.14-19.
72. Daniel J. McCarthy, *Prisoner of War in Germany*, New York 1918, p. 124.
73. PRO, *CO/904*, June 1918.
74. National Archives, *115 5/5/Bodkin Family*, No. 4975499.
75. Fr. Patrick Gaynor, "The Dean of Cashel and the 1918 General Election" in *Tipperary Historical Journal,* 1998, p. 52; See also Browne, *De Valera and the Banner County*, p. 104.

Epilogue.

1. *The Examiner,* 16 December, 1998. Tadhg Moloney, Limerick, the secretary of the Royal Munster Fusiliers Association noted the absence of badges, which contained soldier's rank, serial number and regiment, on the gravestones of the Great War dead when he visited Ennistymon graveyard in 1996, and he began a two year campaign to have Co. Council reconsider the authoritys six year old decision.
2. Jane Leonard, "Getting them at Last" in David Fitzpatrick,(ed.), *Revolution? Ireland 1917-23*, Dublin 1990, pp. 118-127.
3. Ibid.
4. Conor F. Clune, *The Clunes*, p. 18.
5. Michael McCarthy, "Parteen- to organise or not?", op.cit.
6. Sonny Enright, *The Life Of A Cattle Dealer*, Galway 1986, p. 35.
7. Martin Morrissey, *The Changing Years*, Dublin 1992, p. 46. Morrissey goes on to describe the comically unorthodox antics of Mike, which included fishing in bathtubs, in his successful efforts to feign insanity to qualify for the disability pension.
8. Ibid.
9. Staunton, *Royal Munster Fusiliers*, p. 302.
10. *Clare Champion*, 12 October 1918. The infirmary surgeons were not in receipt of the war bonus which was generally available to other surgeons and were seeking to be allowed 6d per head per day for attendance to these veterans.
11. Ibid.
12. Joost Augusteijn, *From Public Defiance to Guerrilla Warfare*, Dublin 1996, p. 97.
13. *Ennistymon Parish Magazine 2002*, p. 99.
14. Civil War papers, courtesy of Christina Finn, Ennis, Co. Clare.
15. This controversial case where Kirby was executed by local IRA men for treason, despite later evidence suggesting he was the victim of republican in-feuding is covered by a display at the South Tipperary Museum in Clonmel.
16. Jane Leonard, *Getting Them At Last*, op.cit..
17. *Clare Champion,* 13 November, 1998.

BIBLIOGRAPHY

PRIMARY PUBLISHED SOURCES:

NEWSPAPERS:
Irish Times, NUIG Special Collections Library.
Clare Journal, Clare Local Studies Centre.
Clare Champion, Clare Local Studies Centre.
Freeman's Journal, NUIG Special Collections Library.
The Limerick Leader.
Gaelic American.
Celtic Times, Clare Co. Library.
Irish Advocate, Iona College Library, New Rochelle, New York.
Nationality, New York Public Library.
The Irish World, New York Public Library.
The Catholic Bulletin, Catholic Central Library.
The Irish Ecclesiastical Record, NLI.
The Examiner.
Clare Advertiser.
Clare County Express.
Sinn Féin NUIG Special Collections Library.
The Leader NUIG Special Collections Library.
Church of Ireland Gazette, Representative Church Body Library, Dublin.

PERIODICALS:
History Ireland, James Hardiman Library, NUIG.
The Irish Sword, NLI.
Studia Hibernica, James Hardiman Library, NUIG.
Irish Studies Review, NLI.
Old Limerick Journal, UCD Library.
Irisleabhar Mhá Nuad, UCD Library.
The Other Clare, Clare Local Studies Centre.
Capuchin Annual, Clare Local Studies Centre.
Tipperary Historical Journal, James Hardiman Library, NUIG.
Irish Maritime Journal, National Maritime Museum.
Sliabh Aughty, Clare Local Studies Centre.

JAMES HARDIMAN LIBRARY, NUIG:
1911 CENSUS RETURN : Province of Munster, County of Clare.

JAMES HARDIMAN LIBRARY, NUIG:
Report of the Department Committee of Agricultural Credit - Ireland 1914 command paper.

NATIONAL LIBRARY OF IRELAND:
Report of Land Commission 1951.

Report of Royal Commission appointed to enquire into the financial relations of Ireland and Great Britain.

Hansard, 1 XXIX, 406, 19 February, 1900.
Hansard, 1 XXX, 135/136 16 March, 1900.

CLARE LOCAL STUDIES CENTRE:
Parish histories of Kilmihil, Kilfidane, Kildysart, Kilmaley, Ennistymon and Kilmurry Ibrickane.

WEBSITES:
www.thewildgeese.com
www.geocities.com/thecullinanefamilygeneaologyproject.website

PRIMARY UNPUBLISHED SOURCES :
Griffin-McCarthy, Siobhan, *The Changing Face of Clare Rural Farm Families,* B. Ed. thesis, St. Angela's College 1997.

Kelly, Tim., *The History of Ennis*. MA thesis, NUIG 1971.

O'Callaghan, Edward, *Bishop O'Dwyer and the course of Irish politics 1870-1917,* MA thesis 1976, NUIG Special Collections Library (microfilm).

McMahon, Deirdre, *Ireland and the Empire during the First World War*, unpublished lecture, Mary Immaculate College, Limerick 2000.

Unpublished memoirs of Joseph Barrett, copy in the possession of author.

Sawyer, R.J., *The Failure of the IPP 1910 - 1918*, Ph.D., Columbia 1966.

Queally, Tom, *A History of the Republican Courts of Justice in the parish of Kilmacduane, 1917-1922,* Clare Local Studies Centre.

NATIONAL ARCHIVES:
Monthly Crime Reports (MCR) and Inspector General Reports (IGR) between 1900 and 1918.

Crime Special Branch Reports (CBS), *Synopsis of Clare Co. Inspectors Reports*.

Registered Papers 1914-1918.

NATIONAL LIBRARY, IRELAND, MANUSCRIPTS DEPARTMENT:
Col. Maurice Moore Papers.

Mac Lysaght Papers, Ms. 2649.

Redmond Papers, Ms. 15258.

LIDDLE LIBRARY, LEEDS UNIVERSITY:
RMF Letter.

IMPERIAL WAR MUSEUM:
Lord French Papers.

ROYAL ARMY CHAPLAINS DEPARTMENT DEPOT:
Catholic Chaplaincy:
Clare Chaplains' Papers.

NUIG SPECIAL COLLECTIONS LIBRARY:

PRO CO/904 Intercepted Letters MI5; Distribution of Seditious Leaflets; Censor's Monthly Reports.

CATHAL BRUGHA MILITARY BARRACKS, ARCHIVES SECTION:

Michael Collins Papers, containing biographical information on Liam Haugh, Michael Brennan and references to other republican figures in Clare.

PUBLIC RECORDS OFFICE:

PRO, Kew, London: CO/904 CI Report 1914.
PRO, Northern Ireland: Wilson's Tour of Clare 1916.
PRO, Northern Ireland: IUA; Annual Report 1912-13, Appendix A; minute book of joint committee of Unionist Associations of Ireland.

CLARE LOCAL STUDIES CENTRE, LOCAL AUTHORITIES RECORDS (at time of research):

Minute Books for:
    Ennis RDC.
    Ennis UDC.
    Corofin RDC.
    Ennistymon RDC.
    Kilrush RDC.
    Ballyvaughan RDC.

KILRUSH TOWN HALL:

Kilrush UDC. (Minute Book)

CLARE COUNTY ARCHIVES:

Clare Co. Council Records. (formerly kept in Ennis Courthouse).

CLARE LOCAL STUDIES CENTRE:

Statement of Andrew O'Donoghue, Mid-Clare IRA brigade.

KILLALOE DIOCESAN RECORDS:

Westbourne, Ennis (Chaplain Records).

CHURCH OF IRELAND, REPRESENTATIVE CHURCH BODY LIBRARY, CHURCHTOWN, DUBLIN 14:

The registers of Baptisms, Marriages and Burials from the Church of Ireland parishes in County Clare.

FRANCISCAN LIBRARY, KILLINEY:

Benedict Coffey Paper.

PEADAR CLANCY LETTERS:

Courtesy of Padraig Shannon, Cranny, Co. Clare.

DR DONAL P. McCRACKEN LETTER:
to the author.

PETER J. POWER- HYNES LETTER, RESEARCHER OF THE CONNAUGHT RANGERS:
letter to the author.

CHRISTINA FINN, ENNIS:
presented WWI photograph and Civil War papers to the author.

JOHN RIDGE LETTER:
letter to the author relating to Irish-American sources.

INTERVIEWS:
Interview with Mr. Falvey, Kilkee, whose father survived the war.
Interview with Josh Honan, Co. Clare 1998.
Interview with Lt. Col. Kenneth Powers, Regimental Historian, 69th Regiment, U.S. Army.
Interview with the late Fr. Michael Hillery,P.P., Kildysart, Co. Clare.
Interview with P. J. Cleary, N.T. Gallow's Hill, Ennis, who kindly furnished the author with family papers on General Lynch.

GREATER JOHANNESBURG LIBRARY SERVICES, SOUTH AFRICA:
Extract of Stanley Monick's *The Shamrock and the Springbok: the Irish impact on South African Military History, 1689-1914.*

STATE LIBRARY OF NEW SOUTH WALES, AUSTRALIA:
MIHILIST and APAIS databases.

NATIONAL DEFENCE HEADQUARTERS, OTTAWA, CANADA:
Directorate of History and Heritage - The Irish-Canadian Rangers, Montreal, 1916.

CANADIAN WAR MUSEUM, OTTAWA, ONTARIO, CANADA:
Source information on the 208th Battalion of Toronto.

COMMONWEALTH WAR GRAVES COMMISSION, U.K. 2 MARLOW ROAD, MAIDENHEAD, U.K.:
Casualty Listing Report for all casualties with Co. Clare in the register listings for the First World War. All Royal Munster Fusiliers commemorated in the Province of Munster for the First World War. For the purposes of the Commission, the dates of the First World War are as follows: WW1: 04/08/1914 - 31/08/1921.

CHIEF OF THE SA NATIONAL DEFENCE FORCE, CHIEF OF PERSONNEL, PRETORIA:

CSF (Documentation Service Directorate) Box 97, File ref. 514/3/4/10/2 relating to Irish Military History in South Africa.

MINISTERIE VAN LANDSVERDEDIGING, 1000 BRUSSELS:

Sources on Belgian WW1 refugees from the Branch Chief of The Historical Service of the Belgian Joint staff.

DEPARTMENT OF THE ARMY, THE CENTRE OF MILITARY HISTORY, WASHINGTON DC.:

Historical Support Branch, history of the 77th Infantry Division.

U.S. ARMY MILITARY HISTORY INSTITUTE (MHI), CARLISLE BARRACKS, PENNSYLVANIA:

Centre of Military History (CMH) files.

SECONDARY SOURCES:

1.   Akenson, D., *Small Differences*, Quebec 1988.
2.   Arensburg, C., *The Irish Countryman*, Massachussets 1937.
3.   Augusteijn, J., *From Public Defiance to Guerilla Warfare*, Dublin 1996.
4.   Bartlett, T. and Jeffrey K., *A Military History of Ireland*, Dublin 1996.
5.   Bence-Jones, M., *Twilight of the Ascendancy*, London 1987.
6.   Blaghd de, E., "Hyde in Conflict", in Sean Ó Tuama, *The Gaelic League Idea,* Cork 1972.
7.   Bohan, Rev.Fr. H. "Economic & Social Trends" *in St. Flannans, 1881-1981*, Ennis 1981.
8.   Bolger, P., *The Irish Co-operative Movement: Its History and Development,* IPA, Dublin 1977.
9.   Bowen, D., *History and the shaping of Protestantism,* New York 1995.
10.   Boyce, D. G., Eccleshall, R. and Geoghegan, V., (eds.) *Political Thought in Ireland Since The Seventeenth Century*, London and New York 1993.
11.   Brady, L.W. *T.P. O'Connor and the Liverpool Irish*, London 1983
12.   Bredin, A.E.C., *A History of the Irish Soldier*, Belfast 1987.
13.   Brown, T., *Ireland - A Social and Cultural History,* London 1989.
14.   Browne, K.J., *Eamon de Valera and the Banner County*, Dublin 1982.
15.   Buckland, P. *Irish Unionism I. 1885-1922*, Dublin 1972.
16.   Búrca de, M., *The G.A.A.: A History*, Dublin 1999.
17.   Byrnes. O., *Memories of Clare Hurling*, Cork 1996.
18.   Childs, P. and Williams, P., *An Introduction to Post Colonial Theory*, London 1997.
19.   Clark, S. and Donnelly, J.S., *Irish Peasants, Violence & Political Unrest, 1780-1914*, Dublin 1983.
20.   Clifford, B., *Ireland in the Great War*, Belfast 1992.
21.   Clune, C.F., *The Clunes from Dalcassian to Modern Times,* Cork 1992.
22.   Collins, M.E., *History in the Making 1868-1966*, Dublin 1996
23.   Coffey, T., *The Parish of Inchicronan*, Ballinakella Press, Clare 1993.

24. Coogan, T.P., *Wherever Green Is Worn*. London 2000.
25. Costelloe, C., *The British Army on the Curragh of Kildare, Ireland, 1855-1922*. Cork 1999.
26. Cronin, M., *Country, Class or Craft?* Cork University Press 1994.
27. Crossman, V., *Local Government in the 19th Century Ireland*, Belfast 1994.
28. Crotty, C.R., *Irish Agricultural Productions*, Cork 1996.
29. Curtis, E. and McDonald, R.B., *Irish Historical Documents, 1172-1922*, Methuen 1943
29. Curtis, L., *The Cause of Ireland,* Dublin 1994.
30. Curtin and Ryan "Clubs, Pubs and Private Houses in a Clare Town", in Curtin & Wilson (eds.) *Ireland from Below*, Dublin 1990.
31. D'Alton, I. "Southern Irish Unionism" in *Cork History and Society*, Dublin 1973.
32. Daly, M.E., *The Buffer State: The Historical Roots of the Department of the Environment*, Dublin 1997.
33. Dangerfield. G., *The Damnable Question*, London 1977.
34. Denman, T., *Ireland's Unknown Soldiers*, Dublin 1992.
35. Denman, T., *A Lonely Grave: The Life and Death of Willie Redmond*, Dublin 1995.
36. Dillon T., *The Banner*, New York 1967.
37. Dinan, B., *Clare and Its People*, Cork 1987.
38. Duggan, J., *A History of the Irish Army*, Dublin 1991.
39. Farmer, T., *Ordinary Lives*, Dublin 1991.
40. Farrell, B., *The Irish Parliamentary Tradition*, Dublin 1973.
41. Feingold, W., *The Revolt of Tenantry: The Transformation of Local Government in Ireland. 1872-1886*, Boston 1984.
42. Fraser, T.G. and Jeffery, K., *Men, Women and War*, Dublin 1993.
43. Edwards, R.D., *Patrick Pearse, The Triumph of Failure*, London 1977.
44. Enright, S., *The Life of a Cattle Dealer*, Galway 1986.
45. Fitzpatrick, D., *Politics and Irish Life*, Aldershot 1977.
46. Fitzpatrick, D., *Ireland and the First World War,* Dublin 1986.
47. Fitzpatrick, D.,(ed.) *Revolution? Ireland 1914-1923*, Dublin 1993.
48. Forde, F., *They Called themselves Irish - The Seventh Cavalry Regiment of the U.S. Army,* Copy in Cathal Brugha Barracks, Archives Section.
49. Gailey, A., *Ireland and the Death of Kindness*, Cork 1987.
50. Garvin, T., *The Evolution of Irish Nationalist Politics*, New York 1981.
51. Garvin, T., *Nationalist Revolutionaries in Ireland, 1858-1928*. Oxford 1987.
52. Genet, J., *Rural Ireland, Real Ireland*, Gerrards Cross, Bucks 1996.
53. Goldring, M., *Pleasant The Scholar's Life,* London 1993.
54. Gwynn, S., *John Redmonds Last Years*, London 1919,
55. Hachey, T., and McCaffrey, L. (eds.) *Perspectives on Irish Nationalism*, Kentucky 1989.
56. Hammond, H., *Readings in Sociology of Community*, Clarendon Press 1968.
57. Hannan, D.F., Katsiaouni, L., *Traditional Families From Culturally Prescribed to Negotiated Roles in Farm Families*, Dublin 1977.
58. Harris, H.E.D., *The Other Half Million - The Irish Regiments in the First World War*, Dublin 1993.
59. Hawkins, R., *Policing The Empire,*. Manchester 1991.
60. Higham, C., *American Swastika*, Doubleday 1985.
61. Hobson, B., *The History of the Irish Volunteers,* Vol.1, Dublin 1918.

62. Hooker, E.R., *Re-Adjustments of Agricultural Tenure In Ireland*, North Carolina 1938.
63. Hoppen, K.T., *Ireland Since 1800: Conflict and Conformity*, London 1999
64. Horgan, J., *Parnell to Pearse*, Dublin 1948.
65. Hurley, M. (ed.) *Irish Anglicanism*, Dublin 1970.
66. Hutchinson, J. *The Dynamics of Cultural Nationalism: The Gaelic Revival and the Creation of the Irish Nation State*, Dublin 1987.
67. Jeffery, K., (ed.) *An Irish Empire?* Manchester 1996.
68. Jalland, P., "Irish Home Rule, Finance, 1910-1914", in W.F. Mandle, *Reactions To Irish Nationalism, 1865 -1914*, London 1987.
69. Kelly, J.S., *The Bodyke Evictions*, Clare 1987.
70. Kennedy, R., *The Irish - Emigration, Marriage and Fertility*, University of California Press 1973.
71. Kerr, P., *What the Irish Regiments have done*, London 1916.
72. Lee, J.J., *Ireland 1912-1985, Politics and Society*, Cambridge University Press 1989.
73. Lee, J.J., *The Modernisation of Irish Society, 1848-1918*, Dublin 1984.
74. Linehan, M., and Tucker, V., (eds.) *Workers Co-operatives*, U.C.C. Bank of Ireland Centre for Co-operative Studies, 1983
75. Longley, E., *Culture in Ireland - Division or Diversity*, Belfast 1991.
76. Lynch, A., *My Life Story*, London 1924.
77. Lynch, D., *The IRB and the 1916 Insurrection*, Cork 1957.
78. Lyons, F.S.L., *Irish Parlimentarv Party, 1890-1910*, London 1951.
79. Mandle, W.F., *Reactions to Irish Nationalism 1865-1914*, London 1987.
80. McCarthy, *D.J. Prisoner of War in Germany*, New York 1917.
81. McCaughey, T.P., *Memory and Redemption*, Dublin 1993.
82. McConville,M., *Ascendancy to Oblivion*, London 1986.
83. McCracken, D.P., *Irish Commandoes in the Boer War*, London 1999.
84. McDowell, R., *The Church of Ireland*, London 1975.
85. McGuann, J., *Sligo and the Great War*, Sligo 1996.
86. McNamara, S., *Mícheál on gCárn*, Clare 1997.
87. MacAonghusa., P., *Ar Son na Gaeilge, Conradh na Gaeilge 1893-1993*, An Chéad Chló, Dublin 1993.
88. MacCluin, An tAthair S., *Cáint an Chláir*, 1940.
89. MacGiolla Choille,B., *Intelligence Notes, 1913-1916*, Dublin 1966.
90. MacLysaght, E., *Changing Times*, Gerrards Cross 1978.
91. Morris, Dr K. R., *John P. Holland, Inventor of the Modern Submarine*, New York 1980.
92. Morrissey, M., *The Changing Years*, Dublin 1992.
93. Morton, G., *Home Rule and the Irish Question*, Longman Group Ltd., 1986.
94. Muenger, E. A., *British Military Dilemma in Ireland, 1886-1914*, Dublin 1991.
95. Mulqueen, N.J., *The Vandeleur Evictions in Kilrush, 1888*, Ennis 1990.
96. Murphy, B.P., *Patrick Pearse and the Lost Republican Ideal*, Dublin 1991.
97. Murphy, Ignatius, *The Diocese of Killaloe, 1850-1904*, Dublin 1995.
98. Murray, T., *The Story of the Irish in Argentina*, New York 1919.
99. O'Brien Sr. P., *The Sisters of Mercy of Ennis*, Clare 1992.
100. Ó Caithnia, L., *Mícheál Cíosóg*, Baile Atha Cliath 1982.
101. Ó Ceirín, C., and K., *Women of Ireland: A Biographic Dictionary*, Galway 1996.

102. Ó Cillín S. P., *Ballads of Co. Clare 1850-1976,* Galway 1976.

103. O'Connor, E., *A Labour History of Ireland,* Dublin 1992.

104. Ó Dálaigh, B.,(ed.), *The Stranger's Gaze: Travels in County Clare 1534-1950,* Clare 1998.

105. O"Farrell, P., *Ireland's English Question,* London 1971.

106. Ó Grada, C., *Ireland - A New Ecomonic History,* Oxford 1994.

107. Ó hAodha, M., "The Iceman Cometh" in *St. Flannan's, 1881-1981,* Ennis 1981.

108. Ó Murchadha, C., *Sable Wings Over The Land,* CLASP 1999.

109. Ó Snodaigh, P., *Hidden Ulster: Protestants and the Irish Language,* Belfast 1995.

110. Ó Tuathaigh, M.A.G. "De Valera and Sovereignty" in Murphy, J. and O'Carroll, J.P, (eds.) *De Valera and his times,* Cork 1983.

111. Rhodes, R.M., *Women and the Family in Post-Famine Ireland,* New York 1992.

112. Rickard, V., *The Story of the Irish Munsters,* London 1921.

113. Roche, D. *Local Government in Ireland,* Institute of Public Administration, Dublin 1992.

114. Rumpf, E. and A.C. Hepburn, *Nationalism and Socialism in 20th Century Ireland,* Liverpool 1977.

115. Ryan, Meda., *Michael Collins and the Women in his Life,* Dublin 1996.

116. Ryan, W.P., *The Pope's Green Island,* Dublin 1912.

117. Sheedy, K., *The Clare Elections,* Dun Laoghaire 1993.

118. Silverman and Gulliver, *In the Valley of the Nore: a Social History of Thomastown, County Kilkenny, 1840-1983,* Dublin 1986.

119. Smyth, J., *Ballads of the Banner,* Dublin 1998.

120. Spellissy, S., *The Ennis Compendium,* Ennis N.D.

121. Tierney, M. *Ireland Since 1870,* Dublin 1988.

122. Townsend, C., *Political Violence in Ireland,* Oxford 1983.

123. Turner, M., *After the Famine; Irish Agriculture, 1850-1914,* Cambridge 1996.

124. Vaughan, W.E. and A.J. Fitzpatrick, *Irish Historical Statistics, Population, 1821-1971,* Dublin 1978.

125. Walker, B.M., Ó Broin, A. and McMahon, S., *Faces of Ireland,* Belfast 1980.

126. White, Rev. Fr. P., *History of Clare and the Dalcassian Clans,* Dublin 1893.

127. Williams, D., (ed.) *The Irish Struggle, 1916-1926,* London 1966.

128. Williams, W.M., *A West Country Village,* London 1963.

Index

212